Mil Mi-24 Hind

Mil Mi-24 Hind

THE ICONIC SOVIET AND RUSSIAN ATTACK HELICOPTER

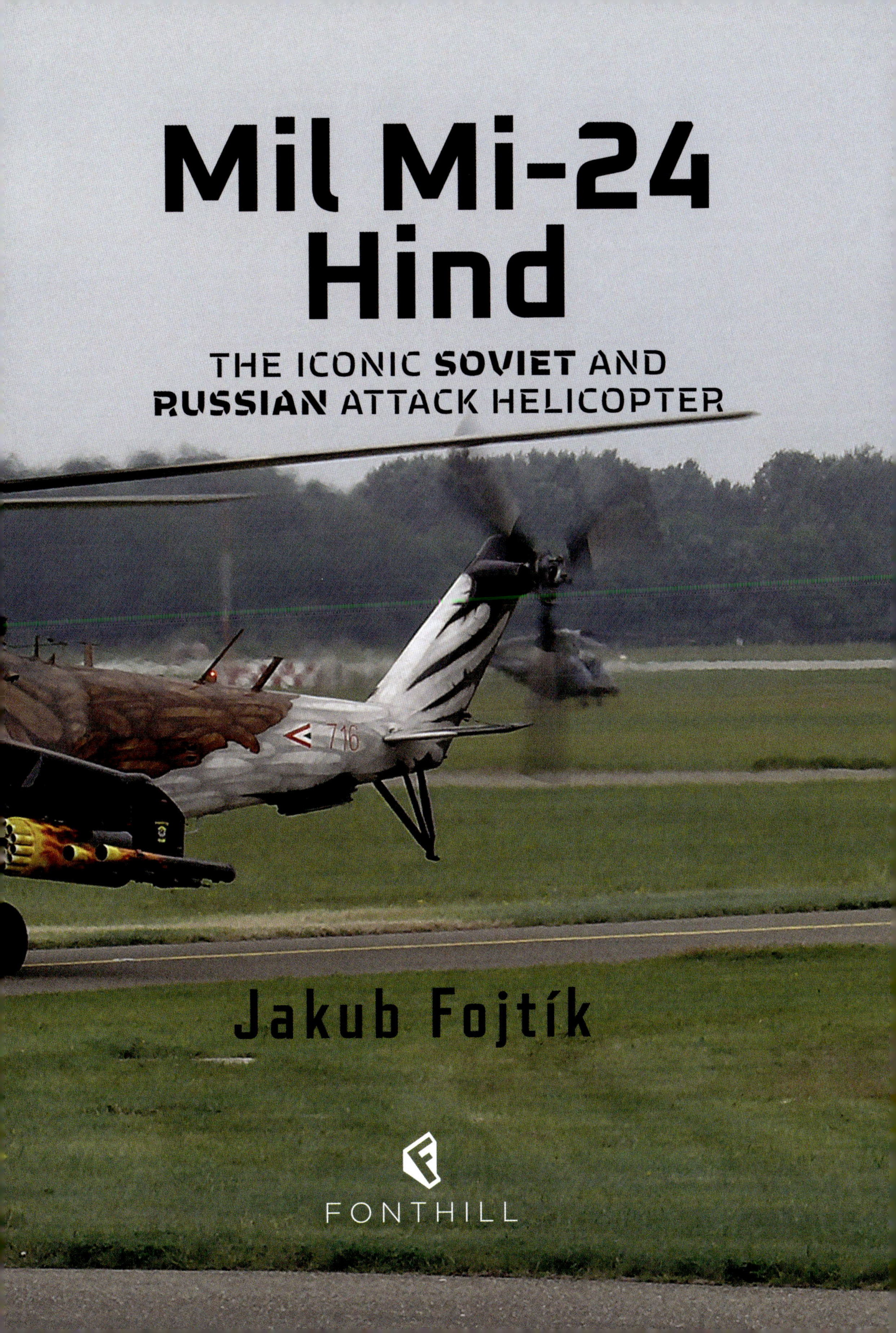

Jakub Fojtík

FONTHILL

Author's note: As the data on Russian helicopters normally varies a lot between sources, the source closest to the Mil Moscow Helicopter Plant was selected for this book. You may contact the author via hind.4ever@seznam.cz email.

First published in Great Britain in 2026 by
Fonthill
An imprint of
Pen & Sword Books Ltd
Yorkshire – Philadelphia

ISBN 978-1-03619-099-6

A CIP catalogue record for this book is available from the British Library.

Typeset in SabonLTStd 10/13 by
SJmagic DESIGN SERVICES, India.
Printed and bound in India by Replika Press Pvt Ltd

MIX
Paper | Supporting responsible forestry
FSC™ C016779
FSC
www.fsc.org

The Publisher's authorised representative in the EU for product safety is Authorised Rep Compliance Ltd., Ground Floor, 71 Lower Baggot Street, Dublin D02 P593, Ireland.
www.arccompliance.com

For a complete list of Pen & Sword titles please contact
PEN & SWORD BOOKS LIMITED
George House, Units 12 & 13, Beevor Street, Off Pontefract Road,
Barnsley, South Yorkshire, S71 1HN, England
E-mail: enquiries@pen-and-sword.co.uk
Website: www.pen-and-sword.co.uk

or

PEN AND SWORD BOOKS
1950 Lawrence Rd, Havertown, PA 19083, USA
E-mail: uspen-and-sword@casematepublishers.com
Website: www.penandswordbooks.com

To my beloved wife Petra, charming daughter Noemi and amazing son Samuel for their great support, patience and joy they bring to my life every day.

Acknowledgements

I would like to express my sincere thanks to all people and organisations who supported this book (in alphabetical order): Bartek Bera, Jan Čadil, Jan Drdák, William du Monte, Thomas Girke, Miroslav Gyűrösi, Andrzej Kiński, Robert Kučera, Petr Kunetek, Jiří Matoušek, Pavel Pánek, Miłosz Rusiecki, Lukáš Syrový, Petr Štefl, Dũng Nguyen, Daniel Vuković, Agence France-Presse, Agência Força Aérea Brasiliera, Arsenyev Production Plant Progress, ATE, Aviakon Konotop, Agentura vojenských informací služeb CIA, Controp, Helicopters of Russia, ITAR-TASS, Kamov Experimental Bureau, Mil Moscow Helicopter Plant, Ministerio de Defensa del Perú, Ministry of Defence of Belorussia, Ministry of Defence of India, Ministry of Defence of Russian Federation, MVZ Mil, RIA Novosti, Rostvertol, Rosvooruzhenyie, Shaam News Network, Terma, TsAGI, Ukroboronprom, US Department of Defense, US Library of Congress, Vertol Systems Company, Vertolet, Vojenský historický ústav Praha and ZVI.

Contents

Abbreviations

AAFSS	Army's Advanced Aerial Fire Support System
AAGM	Anti Aircraft Guided Missile
ADF	Automatic Direction Finder
AF	Air Force
AFT	Auxiliary Fuel Tank
ANVIS	Aviator's Night Vision Head Up Display
APU	Auxiliary Power Unit
ATGM	Anti-Tank Guided Missile
BERP	British Experimental Rotor Programme
CIS	Commonwealth of Independent States
CoMPASS	Compact Multipurpose Advanced Stabilised System
CRT	Cathode Ray Tube
DIRCM	Direct Countermeasures
DOSAAF	Volunteer Society for the Assistance to the Army, Aviation and Navy (*Dobrovolnoye Obshchestvo Sodeystviya Armii, Aviatsii i Flotu*)
DME	Distance measuring Equipment
EDB	Experimental De sign Bureau
EG	Experimental Helicopter (*Eksperimentalnyi Gelikopter*)
ELINT	Electronic Intelligence
ELT	Emergency Locator Transmitter
FAP	Peruvian Air Force (Fuerza Aérea del Perú)
FFAR	Folding Fin Aerial Rocket
FLIR	Forward Looking Infra-Red
FMS	Flight Management System
FSB	Federal Security Bureau of Russia
FSO	Federal Protection Service of Russia
GBU	Guided Bomb Unit

GDR	German Democratic Republic
GPS	Global Positioning System
GTD	Turboshaft engine (*Gazoturbinnyi dvigatel*)
HG	Helicopter Wing (Hubschraubergeschwader)
HF	High Frequency
HMOSP	Helicopter Multi-mission Optronic Stabilised Payload
HOCAS	Hands On Collective And Stick
HUD	Head-Up Display
IFF	Identification Friend or Foe
ILS	Instrument Landing System
IR	Infra Red
LLLTV	Low Light Level TV
LaSK	Ground forces command of the NVA (Landstreitkräfte)
LSK NVA	Army Aviation Air Force of the National Army (Luftstreitkräfte der Nationalen Volksarmee)
MANPADS	Man-Portable Air-Defence Systems
MAP	Ministry of Aviation Industry of the USSR (*Ministerstvo Aviatsionnoy Promyshlenosti*)
MFD	Multifunctional Display
MKR	Marker
NATO	North Atlantic Treaty Organisation
NBC	Nuclear, Biological and Chemical
NVA	Nationale Volksarmee (GDR National Army)
NVG	Night Vision Goggles
OKB	Experimental Design Bureau (*Opytno-konstruktorskoye Byuro*)
OSAE	Independent Mixed Aviation Squadron (*Otdelnaya Smeshanaya Aviatsionnaya Eskadrilya*)
OTBVP	Independent Transport-Attack Helicopter Regiment (*Otdelnyi Transportno-Boyevoy Vertoletnyi Polk*)
OVE	Independent Helicopter Squadron (*Otdelnaya Vertoletnayia Eskadrilya*)
OVEBU	Independent Helicopter Squadron of Combat Deployment (*Otdelnaya Vertoletnayia Eskadrilya Boyevogo Oopravlenyia*)
OVO	Independent Helicopter Detachment (*Otdelnyi Vertoletnyi Otryiad*)
OVP	Independent Helicopter Regiment (*Otdelnyi Vertoletnyi Polk*)
OVPBU	Independent Helicopter Regiment of Combat Deployment (*Otdelnyi Vertoletnyi Polk Boyevogo Oopravlenyia*)
RHA	Rolled homogeneous armour

RPG	Rocket Propelled Grenade
SAR	Search And Rescue
TACAN	Tactical Air Navigation
TsAGI	Central Aerohydrodynamic Institute (*Tsentralnyi Aerogidrodynamicheskyi Institut*)
UHF	Ultra High Frequency
USA	United States of America
USSR	Union of Soviet Socialist Republics
UV	Ultraviolet
V/STOL	Vertical/Short Take-off and Landing
VD	Helicopter for Airborne Troops (*Vertolyot Desantnyi*)
VHF	Very High Frequency
VIP	Very Important Person
VOR	VHF Omnidirectional Radio Range
VVS	*Voyeno-vozdushnye sily* (Soviet/Russian Air Force)
WSO	Weapon systems operator

Author's Note

The Mi-24 Hind seems to be generally well known, so another Hind book may be redundant as dozens of books and profiles in various languages have already covered the topic. However, I believe the opposite is true. Although there have been few limitations in data research in recent years, none of the type's monographs even touch the rationale behind the Hind's development. After all, the Soviet industry was always obsessed with standardisation, and understanding the development legacy of previous models allows for a better understanding of the options selected by Hind designers.

The heritage from its predecessors and limited industrial capabilities are why the Mi-24 is so much different from any Western counterpart, not only by some simple system in it but in its general appearance and concept. Also, when someone researches the topic thoroughly and precisely, they should have direct experience with the type. Luckily, the book you hold in your hands is not my first attempt to capture the timeline; it is the result of two decades of research on the topic, with frequent consultations with pilots, mechanics, historians, and even experts from the OEM. During a significant part of my professional career, I was responsible for the work of an overhaul plant performing Mi-24 overhauls and upgrades. I had a chance to see with my own eyes dozens of Hind modifications and models from Africa to the Far East, including live deployment. I was also fortunate to become familiar with many design features of Mi-2, Mi-4, and Mi-8. I climbed on the Hind's engine cowlings many times, and flew it as well. Consequently, in this book I have tried not only to describe various modifications and introduce the Hind development line, but also to explain the reasons why engineers chose certain approaches, and the benefits or drawbacks of those approaches. After all, since my last book on the topic I have managed to collect new information which, as is the case with any historical research, detail, modify, or even contradict the previously discovered information—including those I published myself. So now all the latest data is embedded here.

I am convinced this book presents a comprehensive summary of the type's history, emphasising technical details and deployment experience with a lot of previously undisclosed information. I hope you will enjoy reading the history of one of the most successful helicopters ever. The Mi-24 deserves recognition as an irrepressible part of aviation history, having a significant impact on all later Soviet and Russian attack helicopter types and battlefield tactics around the globe. The legend of the Mi-24 continues, and this book also covers the export success of the latest Mi-35M and derived models, making it a source that covers all Hind models up to date. This book is also supported by many great photographers who have documented the decades of service of the Mi-24 from various perspectives, capturing beautiful images that you can see on the following pages. I deliberately tried to ignore, as much as possible, the digital era of the type, which is omnipresent and thousands of pictures can be found online. Instead, the absolute majority of the pictures in this book are historical and rarely seen today.

I hope the Mi-24 will impress you as much as it impressed me when I saw it during a low flyover for the first time many years ago. Sitting on a balcony of my parents' home as a small kid, I was stunned by seeing two Czech Mi-24s performing ultra-low pass and vigorous combat exercise on their trip to an unknown destination. Surely not allowed to fly at the treetop level altitude at that time, but so incredibly impressive. I clearly remember that feeling and feel it still when I see the Hinds in the sky. When I had a chance to fly in it, I was mesmerised. Eleven tons of metal flying at tree-top altitude with speeds exceeding 300 km/h while the ship is manoeuvring violently, although with a lot of moments of inertia, definitively leaves an impression that this is the ideal tool for battle.

It is not all good however! Production quality was of a Russian standard where inches do not matter cause harsh behaviour, constant vibrations everywhere, a rubber smell inside, a set of strange noises from the closing landing gear to main gearbox revolutions, buffeting during dynamic deceleration, suffocating heat in the cabin when flying in a hot environment, terribly uncomfortable seats, and deafening noise and shaking when launching the weapons. This is a Hind for everyone who drives it for the first time, and yet it is a legend. As for mechanics, it is still a machine that needs tiring lubrication, constant mechanical adjustment of everything, but which rewards itself with incredible endurance when something breaks—or something hits it. Often the damage is only discovered after landing; often not even the pilot detects it.

Unfortunately, the type was designed to counter NATO tank units, and it recently returned to its original role due to geopolitical shifts and the war in Ukraine. Another war where the ubiquitous Mi-24s are deployed again by both sides of the conflict. Another war in the combat career exceeding five decades. Without much of improvement ... this is THE HIND.

Introduction

The development of the Hind followed the failure of the efforts to arm the Mi-1 and Mi-4 piston types with significant firepower. These designs were never armed as battle helicopters should be, and this weakness handicapped their success as armed transport and liaison types. When the AH-1 Cobra emerged in the Vietnam war and prototype AH-56 was flying, the Soviet generals were immediately aware of the threat the types could pose to Warsaw Pact tank columns. A counterpart was urgently needed, and after the initial ideas to build a Soviet copy of UH-1, a specific attack model design prevailed. It was primarily the available TV3-117 engines and critical lack of time for development that dictated the future shapes of the very first Soviet attack helicopter, the V-24, later in production called Mi-24 and recognised by NATO as Hind. Unlike in the USA and Europe, the Soviet attack type was super heavy—with eleven tons of maximum take-off weight which superseded the US AH-1 type by almost three times! On the other hand, the 2.5 tons weapon-stores capacity was close to the empty weight of AH-1. With a top speed of over 330 km/h, high manoeuvrability, and a large payload capacity, the Mi-24 became a formidable type, capable of significantly threatening NATO tank units, especially in its later versions.

The Mi-24 Hind became a true symbol of Soviet defence technology. On its debut in East Germany in the early 1970s, it was described by the Western press as a heavy attack type with impressive firepower and high battle-damage tolerance. Unlike Western attack types, it represents a category of its own, combining attack and transport roles and making the type always bigger, heavier and visually more impressive when compared with its lightweight Western counterparts. It was the very first dedicated attack helicopter designed on the Eastern side of the Iron Curtain and it became a real legend, influencing the combat strategies of dozens of countries. The versatility with troop transport capability and great firepower made it ideal for a variety of missions which include also artillery spotting, NBC reconnaissance or even protected VIP transport. The long Afghan experience helped to increase the type's qualities and even today it is an inspiration for engineers.

There is no better proof of the type's qualities than the fact that it is still in production almost half a century after its maiden flight, and the currently produced helicopters may reach the milestone of seventy-five years since the first flight of the type. It is also of no surprise that many countries selected a new Hind generation as replacement of the old Hinds. The type will surely reach fifty years of combat engagement and there are still many missions where the type's capabilities may be still widely used. This is possibly because the Hind concept was far ahead of its time and still presents a viable platform on the current battlefield. Another indicator of the type's immortality is that it has been adopted by more than seventy countries, something that will never be beaten among attack helicopters. This gives a clear message that the Hind is able to fly anywhere under any conditions. From the northern and far-eastern cold areas of Russia up to the desert in Algeria or tropical rainforest in Brazil. The Hind is a truly ubiquitous attack helicopter. With at least 2,916 units produced since 1971, of which at least 905 were originally exported by the manufacturer, it is the far most successful Soviet and Russian attack design, which will never be likely outnumbered by any of its successors.

1

How to Find a Hind

The First Dedicated Soviet Attack Helicopter

Shortly after the end of World War II, Mikhail Leontyevich Mil, then a senior designer at the Central Aerohydrodynamic Institute (TsAGI—*Tsentralnyi Aerogidrodynamicheskyi Institut*), began to consider the idea of constructing an experimental helicopter, which he designated EG-1 (*Eksperimentalnyi Gelikopter*). It was intended to verify various technological elements, primarily the rotor and control system designed by Mil himself. On 9 April 1946, Mil presented the project of the three-seat helicopter to the Ministry of Aviation Industry (MAP—*Ministerstvo Aviatsionnoy Promyshlenosti*) commission. After a thorough assessment, the senior representatives informed Mil of the many modifications needed, starting with the recommendation to use a different power unit, changing the cabin layout, and modifying the landing gear scheme. The reason for the changes were primarily the insufficient capabilities of the Soviet industry, as Mil demanded many manufacturing and design solutions that were unavailable at the time.

In the following months, Mil obtained permission to test various construction elements of his project. In March 1947, the director of TsAGI issued an order for the establishment of laboratory No. 5, intended for the research of helicopter construction and associated aerodynamic phenomena, and Mikhail Mil, recently given the scientific title of Doctor of Technical Sciences, was appointed as its head. Approximately twenty people—without any previous experience with helicopters—were transferred to his team, forming the future foundation of the Mil helicopter design office. Mil considered the establishment of the research department as a prerequisite for success and not success itself, although the approval of independent helicopter research was a significant shift in the perception of this technology at the MAP and TsAGI levels. At that time, the State Commission for Scientific and Technical Development received approximately twenty proposals from various aviation design offices and other entities for the development of the 'first' serial Soviet helicopter. This was a response to the semi-official MAP assignment from 1947, requiring the submission of similar projects. The reason for MAP's hesitant approach was primarily the resistance of a large part of the Soviet generality to helicopters and the reluctance to engage in them in a situation where even J. V. Stalin himself did not show interest in them. Slow helicopters seemed to be unusable in the era of the fight for supersonic speeds. On the other hand, the generals did not want to miss anything, especially under the influence of information about the development of helicopters in the USA and thus decided on limited development.

On 19 December 1947, the MAP minister issued an order requiring three designers, Bratukhin, Yakovlev and Mil, to submit a work schedule for helicopters intended for state tests within a month. The very first Soviet helicopter competition was about to begin! The MAP order mentioned the obligation to establish a design office (OKB—*Opytno Konstruktrskoye Byuro*—Experimental Design Office) for helicopters at TsAGI and appointed Mil as its director. This led to the actual establishment of Mil's OKB No. 4, and most importantly, Mil managed to keep pace with much larger competitors also working on fixed-wing aircraft. The first Mil's GM-1 prototype was completed in August 1948 in a situation where the competing Bratukhin B-11 had been flying for two months and was attracting the interest of the MAP leadership. Nevertheless, Mil decided not to rush unnecessarily, and production and initial ground tests proceeded according to plan. At the beginning of September 1948, test pilot Matvey Karlovich Baykalov performed the first tethered hover. Flight tests proceeded very quickly thanks to careful ground preparation, and on 20 September 1948, the GM-1 took off for the first time without tethering ropes. However, it did

Mikhail Leonteyevich Mil, the brilliant mind behind the Hind and other Mil types. He is holding a model of the unrealised Mi-8 high-speed variant. (*MVZ Mil*)

not fly for long, as it was destroyed on 24 November 1948 when the transmission froze during a high-altitude flight. Baykalov bailed out, but died during the flight of second prototype on 7 March 1949, when a welding defect in a tail rotor-shaft caused loss of control. After the tragedy, the unfinished third GM-1 prototype was hastily completed, flown in August 1949, and participated in company tests at OKB-4 until the end of September of that year. It was only in February 1950 that it was decided that the GM-1 met the MAP specifications over Yak-100 and B-11. The GM-1 was adopted into the service as Mi-1, the first Mil type in a long line. Up to 1959 some 597 helicopters were produced at Orenburg plant No. 47, all under the new name Mil Mi-1. It was common in the USSR that the production plant was an independent entity from the design office. It was selected by MAP in order to level the capacities among all plants and so it was in the case of the Orenburg and other plants. In 1957 another plant joined the production, No. 168 plant at Rostov on Don, which built 370 Mi-1s up until 1962, when production finally ended in the USSR and was transfer to Poland. This is how the close relation between OKB No. 4 and the Rostov-based production plant started. In Poland some 1,594 (some Russian sources say 1,597) helicopters under the designation SM-1 were built. Mil's OKB No. 4, renamed later to OKB No. 329, established itself as a major Soviet helicopter design house and in 1951 it accepted the offer to take over the abandoned design and production facilities, which originally belonged to rival Bratukhin's OKB, at the Lyubertsy outskirts of Moscow. It eventually became the final destination of the OKB No. 4 and is used to the present day.

In the late 1940s, the OKB No. 329 design bureau worked on the development of a larger medium helicopter powered by the ASh-62 engine, previously used on the famous An-2 biplane. This engine was one of the best in the USSR in terms of power to weight ratio and it was also available in large quantities. In June 1951 Stalin convened a meeting with leading representatives of the Soviet helicopter design bureaus, namely M.L. Mil, N.I. Kamov, and A.S. Yakovlev (Yakovlev, being a political VIP at that time, later recalled in his memoirs that the heads of the Ilyushin and Tupolev design bureaus were also present, but both refused to work on helicopter technology due to a heavy overload of other projects. Bratukhin is mentioned as well, but his involvement seems unlikely as his OKB was at that time focused on ground support systems only). In the end, however, the meeting was postponed until September of the same year due to the need for Soviet generals to define the requirements for the new type of technology. Stalin and the generals demanded the construction of two types of helicopters: a medium single-engine one for twelve people or 1,200kg of cargo and a heavy twin-engine one for twenty-four soldiers or 2,400kg of cargo. The general staff presented very strict requirements for both new types in terms of performance and required the OKBs to select which type, or both, they were interested in building. The requirements were extremely demanding, given the state of Soviet rotorcraft technology at that time, and so was the deadline, to have an operational prototype within one year. The deadline for OKB's answer was very short as well—the next day. At the meeting, Kamov turned down the project immediately, concerned by the impossibility of building the machine in the unlikely timeline of one year. Mil wanted to use his extensive theoretical work on the project with the ASh-62 engine and signed up to build a medium type, while Yakovlev accepted the development of a heavy one. However, the two offices were supposed to cooperate with use of common aggregates.

As for the engine, the fixed-wing-proven ASh-82 type was selected for the new models, but significant modifications were needed. It should be noted that the ASh-82 model was not entirely a result of Soviet engineering, as it was in fact a licenced copy of the US Wright R-1820 series engine delivered to the USSR in kits during WW II for DC-3 transport planes and later locally produced. The US-proposed Lend-Lease Act helped even long after the war! Minutes of the meeting were signed and on 5 October 1951 the Soviet of Ministers of the USSR issued a request for the construction of the VD-12 helicopter (Helicopter for Airborne Troops, initially called the V-12 with VD standing for *Vertolyot Desantnyi*) designed to transport twelve armed soldiers, a 57mm or 76mm recoilless gun, or a GAZ-67B or GAZ-69 military vehicle, although no details on layout were determined. The document also specified the type's armament, a TBK-481M machine gun with a supply of 150 rounds. It was destined to become the first Soviet helicopter weapon.

After the end of WW II, the main Soviet armaments design bureaus were developing many new machine guns, because their Western equivalents achieved a significantly higher rate of fire. In fact, the main Russian aircraft machine gun, the Berezin UB, widely used during the Second World War, had a theoretical rate of fire of only 850 rounds per minute (in reality, it was below 650). Consequently, the UB machine gun was modernised for a higher burst rate, but it did not bring any significant improvement. At the same time, Tupolev's design bureau was looking for a new machine gun to defend the Tu-4 bomber, a post-war copy of the famous B-29, which the Kremlin considered one of the most important elements of the air force. Therefore, a project to develop a new generation of barrelled aviation weapons was launched. Designer Nikolai Mikhailovich Afanasyev, from the Russian city of Tula, decided to design a new weapon using 12.7 × 108mm rounds; i.e. the same as the UB type. The new machine gun received the factory designation TKB-481M, but later became known also as the Afanasyev A-12.7. The internal army code name was 9-A-016P. Unlike the previous types, the new machine gun was to be powered by the gases collected from the barrel. During trials, the A-12.7 reached a rate of fire of up to 1,500 shots per minute, which was twice as many as with the UB, but the high rate of fire disproportionately shortened the service life of the overheating barrel. After a series of tests that lasted from 1949 to 1953, the designers finally limited the maximum rate of fire to about 800–1,100 shots per minute. This was the only way to achieve an acceptable barrel life of 4,000 shots. Despite many advantages, such as ease of maintenance and low weight, the A-12.7 was unable to significantly outperform the previous UB model. During tests the weapon was selected for use in the new helicopter, where the performance matched the expectations.

The first flying prototype of VD-12 was finished early in 1952 and Mil himself recollected that the engineers and designers were working seven days a week, literally sleeping in the offices and workshops. On 30 April 1952, ground-tethered tests began, during which pilot Vsevolod Vladimirovich Vinitskyi, sitting in the cockpit, tested the individual systems of the helicopter and the engine settings. By the end of August 1952 Mil's prototype workshop delivered a second hand-made VD-12. The second

Above: A-12.7 machine gun in the Mi-4A belly gondola. The gunner was kneeling inside, just under the engine with all the noise and fumes entering his workplace. (*Author*)

Below: The K-10T collimator gunsight in the Mi-4A. Although very simple, it allowed for relatively good accuracy and was adopted for the Mi-24A as well. (*Author*)

helicopter joined the ongoing factory trials, while the Saratov-based production plant No. 292 was passed the set of assembly instructions and put together the third prototype, which was not intended for flight operation but for ground endurance and static tests. In August 1952 factory tests were successfully finished with only minor deficiencies in the design. Although many defects still awaited rectification, production plant No. 292 at Saratov officially launched serial production in December 1952, technically still before the end of the state trials. The helicopter was given the code name Idzeliye 56 (which means Article 56, a typical Soviet-era typology to confuse potential spies as all military products were named 'Article'). In addition to the two prototypes built at Mil's prototype plant, Saratov Factory No. 292 had completed a total of 152 Mi-4s by 1954. However, the Saratov facility turned out to be too busy for mass production and new production locations were scouted. During the summer of 1953 Kazan plant No. 387 was selected for mass production. This is how Mil's attachment to its later major production plant, building thousands of Mi-4 and later Mi-8, started. In total some 3,309 Mi-4s were built in the USSR of which over 700 were exported abroad, with further models built under licence in China.

Although the Mi-1 and Mi-4 types entered the service with the Soviet army, they were used primarily for liaison and transport service and the new ways of using them were yet to be developed and tested. They came in a time when cargo gliders were still on the spotlight. In parallel were the Soviet military experts observing the French activities in Algeria between 1954 and 1962. During this conflict, which was the largest one since the Second World War, the French army aviation deployed on the battlefield several types of helicopters such as H-34A, SO.1221 Djinn, Bell 47G, H-21 and others equipped with various weapons including machine guns, cannons and unguided rockets.

The latest Alouette II model with SS.10 and AS.11 anti-tank guided missiles was available too late to be thoroughly tested over the battlefield. However, it became obvious the armed helicopter can present a very efficient platform for fire support of ground units. Even the US army was heavily inspired and since 1953 experimented with various armament modifications of its types including use of French armament. The Americans adopted similar weaponisations and since 1953 the US army had been experimenting with the H-13 Sioux armament. However, it encountered resistance from the USAF, which was trying to claim fire support. The US army had extensive experience with the deployment of the H-13 in Korea and was fully aware that a similar helicopter could also perform combat missions, especially after receiving the first information about the deployment of helicopters in Algeria. However, it was only in 1958 that it managed to push through the establishment a special unit at Fort Rucker in Alabama, which operated the H-13D, H-13E and H-13H machines provisionally equipped with various types of weapons as part of the test deployment. The first system tested was the XM1 with 7.62mm Browning M37C machine guns and 70mm FFAR unguided rocket tubes; however, it proved to be too heavy. Later, Oerlikon missiles, French SS.10 or AS.11 guided missiles and other armaments including Bazookas were tested. The M2 system, consisting of two 7.62mm M60C machine guns and eight FFAR missiles in each block suspended under the landing skids braces, reached serial production. Each helicopter could carry two blocks, which represented considerable firepower for its time. The system saw deployment in Vietnam, where the helicopter's performance shortcomings became apparent. Nevertheless, combat engagements proved the value of the armed helicopter on the Asian battlefield.

In 1969, armed OH-13s were withdrawn from Vietnam to return to Asia for a year after the army suffered heavy losses of its new OH-6s. These came with an integrated M27 system with a rotary six-barrel M134D machine gun of 7.62mm calibre or other armament in the form of grenade launchers and single-barrel machine guns. M60 series machine guns were also installed on Hiller's UH-12 type, also deployed in Vietnam. In addition to the light types, the US army also worked on arming Sikorsky's H-19D and H-34A models. These were provisionally equipped with side pylons for carrying up to 24 unguided 105mm calibre rockets and four 12.7-mm calibre machine guns. The original 105-mm rockets were later replaced by thirty-two lighter 70-mm rockets on the H-34A. Many modifications were live tested in Vietnam.

Although France actually lost the war in terms of its ultimate goal leading to Algerian independence, the modifications were noted as a way how the helicopters may be used in the future. Based on this experience the Soviet military headquarters issued a directive to OKB No. 329 to prepare a project of upgrade of the current helicopter to verify the feasibility of helicopter air assault. The first updated type became the easily available Mi-1 model equipped in 1958 with twelve TRS-132 unguided rockets of 132mm calibre attached on side weapon racks. The TRS-132 unguided rocket was developed yet in 1943 as a means of increasing the fire power of modern fighters. The all-metal construction of aircraft increased in the Second World War the number of direct bullet hits needed for shooting down an enemy. Instead increasing the cannon calibre, the designers proposed use of aerial rockets. Their explosive charge was expected to damage the aircraft's structure sufficiently to shoot down the plane with a single hit. However, it later proved incorrect as aiming the unguided rockets towards an aerial object proved to be extremely difficult if not impossible. This is why TRS-82 and TRS-132 rockets were originally developed. Both differed in calibre of 82 and 132mm respectively. They were a direct derivate of the RS-82 rocket used during the Second World War on Polikarpov R-5 and Ilyushin Il-2 Shturmovik aircraft. The rockets were not featuring any stabilators and were launched from tubes with rotation of 200 revolution per minute for stabilisation inducted by the launching tube bore. For various reasons those rockets, named finally R-2 and R-3 (and later even S-3 where 'S' stands for *snaryad*—unguided rocket while R for *raketa*—rocket), were not widely used. When used on the Mi-1, they failed to prove any effectivity. The rotor downwash affected the trajectory of the relatively slow rocket and the accuracy was far behind expectation making the real use virtually impossible. Nevertheless, Mi-1 became the very first armed Soviet helicopter.

In 1961, also a modified Mi-1MU variant with four 3M11 anti-tank guided missiles (ATGM) was introduced for testing. This missile was originally developed for ground applications, but due to its compact dimensions and low weight it was selected for such tests. At the time of testing the missile was still in prototype stage. Its development was launched after the initial experience gained with the 3M6 Shmel (AT-1 Snapper in NATO reporting name). The 3M6 type was neither lightweight nor had long range, which made it difficult to use it as portable system and the missile was launched only from specially modified vehicles. Beyond 1 kilometre the guidance

Above: Armed Mil Mi-1M prototype with bomb rack on the side. Note the aerodynamic surface under the nose helping to keep the lateral balance of the ship. (*MVZ Mil*)

Below: Another armed Mi-1M helicopter, this time with TRS-132 unguided rockets of 132mm calibre. Behind the helicopter the FAB-100 free fall bomb is visible. (*MVZ Mil*)

accuracy was troublesome and also the penetration capability was not very high. This is why the new model called 3M11 Fleyta and 3M17 Phalanga (AT-2 Swatter) was developed instead, the former as initial design and the latter as its improved derivate. The major expected use was with the BRDM-type amphibious armoured cars but the lightweight concept was of interest for Mil helicopter bureau.

The design works started in 1957 for the 3M11 and two years later for 3M17 and focused on increased accuracy, lighter weight and more effective warhead. The missile was expected to use radio command line instead of wire guidance. It allowed for higher flight speed due to no trailing of guidance wire although it became naturally more prone to radio jamming. Unfortunately, at the time of testing the guidance system of the missile was still under development and the accuracy was extremely low as was the reliability. The 5kg warhead was potentially capable of penetrating 500mm thick RHA armour, just enough to pierce majority of the tanks from late 1950s. The elevators were in flight powered by pressurised air from the cylinder in the rocket body. The aerodynamic concept with cruciform rudders included small destabilisators in the nose area increasing the efficiency of the command system. Between august 1958 and July 1959 some 100 warhead explosions were tested as well as 84 missile launches. In late 1959, the 3M17 missile renamed as per new coding system 9M17, was cleared for service with army units but officially it was adopted in August 1960. When the Mi-1MU model appeared, it was already in service.

Fully upgraded Mil Mi-1MU prototype, this time with rails for four 3M11 ATGMs. Note the gunsight on the roof of the cockpit. (*MVZ Mil*)

A special non-stabilised optical sight was installed on the roof of the Mi-1MU cabin. In total, sixteen missile launches were performed with detailed evaluation of the accuracy and procedures. The missiles on external outriggers were commanded by the pilot who was both flying the helicopter and managing the weapon. The missile was launched from rails where it was stowed in the X position and once it was flying, it stabilised itself with the + position of the rudders. The rocket engine consisted of boost and sustaining engine. The pilot had to command the missile for all the time of flight and only experienced operators succeeded. The knowledge gained during the tests helped to the missile design office to finalise the updated model 9M17 of which the installation of four was tested on the Mi-1MU.

With multiple fires in 1965 the Mi-1MU again helped to develop the improved 9M17M model, a derivate of 3M11, which was later adopted by multiple Mil's helicopters, and also the lighter 9M14 type was tested. Especially the operational procedures needed for target acquisition and in-flight guidance were verified on the Mi-1MU model. The helicopter launch showed the original maximum range of 2,500 metres can be exceeded when fired from medium altitudes. The system worked, although some issues with the rocket engines ignition occurred but those were not attributable to the helicopter installation. The prototype of the Mi-1 helicopter was also used for testing other types of armament. For example, in 1962, FAB-100 fragmentation bombs were experimentally dropped, and test pilots helped determine suitable flight modes and flight trajectories considering the bomb's drift during flight to the target and the main rotor downwash.

It was the verification of a wide range of armaments on the Mi-1MU helicopter that laid the foundations for the development of later combat versions of Mil's helicopters. Western literature sometimes states that the development of the Mi-1MU was unsatisfactory, and therefore this version did not enter serial production. The Mi-1MU was actually never intended for serial production and regular service but rather for verifying combat procedures and the impact of specific helicopter piloting modes on them. Nevertheless, it was evident that the limited performance of the Mi-1MU helicopter did not allow for full verification of the weapons. The helicopter had low speed and a small power margin and was also very sensitive to balance. It had even to be equipped with an additional aerodynamic surface under the nose for compensating the weapons' use during many flights. Consequently, the tests did not progress further although the Mi-1MU may be considered as the very first soviet attack type.

The basic version of the bigger Mi-4 type was equipped with the A-12.7 machine gun, which proved to be quite handy for low intensity combat operations. Unlike in fast jets, the gunner was able to aim the gun precisely and within the 300 to 500 metres range it was pretty accurate. The aiming was done via a fairly simple K-10T collimator optical gunsight. The gunner was able to move the gun 55°down and 30° to left or right, which allowed him to track even moving objects on the ground. Even the very first army exercises in the early 1950s showed that helicopter fire support could be quite handy and precise. However, the gun's operation, with the gunner kneeing in the underbelly gondola, was not very comfortable and all the smoke from the firing came directly into the cabin. Although the standard ammunition reserve contained 200 rounds, typically less than one third was fired before the gun smoke covered the

Armed Mi-1M helicopter with RBK-250-170M cluster ammunition container—a formidable anti-infantry weapon for such light helicopter. (*MVZ Mil*)

gondola and obstructed visibility. Nevertheless, the smaller Mi-1 or Ka-15 could not accommodate a comparable gun at all, so the Mi-4 solution was considered as vital. Obviously, the load capacity of the large helicopter called for arming it further.

In 1957, a new modification was introduced with six side-mounted tube racks with pylons for UB-16-57UM pods, each containing sixteen S-5 folding-fin aerial rockets of 57mm calibre. These rockets were a direct result of Second World War fighters' experience and were developed on the basis of the TRS-82 and TRS-132 types. At the end of the 1940s, the Kazan-based OKB-16 Precision Engineering Design Bureau, headed by A. E. Nudelman, was given the state task of developing a new type of unguided rocket of 57mm calibre for anti-aircraft fire. The goal was to construct a rocket capable of destroying flying targets at a distance of up to 2 kilometres and at altitudes of up to 20 kilometres. According to the assignment, the rockets were to be used by the MiG-17 fighters being developed at that time but enter the service only with MiG-19. The designers were finally inspired by captured German R4M Orkan unguided rockets, which were developed as an anti-aircraft weapon during the Second World War and briefly used on the Me 262 jets. After the end of the war, the Soviets managed to obtain not only almost complete documentation of the R4M, but also part of the production jigs for these rockets. The result of more than a year of development in the USSR was a new type of rocket called ARS-57. The entire rocket complex was designated AS-5.

The first tests of firing from MiG-15 and MiG-17 showed that rather than against air targets, rockets are significantly more suitable for attacking ground troops, equipment and fortifications. In 1955, rockets were officially accepted into service with the Soviet air force under the designation S-5. The first mass-produced launch pod was the ORO-57K carrying eight rockets, which was used on MiG-19 aircraft. At the same time, the development of a universal pod suitable for use in other types of aircraft was carried out. This eventually became the UB-16-57 pod for sixteen rockets. Thanks to its aerodynamic shape, simple design and operation, it was chosen as armament by the designers of almost all Soviet fighter and attack aircraft as well as helicopters. Since the rocket was literally brand new, the Mil's designers decided to use it to arm the Mi-4. The rocket was stabilised in flight by rotation with 800rpm inducted by the spring-loaded feather-like stabilisers at the rear end. The rocket engine burned only for 1.1 seconds, enough to reach highly subsonic speed for the rest of the flight. The UB-16-57 allowed single or salvo firing. When salvo firing was selected, the rockets were fired alternately from left and right pod with 0.25 second delay (thus 0.5 second delay between two rockets in one block). Compared to fixed-wing aircraft, the missiles' trajectory was significantly affected by the rotor downwash, which is why helicopter blocks were equipped with different front and rear shapes with longer barrels.

Gradually, several variants of missiles emerged, differing primarily in their warhead, but also in their purpose and rocket engine. The most widely used type is the fragmentation warhead, giving the missile the name S-5M (or S-5M1 with a modified rocket engine booster). The warhead of these missiles deforms into 75 pre-fragmented shrapnels after initiation and impact (the S-5MO version then brings additional steel rings around the warhead, increasing the number of shrapnel to up to 360). The S-5M/MO types are usable against unprotected targets and enemy vehicles. The S-5K version with a cumulative warhead is used against armoured targets and can penetrate up to 130mm of homogeneous armour. If necessary, the S-5KO can also be used against manpower, i.e. it is the S-5K type again supplemented with steel rings. The S-5KP and KPB variants are analogous versions with a more sensitive piezoelectric fuse instead of a mechanical one. All missiles proved to be effective against manpower in a point-to-point manner, against which the S-5S and S-5SB versions containing up to 1,100 steel 40mm long arrows were eventually created. These versions achieved great popularity, especially during the war in Afghanistan, where they were able to cause devastating injuries over a large area.

The BDZ-53 weapon racks allowed the carriage of not only the UB-16-57 pods, but also FAB-50 and FAB-100 high explosive free fall bombs. For the aiming of the new weapons a roof-mounted gunsight was selected and it included the trivia PKV collimator gunsight. Firing accuracy depended heavily on range and weather conditions, but one Mi-4 was able to deliver 96 unguided rockets within a minute—at the time an impressive rate of fire power. The first Mi-4s were converted in 1957 under the designation Mi-4AV (V stands for *vooruzhenyi*—armed), but it took eight years to pass state tests and officially accept the type into the Soviet inventory. The reason for the delay was both the need to analyse the recoil impact on the airframe as well as the lack of idea as to how to use the armed type within the army. In 1960, two modified prototypes were involved in extensive state tests. One of them carried eight UB-16-57 pods, the other two pods with six older TRS-132 rotary stabilised missiles.

One of the initial configurations of the Mi-4AV helicopter with six UB-16-57 folding fin aerial rocket pods of 57mm calibre. (*MVZ Mil*)

The TRS-132 was practically abandoned by the air force as it demonstrated terrible accuracy. When twelve rockets were fired from 500m against a target tank during one military exercise, literally zero rockets hit. So its dedication to helicopter use was one idea as to how to utilise the unsuccessful design. Tests proved the S-5 to be more effective and far more accurate and the TRS-132 was dropped.

In 1965, the Mil bureau came up with a new armed model, again designated Mi-4AV. It became the very first serial Soviet Anti-Tank helicopter as it was equipped with 9M17M Phalanga guided anti-tank missiles verified on the Mi-1MU already. It became a miracle of Soviet technology as the type was able to hit a tank with reasonable accuracy from more than 2 kilometres . The new Mi-4AV was equipped with reinforced weapon racks holding six pylons for UB-16-57 rocket pods or free-fall bombs up to 250kg, and on the top four rails for 9M17M ATGMs. The anti-tank missile, officially called AT-2 Swatter in NATO coding, was a radio command missile with a 5.4kg warhead able to penetrate the armour of many post-war tanks. The 9M17M model came up with some improvements as the previous 9M17 type which demonstrated very low reliability. The experience from the Mi-1MU was very useful as a lot of theoretical work was conducted on the topic. In the Mi-4 the co-pilot aimed the missile manually towards the target, using the tracers on its back through the K-4V gunsight. The system somehow worked and allowed the Soviet army to gain its first practical experience with an anti-tank helicopter.

Some 195 helicopters were finished, of which 185 were intended for Soviet army aviation and were basically upgraded from standard transport Mi-4As. These were distributed to European-located regions. The remaining ten aircraft were delivered to Egypt, where they had their baptism of fire against Israeli tank brigades. Within Soviet army regiments the Mi-4 participated in several large military exercises and helped to define the anti-tank role of the helicopter. The Mi-4AV model was operated by only a very few Soviet units, with one being the 688. Independent Helicopter Regiment based near to the Polish city of Legnica. Soviet army gained in the Mi-4AV its first dedicated anti-tank system. The initial experiences of Mi-4AV-equipped units showed that the Mi-4AV suffered from a lack of power and manoeuvrability. When all weapon hardpoints were used, the helicopter's frontal resistance doubled, and due to the weight of the armament, its flight performance significantly decreased. Therefore, pilots could have performed more or less only straight flights without significant evasive manoeuvres, which was in stark contrast to the experiences of crews of armed helicopters deployed in Algeria. Although the Mi-4AV type finally allowed to destroy the enemy tanks from helicopter, it was still far from becoming a serial type.

In the meantime, Mil's experimental design bureau succeeded in the 1950s not only with the aforementioned types but a bit later also with the first Soviet turbine-powered Mi-6 helicopter, a truly giant aircraft originally developed, among other tasks, for nuclear missile transportation. It was powered by turboshaft engines, which allowed a significant boost in rotorcraft performance. It was no surprise when Mil

Full configuration of the Mi-4AV with UB-16-57 folding fin aerial rocket pods and four 9M17M ATGMs on the launching rails, as well as an A-12.7 machine gun in the belly gondola. (*MVZ Mil*)

looked for other areas where the extensive experience with such power plants could be reused. An increase in helicopter performance was not feasible with piston engines, as they required more bulky space when higher output was needed. However, this understanding was familiar only to Mil, while army officials were not willing to listen to it. This is why Mil's plan to build a new helicopter was first presented as a modernisation of the legacy Mi-4 model.

Initially, only a plan to install two turboshaft engines into a modified Mi-4 fuselage was envisaged, retaining the majority of helicopter systems. The installation of turboshaft engines required a complete redesign of the helicopter's nose section, with engines installed above the flight deck. This arrangement would allow for increase of the pilots' view from the cockpit as well as a more spacious cargo cabin. Finally, the new type of engine was expected to bring significant benefits in smaller dimensions, lower weight, better safety in case of one engine failure with doubled systems, and better climatic tolerance allowing low-temperature starts without pre-heating. The new cargo cabin was designed to accommodate the latest army hardware, including GAZ-69 jeeps, artillery howitzers, or up to twenty fully equipped soldiers. With such an arrangement, the new model should have drawn the attention of army officials as a seriously improved means of rotorcraft surpassing the Mi-4 in all aspects. From the beginning, Mil expected to design the new type in a modular way, allowing easy production of transport, armed, naval, and VIP transport variants. Especially the last one mentioned was of huge interest as it was obvious that added value in terms of safety and comfort for Soviet state officials could be an important reason to support such an initiative. This is why the Ministry of Transport Aviation was also involved in the project.

With Soviet leaders' comfort in focus, Mil finally reached at least limited state support for such rotorcraft modification concept development. In 1958, after many meetings between OKB No. 329 officials and state authorities' representatives, the Soviet ministerial council issued a directive requiring a new V-8 helicopter to be built, powered by a single Ivchenko AI-24 engine. The engine, designed by OKB No. 478, was originally developed as a turboprop for An-24 cargo planes. For the helicopter, it was supposed to be modified into a turboshaft variant with a shaft going through the exhaust pipe to the main gearbox. The expected output was set to 1,416 kW with an empty weight of 600kg, while the original Mi-4's piston ASh-62 type reached a maximum of 1,267 kW with a weight of 980kg. The maximum take-off weight was at the same time expected to rise from 7,500kg of the Mi-4 to more than 11,000kg with the V-8. On the other hand, the engine suffered from high fuel consumption, and engineers did not stop thinking of a twin-engine configuration with higher safety. Nevertheless, there was no such engine available for twin installation, and the work on the single-engine V-8 proceeded. In late 1959, the project was officially launched after internal opposition.

In contrast to the original Mi-4 modification plans, the V-8 was an entirely new type with a different arrangement than the Mi-4 and Mi-6. It featured an extensively glazed cockpit section with great visibility for the crew and large clamshell doors at the end of the fuselage. Rotors and many other systems were transferred from the Mi-4 type to limit both development time and risk. Despite the lack of suitable engines for the twin-engine configuration on the market, Mil himself started to talk with the Leningrad-based OKB No. 117 engine bureau led by Sergey Petrovich Isotov. As a result of various consultations, Isotov proposed a new engine to be developed together with a brand-new gearbox. Such a proposal from a well-known design bureau was accepted by the Soviet ministerial council, and Mil was granted in 1960 with a directive to develop in parallel both single-engine and twin-engine V-8 variants. The 1960 directive tasked OKB No. 117 with developing a TV2-117 turboshaft engine with 932 kW output as well as a VR-8 main gearbox. As the projected V-8 model became heavier during design work, two engines with a total output of 1,864 kW seemed to be a better fit than a single 1,416 kW engine. On the other hand, compared to the Mi-4, to reach the same range, twice as much fuel had to be carried. This is why external fuselage tanks were designed, a feature never used on Mi-4s. In parallel, since 1959, Mil EDB worked on a V-8G (*gidro*—water) project of a helicopter intended for submarine localisation and destruction.

The first V-8 prototype was finished in the summer of 1961 with ground tests at Panki and flight untethered tests initially performed at Ismailovo airport. However, such an airport was soon closed and used for building new houses. This is why the maiden flight took place at Tushino airfield. The maiden flight of AI-24-powered V-8 happened on 24 June 1961. In the summer of 1962, the OKB No. 329 received the

V-8AT prototype, in serial production called Mi-8. Although with passenger interior, on the nose there is a mount for the A-12.7 machine gun and the weapon racks could have been installed on sides. (*MVZ Mil*)

UB-16-57 folding fin aerial rocket pods of 57mm calibre on the Mi-8T helicopter. Basically, every transport Mi-8T was theoretically capable of carrying weapons. (*Author*)

first set of TV2-117 engines and VR-8 three-stage planetary gearbox. One V-8 was therefore converted into the V-8A modification with new powerplant arrangement. The first hovering took place on 2 August 1962. The twin-engine variant prevailed and entered the serial production as Mi-8, becoming a real workhorse of the Soviet army aviation. As a main production plant the Kazan aircraft production facility No. 387 was selected and the Mi-8 replaced the Mi-4 there. The first Mi-8 drawings of production jigs were released to the company in early 1964. Because only limited overlap of Mi-4 and Mi-8 production was expected, the later type utilised many of the Mi-4 shops in the production company and in 1966 phased out the earlier type entirely. Some five years later another parallel plant was selected for Mi-8 production in order to meet the high domestic and export demands for the new type. This time the Ulan Ude Aviation Plant No.39 near Baikal Lake was selected. For the Mi-8 type many new on-board systems were developed and used on following types later. After several years a specific armed model named Mi-8TV with the Mi-4AV armament set was approved for production.

The parallel V-8G project was intended to replace the piston-powered Mi-4M naval helicopters. Their performance did not allow for further expansion of the carried equipment. Therefore, Mil decided to build a new helicopter designed for anti-submarine warfare. The helicopters were not to operate from ships, but from coastal bases. In the elongated nose section, the helicopter was supposed to carry a surveillance radar. It was planned that the helicopter would carry gondolas for retractable landing gear on the sides of the fuselage. The aircraft was supposed to be able to land on water in an emergency. However, in 1962, Soviet authorities decided to change the project. It was no longer to be an installation of equipment into an existing helicopter, but the construction of a purely amphibious aircraft equipped with special means and much increased performance. The project was designated V-14. Mil received the exact assignment on 14 April 1965. Mil wanted to speed up development and production as much as possible, so he used as many parts from an existing Mi-8 helicopter. Even the V-14 airframe came from this type no matter it was heavily modified for amphibious operation. The solution proved successful and shortened the development of the prototype to just two years. Because the anti-submarine equipment including means of submarine destruction was very heavy and the integration of the boat-shaped fuselage also increased the helicopter weight, Mil's designers had to find ways to increase performance. The use of a third TV2-117 engine was considered, but this would have required a complete reconstruction of the dynamic system with many penalties in terms of complexity and weight. Therefore, the project of a new engine, which was being considered at the Izotov's design office OKB No. 117 yet without state authorisation, was preferred. This engine was named TV3-117 and offered a 30 per cent higher performance with slightly lower weight and practically the same installation requirements. However, at the time of completion of the first prototype, it was still not available, so the first V-14 had to use the older TV2-117 engines. The first flight of the V-14 was made on 1 August 1967. It was not until September 1967 when the manufacturing plant delivered four prototype TV3-117 engines, and the designers installed two of them in the airframe of the fourth prototype. Their installation required the replacement of the main gearbox with a new type called VR-14. The tail rotor remained on the right side, only to be moved to the left during testing as the analyses showed its higher efficiency in the new position. With the TV3-117 engine, and from 1969 TV3-117M, the V-14 underwent most of the factory tests. This is how Mil got to the TV3-117 turboshaft engine, which is powering the majority of its models up to now.

The TV3-117 turboshaft engine may be considered as a marvel of Soviet aviation engine engineering. Unlike from other Soviet jet engines this type was powerful, lightweight and fuel efficient, while those attributes can be hardly found with contemporary Soviet engines. Its design was launched in 1964 as an internal project of the OKB No. 117. In April 1966 a detailed specification was finally drafted for prototype engine parts to be built and in December that year the first engine was finished. Its initial weight of 216kg dry weight of the core and 295kg with accessories was far below 334kg of the previous TV2-117 type with 30 per cent extra power. To achieve 1,491 kW of the take-off regime and even 1,640 kW of emergency regime, which was dramatically exceeding the 1,118 kW of the TV2-117A model, meant to use brand new materials and technologies. The TV3-117 engine became the very first one in the USSR helicopter industry to use titanium parts compromising almost 50 per cent of the parts, graphite sealing elements, analogue control system with hydraulic back up or inlet vane guides

Above: Mil Mi-14PL anti-submarine helicopter operated by the Soviet naval aviation. This was the first helicopter to use TV3-117 family engines. (*MVZ Mil*)

Below: TV3-117V engines of the Mi-24V helicopter. Note the massive hydromechanical control units and air starters on the top. (*Author*)

for four stages of the compressor. It became also the very first Soviet engine benefiting from machine-controlled welding during production. Yet still the engine had significant power safety margin as the design was calculated for 1,938 kW shaft output power. Since the first engine was finished, it took five years to reach the design goal and get the final type. Curiously the state committee formalised the development no sooner than on 6 May 1968, when the engine was already under testing.

During the later stage of the development ten engines were passing 300 hours endurance tests simultaneously but the turbine over-torque occurred and the test had to be repeated after technical remedy of the error cause. The 300 hours endurance tests were finally finished in August 1972 and total of sixteen test engines run 15,855 hours on the test benches and 2,755 hours in the V-14 and V-24 prototypes as well as in the initial series of Mi-14 and Mi-24 models. The TV3-117 became the most thoroughly tested soviet helicopter engine in the history. Yet before the end of the state tests the serial production was officially launched on 9 September 1970 at the Zaporozhiye engine production plant (now the Motor Sich company, heavily destroyed by the Russian forces during war on Ukraine). The initial production was labelled as 'verification series' while from 1973 it became regular serial production. Altogether some 200 engines were delivered till end of 1972 and all were named as '1st serie' and were operated usually only within 50 hours service life. All were later scrapped without any option for their overhaul or refurbishment. In the '2nd serie' of engines some 2,000 units were produced till 1976 and those remained in operation with initial time between overhaul of 300 hours gradually increased to 500 or 575 flight hours.

In 1977 the '3rd serie' was launched in the production with 750 and later series with 1,000 and even 1 500 hours of time between overhaul were introduced. Also, the service life of the engine was gradually increased from the initial 600 hours up to the total value of 4,500 flight hours. The TV3-117 engine became real engine of choice which proved its excellent parameters in thousands of copies flying worldwide in no less than 5 helicopter types. The engine was designed and tested with a very wide involvement of Mil design office experts, who contributed significantly to its final success. Its creation helped to solve one of the key issues of all helicopter designers—to have light yet powerful engine.

Simultaneously, there was progress in the development of combat helicopters abroad, particularly in the USA. The concept of aerial calvary became irrepressible and Soviet air force, which was back then operating Mi-1 and Mi-4 helicopters, was falling behind its major geopolitical rival. In 1965, the prototype of the Bell Model 209 helicopter was introduced in the USA, and two years later, its deliveries to the US army under the name AH-1 Huey Cobra started. The Americans, increasingly drawn into the Vietnam War, ordered over 500 combat helicopters, and in 1967, these machines first appeared in combat deployment in Asia. However, part of the Soviet general staff did not see the AH-1 model as a threat and considered the AAFSS (Army's Advanced Aerial Fire Support System) competition, officially launched in 1964, to be more significant. The winner of this competition was announced in 1966 as Lockheed with its heavy combat model YAH-56 Cheyenne. Compared to the AH-1, it was a very sophisticated type, adapted for flight not only at night but also in adverse weather conditions, capable of flight speeds exceeding 350 km/h. From a design perspective, the AH-56 was relatively conventional, but it contained many new technologies. For example, titanium elements in the main rotor head, including the blade construction, were designed by the famous Skunk Works workshops. The helicopter had a four-blade main rotor and a four-blade tail rotor. At the end of the tail boom, there was also a pusher propeller, which at high speeds was the main element creating propulsion force. During fast forward flight, most of the lift was generated by the wings, and the rear propeller took up to 85 per cent of the engine power. The rear propeller could also create reverse thrust, allowing the machine to fly forwards or backwards without having to lower or elevate the nose. The cockpit was very advanced. Due to strict requirements in the army's specifications, the pilot had access to an advanced avionics system with CRT screens, and the AH-56 was among the first helicopters in the world with such equipment. The operator sat in a special rotating seat coupled with the weapon aiming system, and when the 7.62mm machine gun under the fuselage moved, the seat rotated in the direction of fire.

The first prototype was completed in May 1966 and four months later, on 21 September, the second prototype took off for the first time. During the first flights, the ship achieved good performance and speeds exceeding 230 km/h and amazed all observers with the helicopter's excellent manoeuvrability. On the other hand, the ship suffered from vibrations and other stability issues. After factory flights, Lockheed decided to undergo civil registration with the US Federal Aviation Administration. Although the AH-56 was a military type, it was supposed to be the first mass-produced helicopter with a rigid rotor that could also find use in civilian applications. Although the AH-56 tests continued, the army did not have enough funds in the budget to purchase helicopters, as a significant portion of the expenses was drained by the Vietnam War expands. Despite all the difficulties, at least some money was found for the preparation of the production line. The army considered an order for 375 machines, which was a quarter of the originally expected amount. Before its issuance, however, there was a fatal accident of the third AH-56 prototype. After familiarising with its causes, US army representatives demanded the elimination of problems with vibrations and rotor oscillations. Although Lockheed tried to resolve the deficiencies, the US army stopped development in 1969, stating that the AH-56 did not meet the requirements in terms of weight, some performance and safety indicators, and the ability to operate at night and under difficult conditions. It is paradoxical that, for example, the stabilisation system developed by the manufacturer later eliminated most of the deficiencies. Instead in 1972, the US army announced a new tender for a combat helicopter, with high speed no longer being a decisive criterion. The winner was the AH-64 Apache type.

By the end of the 1960s, the AAFSS project was still in full swing, and from the Soviet perspective, it seemed that the AH-1 was a type intended for immediate reinforcement of units in Vietnam, while AH-56 helicopters would be deployed in large numbers in Europe. American advancement firmly formulated need to develop a brand-new Soviet attack helicopter able to cope with the US threat. The lack of attack type in the inventory of the Soviet army was something of constant stress for a part of the Soviet military headquarters. While some high rank officials preferred ballistic weapons, others understood the need to have such conventional weapon mean. The modification of Mi-4 model was effective way of utilising old airframes, but it was unable to compete with the latest US counterparts in terms of firing accuracy, reliability, robustness and tolerance against battle damage. Neither the adoption of the Mi-4AV weapon system on the Mi-8TV was fulfilling the expectations. An idea to launch a work on the creation of a brand-new attack type was started to be accepted. This is how the fundamental requirements for the Mi-24 were laid down although yet not accepted by all generals. The AH-56 was perceived as the main future adversary for the new Soviet attack type and the new Soviet model was expected to overcome its American counterpart in many areas. The information about the AH-56 project cancellation came too late to change this course. In the Soviet army a successful parallel was found. The BMP-1 infantry fighting vehicle was recently introduced and it combined troop-carrying capability with substantial fire power, something what was considered as ideal even for the rotary wing aviation. The Mil's team even visited the BMP-1 trials to see the value of the type for the army and its tactics. The first dedicated attack helicopter considered by the Mil Design Bureau was intended primarily for fighting enemy tanks and infantry vehicles. However, the troop-transport capability remained an essential task in the minds of soviet generals and therefore a 'flying infantry vehicle' was designed instead of pure attack type. Such approach allowed to build a versatile rather than single-purpose type with lower risk of rejection from the General Staff. After all, everybody was able to find his key role in the new design, which was able to fight with the enemy's tanks and infantry, transport troops or evacuate wounded soldiers like the novel BMP-1 infantry vehicles did. Additionally, there was no direct counterpart in the West and Mil fought for the idea of going own way. Several parallel options were under consideration such as modification of the Mi-2 or Mi-8 types, but all were rejected.

Integration of armour protection basically required a new helicopter to be build and so did the General Staff require at the end. Two brand new projects were prepared by Mil Design Bureau based on recommendations and comments of all officials. The first was a 7-ton helicopter powered by a single AI-24-type engine (like the V-8 prototype) with increased power, while the second project envisaged 10.5-ton helicopter with two TV3-117 engines. In total three different mock-ups and five nose sections were evaluated before a final configuration was selected.

In 1966 a brand-new mock-up of the 7-ton type designated the V-24 with appropriate '24' fuselage code was revealed by the Mil OKB (some sources call it V-22, but it seems to be incorrect as the mock-up fuselage code usually matches the type name). It resembled the US UH-1 helicopter in many aspects with clear heritage from the V-8 type revealed by its very long tail boom creating almost half of the total length. It had a cockpit for two pilots with side-by-side seating, in front of a large cargo cabin for eight troopers. The helicopter was supposed to be armed with a GSh-23 twin-barrel cannon and four anti-tank guided missiles of new type. Like the Mi-6 it was equipped with a wing taking some of the load of the main rotor and also providing for weapons carriage. The helicopter was expected to be powered by a single AI-24 engine (some sources say TV3-117 but it was not mentioned in available Mil's notes) installed above the cabin. The engine powered three-bladed main rotor and three-bladed tail rotor. The concept included armouring of the engine and main gearbox, which actually came from the V-8 prototype to save time and effort, as well as of key elements of the control system. The pilots were sitting behind flat glass panels made of multilayer ballistic-tolerant glass. Because of use of metallic armouring, no low-segment visors were incorporated into the concept. This mock-up was displayed to several top Ministry of Defence officials. A large number of those led by the minister Marshal Rodion Y. Yakovlevich Malinovsky himself rejected it, favouring more traditional weapons, but Mikhail Mil managed to persuade some younger top-ranking officers to back the idea. Among those, the first deputy Marshal Andrey A. Grechko was the major supporter who liked the idea of having a dedicated attack helicopter. However, even so the proposed mock-up was rejected as 'not sufficiently advanced'. It was so serious that one of the top-ranking generals said that Mil himself shall be sat into a helicopter and sent to combat to see what kind of nonsense he presents. The V-24 concept was in some reports even described as 'useless due to apparent superiority of the existing armament of the major opponent'. It looked like Mil and his team had to start from scratch, but quite opposite was actually true. Some engineers later recalled in their memories that it was the Mil's brilliant mind who created this almost fake display. In reality, there was no real plan to neither design in detail nor produce the V-24 like it was presented. It was Mil himself who decided to show to the general staff a project, which was significantly lagging behind the development in the USA. At the time of the V-24 mock-up presentation, it was still uncertain whether any development of a Soviet attack helicopter would take place at all. Viewing the V-24 mock-up, including Mil's own commentary highlighting the advancements of the American AH-56 model using posters carefully prepared by his colleagues, left an indelible impression on the minds of Soviet generals about lagging behind the USA. Marshal Andrey A. Grechko, although very friendly to Mil, had to interrupt his excited speech with a subsidy to leave on the army experts to make their own idea about attack helicopters and potential of their battlefield deployment. Also, some design features of the presented V-24 mock-up were at least problematic such as landing skids, while all Soviet army helicopters up to that time used wheeled undercarriage for easy moving of the ships even on the grassy field. The final decision of the general staff was eventually not about whether a new attack helicopter should be developed or not, but finally what it should be like. Mil unequivocally won because he managed to push through the proposal for the development of an attack helicopter with this small ruse.

Luckily for Mil, Marshal Malinovsky left his position with Marshal Grechko being nominated as Minister of defence in 1967. Based on the smart negotiation led by Mil himself, a state competition was launched personally by Marshal Grechko on 29 March 1967 for a new attack type. The proposition required a new helicopter capable of destroying enemy tanks as well as fortifications or even soldiers. The alternative role was supposed to be to carry eight fully equipped soldiers and support them with fire after disembarking as well as insertion of diversion units behind the enemy lines with capability to defend itself against any threat. Another task was medical evacuation of two patients on stretchers and two sitting patients with one medical attendant. The new type was supposed to reach maximum speed of at least

Above: The 7-tonne class V-24 helicopter mock-up—the inspiration in the UH-1 Huey is more than visible. Note the GSh-23 twin-barrel cannon under it as well as dummy anti-tank missiles. (*MVZ Mil*)

Below: Another shot of the initial V-24 mock-up with a line-up of the eight troops it could carry. The model resembled the UH-1 with extremely long tail boom inherited from V-8 prototype. (*MVZ Mil*)

315 km/h and ideally 320 to 350 km/h, have hovering ceiling in hot environment of 1 500 metres at least and 3,000 metres in standard atmosphere, have the capability to reach a maximum G-load during mid-speed manoeuvring up to 1.7g and to reach 45° bank angles and 30° angle of attack flights. The cabin and selected components were expected to be ballistically protected from hits from up to 12.7mm bullets. The desired armament was consisting of S-5 unguided rockets, free fall bombs, cluster submunition cannisters and machine gun in a turret. For destruction of enemy tasks the in-development Shturm missile was required to be integrated. Mil naturally joined the competition with the below mentioned V-24 project and so did Mil's main rival, the Kamov design bureau.

The Kamov Ka-25F attack helicopter, presented only through small model and drawings, was a substantial modification of the Ka-25PL naval type. When the competition for the new Soviet attack type was opened, the Ka-25PL was already in service, and this was considered as a strategic advance by the Kamov team as it significantly lowered the development risk. Last but not least, the Ka-25F project was proposed for less than two thirds of the projected unit cost of the V-24. For the attack Ka-25F, basically just the platform with the engines, main gearbox, transmission and tail boom were kept, while the entire fuselage was expected to be designed and built

Kamov Ka-25F model showing the GSh-23 twin-barrel cannon of 23mm calibre in a turret under the fuselage. The model presents transport configuration and lacks anti-tank weapons. (*Kamov*)

brand new. A crew of pilot and weapon-system operator sat in the front cockpit, while behind there was a space for up to eight fully equipped soldiers. The cabin was expected to be lightly armoured in the primary construction. Instead of the original wheeled undercarriage, large skids were proposed as a solution, enabling landing in a variety of environments—no matter that the ground handling on grassy airfields would be problematic. The concept was clearly inspired by the American UH-1 helicopters and presented a deviation from the traditional Kamov scheme. The powerplant consisted of two GTD-350F turboshaft engines, retained from the original type. The layout with counter rotating rotors and no tail rotor was marketed by Kamov as a major advantage as it removed the risk of tail-rotor hit and helicopter loss, a typical scenario in combat. The armament was to consist of an under-belly turret with GSh-23 twin barrel 23mm cannon, six UB-16-57 blocks for S-5 rockets and 9M17 ATGMs and below described Shturm ATGMs as well as free fall bombs. The weapon array was expected to be extended in the future. All the weapons were detachable and the helicopter could serve either in the transport or attack role.

Mil proposed another model marked V-24—this time resembling the Mi-24 as we know it now. It was a dual-purpose transport and attack type built around components already extensively used on the Mi-8 and Mi-14 family. It was a conventional helicopter with a five-bladed main rotor and a three-bladed tail rotor, powered by two TV3-117 engines. The maximum take-off weight was to exceed 11 tonnes, but this was not a problem for the two most powerful engines at the time. The main VR-24 gearbox was developed by modifying the VR-8 and VR-14 types from the Mi-8 and Mi-14 helicopters. It was reducing the nominal 1,500rpm of the engine output shaft to 240rpm to the main rotor shaft and 3,237rpm to the tail rotor gearbox. The ratio changed when the engine was spooled up to take-off revolutions.

Mil tried to make maximum use of established components, so the dynamic system of the Mi-24 is similar in many details to that of the Mi-14. This fact defined the dimensions of the future helicopter as the engines are located in front of the gearbox, determining the dimensional proportions of the entire machine. The V-24 was to receive completely new rotor blades optimised for high-speed flights. However, these could not be completed due to a large number of problems encountered during wind tunnel measurements. The nose of the helicopter was designed to be extensively glazed, and in Mil's design office, it was given the working designation 'veranda,' referring to the extensive glazing. This was designed to ensure the best possible view for the weapon systems operator sitting in the front and the pilot sitting in the back. The shape of the cabin was optimised for a long time to have the lowest possible frontal resistance and to help achieve high cruising speeds. In the transport configuration with empty underwing hardpoints, the frontal area of the helicopter was 2.12m^2, while in the combat configuration with armament stores it was 2.75m^2, which was still less than values of the purely transport Mi-8T with a frontal area of 3m^2 (and almost 5m^2 when weapon stores were installed).

The middle section of the fuselage and the tail boom were interestingly tilted 2°30' to the right (when viewed from the rear) for aerodynamic reasons, as well as the main rotor shaft being tilted 4°30' forward. The side tilt partially compensates for the reaction torque of the main rotor, and as a result, the wings are in a level position during flight. This adjustment significantly impacts the firing accuracy of the weapons mounted on the wings. Behind the pilot's cabin was the cargo cabin, designed to transport up to eight fully armed soldiers, or cargo weighing 1,300kg, or alternatively two auxiliary fuel tanks with a capacity of 850 litres of fuel each. Access to it was secured by double-wing doors on both sides, which opened with the top part upwards, and the bottom part downwards. The lower part also served as a step for soldiers to board and contained an armour plate that protected the soldiers when in the closed position. The upper part of the door had two windows, and the cabin behind it had two more on each side of the fuselage. All windows were openable, and below them were foldable pintle mounts for the personal weapons of the transported soldiers. This allowed them to cover the helicopter with fire during flight or landing. The portside door was by some 3cm higher to allow installation of internal auxiliary fuel tanks. The cabin, like the cockpit, was hermetically sealed so that the helicopter could fly in contaminated environments. The tail boom had a large cross-section and was designed to smoothly transition into the fuselage. It ended with a keel beam with an enormous area of 2.8m², which provided up to two-thirds of the force needed to counteract the reaction torque of the main rotor during high-speed flights. Due to the significantly

Mil's final V-24 concept mock-up. Note the UB-32-24 rocket blocks behind as well as auxiliary fuel tanks and bombs of unknown type under the wing. (*MVZ Mil*)

higher speed, the keel beam is much larger than that of the Mi-8 or Mi-14. The V-24 helicopter also had a distinctive feature—a straight un-swept wing. This wing was designed to offload the main rotor during high-speed flights. Additionally, it allowed the helicopter to carry four hardpoints for unguided weapons. A lot of attention was paid to the serviceability of the helicopter in field conditions. The engine and main gearbox cowlings were designed in such a way that when opened, they served as a working platform for the mechanic. The main and tail rotor blades as well as wings, were designed for quick disassembly so the helicopter could easily and swiftly be loaded onto a railway transport platform or into a cargo aircraft.

One of the most complex elements of the V-24 helicopter was the landing gear. To achieve the required speeds a fixed landing gear could not have been used. In accordance with established Soviet aviation procedures, Mil did not want to use skids which would not be advantageous for a heavy type for many reasons. Therefore, the landing gear was designed as a three-point retractable system. Although it made the landing gear relatively heavy, it came with minimal drag when retracted. Due to the size of the low-pressure tyres they are not fully accommodated in the fuselage when retracted and so bulges on the lower fuselage are typical when retracted. The landing gear was designed to be hydraulically operated and can be deployed even in an emergency situation after a hydraulic system failure. The helicopter's armament was to consist of a movable turret with GSh-23 cannon of 23mm calibre and UB-32-24 pods for unguided S-5 rockets of 57mm calibre, bombs weighing up to 250kg. Mil's design bureau had access to the development data of the new Shturm anti-tank missile and the helicopter design team was in close contact with the missile OEM from the time of the Mi-1MU and Mi-4 tests, which allowed for frequent consultations.

The Shturm missile was developed in two variants—Shturm-S for ground application and Shturm-V for aerial craft such as helicopters. It was designed by KBM design bureau from the city of Tula. It took into account the previous experience with older missiles, developing the requirement for supersonic speed for technological and timing reasons. The subsonic speed of previous models meant the weapon operator had to hold the aiming cross on the target for the whole flight of the missile, which could be more than 30 seconds for the maximum range. Enough time for the tank to deploy a smoke screen or execute an evasive manoeuvre to hide. The very same problem was faced by Western designers as well and it was not until mid-1970s when the American AGM-114 Hellfire missile, with a supersonic speed of Mach 1.3, occurred.

The supersonic capability of lightweight missiles was not easy to achieve. The Soviet military industry had tried to tackle the problem since 1967 and the Shturm missile was supposed to break the sound barrier. The design goals asked for speed of 2,016 km/h. That would allow to reach the 5 kilometre maximum distance in little over 10 seconds! To achieve such high speed, the missile was designed with minimum frontal resistance and a very sleek body, which was equipped with wrap-around spring-loaded fins at the rear end, inducting the rotation for better accuracy, and pop-up elevators in the front section. To save weight, the missile could use only one guidance radio channel and the programming and pairing on the level of its launching helicopter had to be done when hooked on the pylon. The helicopter coding sequences allowed for maximum of ten helicopters to be deployed simultaneously without risk of improper commands.

To avoid the handover, the infrared tracers used some coding which needed to be paired with the simple electronics of the guidance system. The missile was launched from a special sealed tube container made of fibreglass. It worked as a launch tube as well as a storage container, allowing the missile to remain maintenance free for ten years. The speed of the missile flight and increased accuracy of the guidance system allowed for the launch in fast flights instead of hovering or slow speed flight like with the 9M17 type. The missile weight was 31.4kg, including a 5.3 high explosive anti-tank warhead. It could penetrate up to 650mm of rolled homogeneous armour or equivalent, and the final supersonic speed was 1,240 km/h. This distinctly shortened the time the helicopter was exposed to enemy fire while guiding the missile towards the target. On the other hand, the higher speed was achieved at the cost of higher drag and fuel consumption. This was why the 9M114 diameter was much smaller and there were two motors to ensure a reasonable range. The 9M114 could be used not only against armed and stationary targets on the ground, but also in non-contact (proximity) mode against slow-speed flying targets such as helicopters and transport planes. However, the Shturm missile was not available at the time of V-24 helicopter development. During one of the discussions with the army command, Mil was also advised to use a machine gun with a high rate of fire instead of the cannon. The destruction of hardened targets or armoured vehicles was supposed to be done via the unguided rockets, while the cannon in a turret could be used for destruction of human targets and soft-armoured vehicles, or even helicopters. Mil proposed a provisional weapon kit for the V-24.

The projects of both Mil and Kamov were seriously considered, although the evaluation was only in terms of paper exercise. Kamov defended his project as more agile with a lower development and production cost—and it must be noted that the avionics of Ka-25PL significantly exceeded those of Mi-8. However, although the naval Ka-25PL models had performed quite well in service, the Ka-25F was rejected. Mil apparently pulled all the strings available to him through his previous work with the army and the committee selected his design. This is how the very rigid specialisation of Kamov for naval helicopters and Mil for army helicopters was confirmed. It was even told in some unofficial sources that Mil then decided not to continue in the development of amphibious helicopters and focused on those for the army only. Mil won, and the V-24 was about to be produced. It dramatically differed from the above-mentioned mock-up. The is how the Mi-24, as the initial serial variant was called, was born. Kamov did not give up and used the experience gained in the Ka-25Sh attack model introduced in 1975. This helicopter was intended to be a low-cost solution to convert older Ka-25PLs into a transport-attack type for marines, while newer Ka-27s were delivered to the navy. However, this project also failed. Kamov still persisted and in the late 1970s promoted other combat concepts such as the V-50 tandem model and later V-80 coaxial project, which finally reached serial production in the 1990s as the Ka-50 and, later, Ka-52. Those models were, however, competitors of the Mi-28, not the Mi-24.

On 6 May 1968, a government directive was issued requiring V-24 full design and prototype work to begin. The V-24 concept was officially accepted in August 1968, and work on a prototype was launched. After the death of Mikhail L. Mil in January

Kamov Ka-25Sh—an attack conversion of a naval helicopter which was abandoned as not even levelling the Mi-4 capabilities. (*Kamov*)

1970, his deputy, Marat Nikolayevich Tischenko, became the chief of design. The official order for prototype construction was also signed in May 1968. Many technical solutions such as the swashplate, scheme of the transmission shaft and main gearbox were adopted and modified from the Mi-14 model which was undergoing trials at that time. In some sources TV2-117 engines are mentioned as the powerplant of the V-24, but this is incorrect. Those engines were electrically started and required no APU, but they also had a different length and exhaust tailpipe shape. The dimensions of the dynamic system hampered design work considerably. For the new helicopter, engineers wanted to develop new rotor blades, but the design work on this element progressed poorly. Due to expected maximum speed of 350 km/h, Mil had wanted to create a new type of rotor blade with asymmetric airfoil and specific blade tips. The theoretical works supported feasibility of the ultra-high speeds, but not so the aerodynamic tunnel tests. The main rotor blade with titanium spar and aluminium honeycomb covered by glass fibre did not have the expected stiffness and twisted under heavy loads, with subsequent stall. Therefore, a temporary solution was adopted and eventually the rotor blades for the Mi-24 were created in a very interesting way—the manufacturing plant took the rotor blade from the Mi-8, used its spar and leading edge, and took the trailing edge from the blades for the Mi-4. This approach led to the rapid creation of a usable rotor with a diameter 2 metres smaller when compared to the Mi-8, but greater blade depth by 20mm. However, it also led to the deterioration of some flight characteristics. This is why, for example, the Mi-24 in Afghanistan and other places achieved much worse flight parameters than the Mi-8MT powered by the same engines.

The rotor blades for all prototypes were made at Kazan helicopter plant, where the production of the honeycomb design was fully mastered. As in everyday life, such a provisional solution turned out to become permanent, and all serial Mi-24s ever since were using such design. Although the development of new rotor blades was ongoing, the concept of a planned economy of the Soviet aviation industry prevented any experiments with new technologies, putting the bonus scheme of all involved workers at risk.

Marat Nikolayevich Tischenko, respected hard worker who fine-tuned the Mi-24 concept to perfection and serial production. (*MVZ Mil*)

The V-24 fuselage was narrow with a cockpit for the pilot and weapon systems operator in a common cabin in front of the fuselage. Behind it there was a cargo cabin with a large stub wing on each side serving as a platform for weapons carrying with four hard points. The fuselage continued with a large tail boom with tail fin, and three-bladed tail rotor. The wing helped to reduce load on the main rotor during high-speed flight by up to 25 per cent. The wing aerodynamic analyses were already available from the giant Mi-6 type which used similar devices. Because the fuselage was quite long, a large stabiliser was attached to the tail boom. It helped to maintain the lateral balance. The dynamic system included hydraulic boosters to reduce control forces on the sticks. The design was in daily management led by Tischenko in behalf of the Mil Design Bureau. The office was further supported by other governmental entities. The Zhukovskyi-based (city south of Moscow) GK NII VVS Flight Research Institute of the air force helped with aerodynamics and overall design; a Red Banner Scientific Research institute was responsible for the cabin design in respect of the instruments integration; Moscow-based NII AS MAP scientific research institute for aviation systems dealt with the combat survivability measures; Lyubertsy-based (same location as Mil's office) NII ERAT scientific technical institute worked on aircraft operation and serviceability, including camouflage; and finally, Zhukovskyi-based TsAGI institute was responsible for the aerodynamics and specific aeroelasticity and other tests. All departments were supported by the air force specific departments which verified the work progress and results.

Originally, a turret with GSh-23 twin-barrel 23mm cannon was selected, but it was later rejected in order to comply with the requests of some Soviet generals. Instead, a new machine gun of 12.7mm calibre (9A-624 machine gun) was intended for integration, but it took too long to develop, so the easily available and proven A-12.7 machine gun of 12.7mm calibre was selected, although it did not bring any substantial battle value. It was fitted with simple K-10T collimator gunsight. For the V-24 a brand new NUV-1A mounting was developed from the K-4V aiming system borrowed from the Mi-4. The NUV-1 was not ready at the beginning of the V-24 testing, so the system was installed later and the initial flights occurred without it. The NUV-1 system was operated manually with a grip much like that on a bicycle handlebar by the weapons operator. Although the viewing angles were perfect, the smoke from the gunfire penetrated the cockpit and soon after the firing started the canopy was filled with smoke. On the other hand, the detachable cowling allowed the operator to reach the gun in case of shell jamming and he could fix such an issue in flight. As the main type of weapon the S-5 missiles were selected with a total of four UB-32-24 FFAR blocks, each with thirty-two rockets. In total, one helicopter could potentially carry up to 128 rockets. It doubled the capacity of previously used UB-16-57 blocks with sixteen rockets only, which could have been hooked as well. Both blocks were specialised for rotary wing platforms. During initial operation of the block it became obvious that the launched rocket suffered from the rotor downwash and so longer launching tubes were selected. Another option was the carriage of free-fall bombs in 50, 100 and 250kg weights on all pylons, and 500kg on the inner pylons only. There were several variants of bombs able to use the same racks. The options included general purpose FAB bombs, and high explosive and fragmentation OFAB bombs in all the aforementioned weights, ZAB-100 and ZAB-250 napalm bombs and SAB-100 and SAB-250 flare bombs. All those weapons were previously thoroughly tested on other types of aircraft and only needed accuracy and compatibility tests before being cleared for operation on the V-24.

The main missile weapon of the new helicopter should have been the new generation Shturm ATGM, but its development took longer than expected. Therefore, an alternative solution based on existing technology was selected. Eventually, to counter tanks and armoured vehicles, four 9M17M Phalanga ATGMs of the 9P146 system were installed on rails attached to the fuselage sides. Already during initial tests it became obvious that this location was not ideal. The missile was not very stable in the initial stage of flight and there were fears it might hit the fuselage. Additionally, during some tests it became apparent that when the helicopter climbed during S-5 salvo firing, some of the rockets could hit the tail surfaces of the ATGMs. Last but not least, when the ATGM missiles were installed the cargo cabin door could not be fully opened. This was not a problem initially, as the anti-tank and troop-transport roles were not expected to be performed at the same time. Although later it became a limiting factor, due to compliance with the original requirement it was not considered a dealbreaker. If the Shturm missiles had been ready with the compact launching tubes, there would have been no problem. The weapon systems operator commanded and guided the missile via a gunsight inside the cabin. Because of the lack of time, this solution was accepted with the expectation it would soon be updated.

The full-scale mock up with the appropriate fuselage code '24' was unveiled in February 1969. The prototype OP-1 followed just a few months later when it was towed from the prototype shop for its first engine run in mid-June 1969. Mil apparently did not wait for the state committee comments to the mock-up which was quite unusual and even little risky. The company flight tests of the OP-1 started on 15 September with ground runs. The first untethered flight occurred on 19 September 1969 with pilot German Vitalievich Alfyorov at the controls. The maiden flight occurred without the stub wings and with large measurement probe on the nose. Alfyorov was selected

The first V-24 prototype during late stage of testing, with the A-12.7 machine gun removed. Note the car-style entry door to the pilot's station. (*MVZ Mil*)

for his detailed approach and broad methodological preparation for each flight. He had previously been the second pilot in the Mi-6 maiden flight, solo pilot in the Mi-2 flight and large Mi-10K, and also second pilot in the giant V-12 twin-rotor helicopter. Some of Mil's test pilots later recalled that Mil himself insisted on selection of the test pilot while in the design phase. The pilot, after all, should know all about the helicopter he is about to fly not when it leaves the prototype shop, but while it is being born. Also, Mil preferred young people and so all the engineering sections were led by people in their early 30s, but not so with test pilots. As Mil allegedly said, a test pilot should have grey hair because that is the only evidence he did his job correctly. He added that another requirement was 'the luck needed for the demanding job'.

Several Soviet generals came to witness one of the initial flights and were very satisfied with the result. Even the then Soviet leader Leonid Brezhnev was informed about the successful flights. Such attention to company tests was unusual and may be understood as the sign of importance of the attack helicopter programme for the Soviet leadership. The first prototype was a giant attack type when compared to American counterparts and Mil knew how to present it properly. He left to tow out the unfinished second prototype OP-2 out of the assembly hall when the generals came and displayed it with all the weapons around it. The wide weapon array was more than impressive as it was in the area of unguided weapons more or less the same one like the frontline fighters used.

Both prototypes were built by the Mil's experimental shop at Panki near Moscow. The design was managed by Mil and Tischenko, the actual design work was managed by V.A. Kuznetsov as Tischenko's deputy (Tischenko was overwatching other programmes as well). Major design and management part was performed by engineers V. M. Olshevets, V. D. Zernov and B. V. Smyslov, all Mil bureau veterans with a vast experience from design process of Mi-1 and Mi-4. By the end of the year some forty flights had been achieved. In 1970, the loss of the first OP-1 V-24 prototype helicopter occurred during a flight demonstration, with three experienced crew members being killed. Pilot M. A. Materialnyi was trying to show the very best of the helicopter performance and unfortunately hit the ground during recovery from the combat manoeuvre. The helicopter hit a nearby textile production facility and burst into the flames with all crew members killed instantly. The position of the first prototype was taken over by the OP-2 ship, which was then used for the company tests. It was the very first ship which suffered an in-flight engine surge and was also experiencing significant engine-blade erosion during hot climatic trials. It became apparent the engines required dust and debris protection because without it there was a possibility that overhaul would be needed after only a few flights.

After two V-24 prototypes had been built by Mil's experimental shop, the Soviet Ministry of Defence granted an order for initial production of a total of ten more

The very first V-24 prototype during display of its armament with UB-32A-24 rocket pods and 9M17M anti-tank missiles. (*MVZ Mil*)

helicopters of which not all were designed for flight operation. In such configuration was the type given Izdeliye 240 internal serial code and yet unofficial designation Mi-24. However, the initial air force cadre immediately nicknamed the type 'Crocodile', referring to the shape of the main landing gear legs and silhouette of the original nose. The nickname stuck and is still used in Russia today. In total, five helicopters were made by the experimental shop of the Mil Design Bureau and five more by the Arsenyev production plant. Four of the craft were intended for flight tests, one prototype for weapons tests, two for static tests, one for fatigue tests and the remaining two were intended to become patterns for serial production. As NATO observed the Mi-24 after spotting the below mentioned Mi-24A variant, it was given the Hind B code by the NATO Air Standard Coordinating Committee.

The Arsenyev production facility with the official name Aviation Facility No. 116, which was generally called 'Progress' and years later named after its post-war long-term general director N.I. Sazykin, was founded in 1936 in the Far East city of Arsenyev, well protected from the German troops. Mainly due to Sazykin the plant mastered the production of An-14 utility craft and improved its technological park. Unfortunately, the An-14 failed to replace the ubiquitous, legendary An-2 biplane and the production ended after some 332 units produced. The end of An-14 production was apparent to the company management well in advance, and Sazykin bet all on the new technology—attack helicopter.

Sazykin proposed support to Mil in terms of offloading his design department and developing and designing the production tooling on his own. Although it was the state committee of MAP who decided how the military production would be distributed, Sazykin managed to create conditions that could not be omitted when the planning took place. When the committee was deciding the location for the Mi-24 production, the Arsenyev plant already worked on the initial series of the helicopters and proposed by far the shortest delivery time. It was a heroic job of the Arsenyev general manager to secure the rotorcraft project.

The first Mi-24 built by the Mil Design Bureau was basically an unequipped airframe destined for full-scale fatigue tests, finished in 1970. They were performed by TsAGI and the prototype passed the tests without any issues with the original service life of 3,000 flight hours confirmed. The second and third Mi-24 helicopters built by the Mil Design Bureau were used for various flight tests and were supporting the weapons' trials later. Many improvements taken from the passed tests were incorporated in their design. After the end of the test programme, both were used for training purposes and were eventually passed to the military aviation college. In the late 1980s one was moved to an airplane junkyard and later scrapped. Finally, the fourth and fifth ship were designed for 9A-624 machine gun and Shturm ATGM testing including the 9S475 guidance system. The first Arsenyev-built helicopter missed many of the improvements introduced on the Mil-build ships as the launch of the production took some time and their incorporation became too demanding. So in reality it reflected the V-24 ship standard and was never finished up to the flyable condition, although it was almost complete. It served as a ground test bench for aggregates and some fatigue tests were performed on it as well. The second, third and fourth ships were used for flight tests and mainly training of the initial flight crews of the air force. They

The very first Mi-24 helicopter is being towed out of the final assembly hangar at the Arsenyev production facility. It was a major milestone in the programme. (*Progress*)

also participated in climatic tests and were operated in the northern Arctic areas as well as in southern deserts. The last Mi-24 served as testbed for 9A-624 machine gun with USPU-24 turret and Shturm ATGMs, but both systems were verified on other Mil-built prototypes as well.

The Mi-24 project gained a lot of attention from the Soviet top-level politicians and army officials. Therefore, many demonstrations were performed. Mil even showed the Mi-24s in combat-like scenario with live firing of unguided and anti-tank rockets. It was again supported by clever marketing when the target tank ended its career in an enormous fireball due to the full fuel drums hidden behind it. The Soviet generals were impressed—during one of the demonstrations one helicopter was able to hit three tanks, all with spectacular explosions. The Mi-24 was also presented to the foreign delegations, the first of which first saw it in early 1970. It became obvious that the type was about to face significant market interest. The Middle East and African countries were particularly impressed when the saw the aerial display and combat power. However, the Soviet MAP did not plan the export production before 1975 originally.

Manufacturer's trials were followed by state trials, which were launched in June 1970 and were managed by the chief engineer of the Soviet Air Force Flight Research Institute, S.K. Atabekyan. Testing showed that Mi-24 was a very agile helicopter with extreme speed and acceleration when compared with legacy Mi-4s and Mi-8s. The engines were found to be very reliable, though vulnerable to attrition from the sucked dust when operated in the dusty environment. The weapon trials confirmed the A-12.7 machine-gun accuracy, but its short range, low rate of fire and very low penetration capability. Due to the delay of 9A-624 machine gun, it was decided to approve the serial production with this weapon. The S-5 rocket launches showed the original UB-32-24 blocks were inadequately shaped and the accuracy was far behind the Mi-4AV model due to influence of the high speed-inducted vortexes and rotor downwash. As a solution, a new type of the block called UB-32A-24 was designed with carefully shaped rear part and different nose. The new shape helped to increase the accuracy. The 9M17M missiles were launched from 10 to 3,000 metres altitude and showed sufficient accuracy, range of up to 4,000 metres, but low reliability. The missile guidance system was evaluated as requiring the weapon systems operator to focus heavily. The manual guidance required low vibration and a relatively stable flight profile, which could hardly be guarranteed during combat. The guiding antenna was installed in the right section of the nose, next to the machine gun. This position was not ideal due to fixed installation with narrow field of view. The solution was found in the upgraded 9M17P missile variant with semi-automatic guidance system, mainly with the guidance antenna on the rotating platform allowing to track the targets even if not located directly in front of the helicopter. The KMGU cluster munition was not tested for timing reasons but was expected to be introduced as well.

State tests revealed several technical drawbacks of the new type. Those tests were not performed by Mil bureau test crews, but by the most experienced air force pilots from the Lipetsk-based test unit responsible for combat deployment tactics. Pilots complained about the poor view from the cockpit, insufficient directional control and stability problems in high-speed regimes. The canopy glazing limited the viewing angles, especially when the helicopter was taking off or landing, and the pilot lost the visual contact with the ground due to nose shape. Also, sitting a little left to the centre of the fuselage, the right side visibility was far from ideal. The worst visibility conditions were experienced during night landing where the flat glass panels created many confusing reflections, and the spatial orientation became very difficult. As Mil hesitated to redesign the plane, it was the Lipetsk unit report signed by the most experienced test pilots which ended any discussions. One of them, F. F. Prokopenko, a Second World War ace with nineteen aerial victories according to Russian sources, described the view from the cockpit as 'absolutely unsatisfactory', and since he held the title Hero of the USSR, nobody doubted to think differently. Prokopenko, who was flying Mi-1 and Mi-4 helicopters within the Lipetsk centre, was one of the most active test pilots helping to define the standard combat manoeuvres. His comments helped him to be valued by Mil design experts and from 1976 he worked in the Mil Design Bureau as a flight methodologist. His signature can be seen in every flight and operational manual published by Mil company ever since.

Prokopenko was supported by test pilot V. S. Elisyeev, another Second World War ace with fourteen aerial victories, who was well familiar not only with Mil helicopters, but also Ka-25. He provided to the Mil's team with a very extensive list of recommendations about how to make the control system and cockpit layout more pilot-oriented. During side flights or flights with cross wind, the tail rotor proved not to be sufficiently effective and the hovering and landing became very difficult in those conditions due to lack of the directional authority. When flying 200 km/h and more, a Dutch roll occurred and the pilot had to take constant corrective actions which was very tiring. The Dutch roll, an unintentional combination of roll and yaw movements with sideslip, looked from outside truly like an impressive ballet of the helicopter to the viewers on the ground, but of course it had to be corrected. Also, the overall performance in hot and high environments was a big disappointment. When tested at the southern areas of the USSR, the hovering ceiling in +30°C was less than 800 metres and in +40° it did not exceed 600 metres. What was more, the design of the main rotor in certain combat manoeuvres led to freezing of the controls as the hydraulic boosters were undersized to provide enough of power for overcoming the swashplates forces. Otherwise, the performance was phenomenal, and the test crews reached over 360 km/h in dive. It was not possible to remedy all the complaints without significant redesign of the helicopter, so Mil launched a development of the improved variant Mi-24A described below, which was the first version to reach full-scale serial production. Despite this, the Mi-24 Izdeliye 240 model became the first to be officially adopted by the Soviet army.

The original Mi-24 sans suffix fleet was used for various testing and Mil continued to work on proposals of various modifications. In 1970 a new Mi-24 project was considered for a prospective naval attack type. The initiative was granted with official state support and received the internal code name Izdeliye 247, with the expected in-service designation Mi-24M. The main task was anticipated to be the transport of crews from assault ships with following fire support. The initial study proposed foldable rotor blades and even tail boom, as well as TV3-117M engines with salt-water protection from the Mi-14 model. It was expected to use the flotation gear like the Mi-14 did. However, it was Tischenko who personally decided not to proceed for several reasons. At first he did not want to harm the Kamov design bureau efforts, as a part of the compensation for being unsuccessful in the V-24 competition, and also because he did not want to commit too much design capacity for such a project at a time when several Mil helicopters were being introduced into the service and required a lot of attention, not speaking about the Mi-24 itself facing a lot of problems. In spite of this decision Mil had to follow the governmental directive of 1973 requiring the prototype of a mine sweeping variant.

Even in this case he managed to strike a deal and presented his model as naval, yet with no capability to be operated from a ship's deck. This Mi-24 modification was given the designation Mi-24BMT, with Izdeliye 248 internal code. Its design was tasked as an emergency solution for Egypt who sought any means to de-mine the Suez channel. The new model, derived from V-24 prototype, completely lacked the weapon system with only two 350-litre auxiliary fuel tanks attached to the wings. Another fuel tank was installed in the cargo cockpit. To lower the weight the landing gear was blocked in the retracted position. Inside the rear part of the fuselage a special reel with a cable for a minesweeping device was installed with the sweeper attached to the rear underside when not in use. The mine-clearing device was to consist of two types of net—MT-34 for contact mines and SEMT-1 for non-contact magnetic ones. The cargo cabin was shortened, with the rear face now behind the third pair of windows. Both cockpits lacked all weapon systems, and the crew was to wear special protective inflatable suits. Only a single experimental model was finished in a form of one Mi-24 conversion and allegedly briefly tested at Fedosia on the Crimean Peninsula on the Black Sea coast. It was not adopted for regular service.

In the mid-1970s, Mil Design Bureau explored various ways of increasing the Mi-24 tail rotor's efficiency to both cope with insufficient directional authority and to reduce its vulnerability to ground fire in combat operation. One interesting variant was the Fenestron shrouded tail rotor. After careful evaluation of the French Sud Aviation SA 340 Gazelle concept and research on the design of the Aérospatiale SA 360 concept under development, the decision to elaborate on the shrouded tail rotor was taken. The new concept of tail rotor, later known worldwide as Fenestron (term for 'small window' derived from the Occitan language of Provence, so-named by the Aérospatiale team), seemed to propose both reduced drag and increased effectivity as well as lowering the vulnerability both to enemy fire and ground strike during combat landing. After detailed theoretical work, a decision was made to build a similar device and test it on the Mi-24. It should be noted that although the French helicopter company is generally recognised as the originator of the Fenestron, the first patent came from United Kingdom where the company G. & J. Weir Aircraft Department Ltd. patented a similar solution in 1943, but never manufactured it. At first a ground test rig utilising the Mi-24 airframe section from the static test was installed on a test bench in 1973 where experiments with various modifications were made. In 1975 a full-scale tail section was manufactured and attached to one of the Mi-24 prototypes. The seven-blade rotor was attached to a three-bladed stator. The tail section was heavily modified, including control rods. The prototype did not have wings, as high-speed flights were not expected during initial testing. Under the shrouded rotor a small skid was installed to prevent damage in case of tail strike during testing. The prototype made its maiden flight in December 1975 and proved the viability of the concept. However, the weight of the modification had a negative impact on the centre of gravity, resulting in the need to install a counterbalance weight in the nose. During some flights a simplified vibration damper was installed on the main rotor head. After several flights the project was stopped, as it was apparent it was not meeting the expected performance. In parallel, other much simpler approaches, as described below, were examined and eventually prevailed.

An Mi-24 converted with Fenestron tail rotor. It lacks the wings, the attachments of which were used for tethering the helicopter during ground tests. (*MVZ Mil*)

Detail of the Fenestron. Compared to the original French design, its efficiency was considerably lower. A relocation of the tail rotor was decided upon. (*MVZ Mil*)

When the Mi-24 type was created, it was obvious that this very powerful helicopter could be a good platform for record breaking, an activity frequently carried out by the USSR—particularly in competition with the USA. In the mid-1970s, another Mi-24 prototype was upgraded for this purpose. The ship is referred to as c/n 020024, but this seems to be to confuse spies because of the need to declare the details of the ship for international recognition of the record. By the sequence it can be interpreted as being the twenty-fourth aircraft of the second series, while in total only twelve ships of similar design were finished. The helicopter was streamlined in many areas with parts such as windshield wipers and tail skid deleted. Also the stub wings were deleted, with aerodynamic fairings over their roots. The complete military hardware and non-essential front cockpit equipment were deleted in order to reduce weight, and so major part of the navigation system and all military installations were deleted. TV3-117 engines were tuned for higher performance, at the cost of lowered time-between-overhaul limits, and on the head of the main rotor a large vibration damper from a passenger Mi-8 was added. The ship retained the standard then-Soviet camouflage with large red stars, but lacked any fuselage code. For the record flights the fuel quantity in the tanks was reduced as well. The helicopter gained the company designation A-10, used for documentation purposes. As performance during the first tests was disappointing, it seemed no records would be attempted. The Mil bureau test pilot team proposed to start with the first public flights performed by an all-woman crew as fewer records had been set in that category and it was easier to beat the world record there. Some senior test pilots such as Felix Vorobyov, who had a vast experience from flights with the V-12 giant helicopter as well as with Mi-24 and Mi-14, proposed young female pilot Galina Rastorgooeva, serving under the Flight Research Institute. She had logged over 1,000 flight hours in total before she attempted the record. She volunteered for the record flight, and took the initiative to send a personal letter to the minister of MAP and DOSAAF air club commander suggesting she take the record flight. She was endorsed by the Mil test pilots and the minister liked the idea. She got the job and selected Lyudmila Polyanskaya as her navigator. Both women represented the Soviet Central Aero Club named after Valery Tchkalov from Tushino airfield. They then started to familiarise themselves with the helicopter. On 16 July 1975, Rastorgooeva and Polyanskaya reached 341.35 km/h (184.51 knots) on a 15/25 closed circuit. Two days later the same crew reached the speed of 334.464 km/h (180.79 knots) on a 100 kilometre course. On 1 August 1975 Lyudmila Polyanska, as pilot, reached 331.023 km/h (178.93 kts) speed over a 500km course, while on 13 August Rastorgooeva reached 333 km/h speed (180.0 knots) over 1,000 kilometre. On the 7th of the same month Galina Rastorgooeva climbed to 3,000 metres (9,843 feet) in 2 minutes and 33.5 seconds, while on 26 August the helicopter climbed into 6,000 metres (19,685 feet) within 8 minutes and 31 seconds. All those were international women's records in the Class E section, and in total eighteen records were set by the female crew on A-10. Some of the flights were definitely not easy. During the long 1,000 kilometre flight, with both engines running continuously on take-off regime, otherwise limited by fixed interval to less than five minutes, the speed-induced vibrations released the fuel pipe and fuel spilled into the cockpit. Rastorgooeva swiftly consulted the situation over radio and on her own decided to finish the record flight, which broke even the then-absolute speed record by 84 km/h (45.36 knots).

After three years of upgrades, the company test pilot, Gourguen Rubenovich Karapetyan, reached a maximum speed of 368.4 km/h (199,13 knots) on 21 of September 1978, setting the absolute helicopter world speed record. To achieve it, even the crew was reduced to a single pilot and all the equipment from the front seat was removed. It should be noted that Karapetyan knew the ship quite well as he led the autorotation tests of the type and helped to elaborate proper techniques for one engine inoperative and both engines inoperative situations. When author of this publication had a chance to talk to him in Moscow more than decade ago, he mentioned that the most difficult flights were the tests of the Mi-24 flight envelope edges. To determine the necessary safety margins, pilots had to perform much more than is allowed and he recalled even a barrel roll performed with the Mi-24. Bank angles of 60° and more were regularly tested. In one of the test flights he even encountered blade chord flutter—one of very few test pilots in the world to do so. The A-10 record flight was, as per his own words, not somehow special, only the level of vibrations was higher. Prior to the record flight specific descents from high-speed flight with one engine inoperative were trialled. When the below described variants of the Mi-24 were deployed in Afghanistan, Karapetyan helped to train the crews on evasive escape manoeuvres and even tested the take-off in mountainous terrain with the front wheel rolling on the runway, unless the lift of the main rotor allowed climb. It also showed the high-speed dive with 360 km/h and more. In 1986, he volunteered to pilot helicopters over the Chernobyl nuclear plant and helped to lay down a lid over the melted reactor. His ultimate Hind speed record was broken by Westland Lynx with BERP (British Experimental Rotor Programme) rotors in 1986 with value of 400.87 km/h (216.45 knots).

The A-10 record-breaking shop with wings and tail skid removed. Note the anti-vibration damper on the main rotor head. (*MVZ Mil*)

2

New Kinds of Hinds

The Family Expansion

When the first Mi-24s entered state trials, plans for a new variant with 9A-624 four-barrel machine gun were in place, and it was expected to feature a redesigned cockpit for better visibility as well. It was eventually named Mi-24B with the next in line internal designation Izdeliye 241. Its main modification was a slightly redesigned nose with increased outward visibility for the pilot, and also more space for the installation of all necessary guidance systems inside. The front cockpit was equipped with emergency controls for piloting the helicopter from the front seat if necessary so the weapon systems operator could take over the ship control should the pilot be hit. The nose had also been reshaped to reduce dazzling by the landing lights' reflections at night. The sides of the fuselage now included armour plates with an option for the crew to wear special ballistic flak vests and helmets. The original car-type entry doors were replaced by a large sliding blister, with a shape that allowed at least some downwards visibility, with optional armouring panel in lower segment. The cockpit and cargo cabin were pressurised for operation in a high-altitude environment, and also for operation over radiation and chemically polluted areas.

The new shape slightly reduced the maximum speed due to its increased frontal resistance. Another important improvement was the upgraded Phalanga-P ATGM missile system with Raduga F guidance system selected because the so-long expected Shturm system was still not available. The letter 'P' in the name of the missile refers to self-automatic guidance capability provided by the Raduga system. The new guidance device was able to guide the 9M17P missiles during firing even when the helicopter was manoeuvring, which helped to increase accuracy significantly. While with the original Mi-24 the guidance antenna was in a fixed position on the right side of the nose next to the machine gun, with the Mi-24B a specific housing was designed under the left side of the nose. It had a turning base, so the antenna could rotate to track the target when the ship manoeuvres. It was a dramatic improvement of the system accuracy. The Raduga system was stabilised and worked well at night. While with the 9M17M the Weapons Systems Operator (WSO) had to control the missile during flight all the way to the target by commanding the missile, with 9M17P he just had to keep the aiming cross of the guidance optics on the target and the missile flight trajectory was corrected automatically.

One of the new systems introduced on the Mi-24B for the first time was the 9Sh121-01 optical sight with wide and narrow field of view for optical guidance of the 9M17M ATGMs. The sight, derived from the Zarnitsa sight of the BRDM armoured vehicles, together with the missiles and 2P32M/K-4V launching rails was the core of 9P146P Phalanga P anti-tank system (sometimes referred to as 2K8). In the Mi-24 the 9M17M missile was guided through a manually controlled sight attached to the cockpit frame. It was on the right side of the cockpit and its non-central position made its operation very difficult, like the limited field of view and potential reflections from canopy windows did. Because of lack of the sighting system stabilisation, the Mi-24 missile firing accuracy barely exceeded 30 per cent, while Zarnitsa proposed significant increase. Integration of this more sophisticated ATGM guidance kit was one of the major reasons for the canopy redesign because the original cockpit lacked space for its positioning. Selection of Zarnitsa was more necessity than choice for Mil.

When Mil and his deputy visited the MAP minister P. V. Dementeyev with the request for development of a specific combined sight for guided and unguided weapons, he absolutely refused it. Having fresh experience with excessive development requirements of the frontline fighter Su-24 and its specific guidance system, development of which delayed the whole programme and caused the capacity of many design bureaus to be exceeded, he clearly told Mil that he must select from the existing hardware inventory. This is how the Zarnitsa sight was selected, as well as the OPB-1D bomb sight and KPS-53AV machine-gun sight for the planned machine gun. The bombsight was a direct derivate of the OPB-1 type designed for the Petlyakov Pe-2 bombers used during the Second World War, and KPS-53AV was derivate of KPS-53 sight of the tail gunner in the Tu-16 bomber. This MAP decision caused several independent and not connected guidance systems were installed in the helicopter.

In total the weapon systems operator used three completely independent sighting systems—the K-4V, 9Sh121-01 and OPB-1R—for each weapon type. Switching between weapons during combat was complex, as the operator had to shift between separate sighting systems located in different areas of the cockpit. As a result, many crews pointed out the necessity of a single, integrated sight. Pilots used a fourth guidance system—the simple K-10T collimator gun sight used to fire S-5 FFAR missiles from UB-16-57 and UB-32A-57 blocks. So the forward-firing unguided weapons were controlled by the pilot, while the weapon systems operator controlled the ATGMs, machine gun and bombs. New sensors were installed under the nose, and the moveable guidance antenna was installed on the helicopter's underside to the left, while under the starboard side the guidance optics were located. The externally installed optics with higher sensitivity were significantly more accurate than the original version fully stowed in the confined cockpit. For unguided weapons, a brand new SPSV-24 automatic firing system for the weapons was installed, which also helped to improve accuracy without limiting the manoeuvrability of the helicopter during attack. The integration of turret with the new machine gun was first demonstrated on the V-24 wooden mock-up which was rebuilt for that purpose and helped to determine the new arrangement of the cockpit.

Mi-24B modification as presented on the V-24 mock-up. The Mi-24A was put in production instead due to delays of weapons development. Note the black panels showing the added external armour. (*MVZ Mil*)

However, neither the 9A-624 machine gun nor the 9M17P ATGM guidance kit with SPSV-24 system were available in time and their development was delayed. The first serially produced model, therefore, became another 'provisional' variant, the Mi-24A with internal code Izdeliye 245 (and Hind A NATO code as it was revealed before the Mi-24 sans suffix variant). It had the new shape of flight cabin, but Mi-24 sans suffix armament. It shall be noted the Mi-24A or Mi-24B version names were usually assigned much later when the full design work was almost ready, so the predeceasing of the A letter before B and V (like the A, B, V, G, D ... sequence in the Cyrillic alphabet) does not mean they were designed in that sequence. The Mi-24A design was launched after the Mi-24B, as is visible from the Izdeliye code above which was assigned at the very beginning of the design effort. Mi-24A was a direct derivative of the Mi-24 model with several modifications only in order to field the helicopter with the first units as quickly as possible. The rush to bring the aircraft into service was caused by the evolution of US army aviation, which had already started accepting first AH-1 Cobra attack helicopters in wide scale and even deployed them in the Vietnam

The Mi-24A model used by TsAGI for aerodynamic measurement in the wind tunnel. Note the final shape of the wings and the strings used for airflow visualisation. (*TsAGI*)

war. Such experience, and the very existence of a highly modern, dedicated American attack type was a cause of serious worries to Soviet generals. Using of large fleet of Cobra helicopters might have had very significant impact on the offensive tactics of the USSR, which had limited means of dealing with the threat posed by the Cobra. Therefore, the Mi-24A was put into production regardless of the fact that it needed many improvements. The helicopter was designed in three major modification states specific to particular roles. The first was for the attack role, while the second was for troop transport, and the third for evacuation of wounded soldiers ('CASEVAC' in Western parlance). Delay of the weapon equipment caused further slips in the family development. The planned following model Mi-24V Izdeliye 242, finally equipped with Shturm missiles, and Mi-24P Izdeliye 243 model with GSh-30 30mm calibre cannon were delayed as well as was the training model Mi-24U Izdeliye 244 which was expected to carry neither machine gun or cannon nor ATGMs.

The first Mi-24A prototype was based on the Mi-24 model and included several brand-new items next to the new cockpit design. The ATGM guidance antenna was removed from the nose position and positioned in the centreline with much better field of view. Unlike the plans for the Mi-24B, it was still fixed with no rotation possible. It helped to increase the 9M17M firing accuracy a bit. Another major visual difference of the Mi-24A was the new anhedral wing. This was the result of experience with V-24 and Mi-24 wings which were subject to instability during flight in high-speed regimes. The new reversed V-shape helped to eliminate the instability completely. Vertical end pylons were added for lateral stability and those also allowed the installation of the ATGMs under them. The wing anhedral angle of 12° helped to better distribute the main rotor downwash, and the 19° incidence supported better lift generation during high-speed flight when the helicopter was flying in nose-down position. The new ATGM position was no longer limiting the use of the cargo cabin and it became very efficient. Missile rails on both ends were installed with incidence of 2° and offset 3°30' to the longitudinal axis of the helicopter for the starboard, and 0°30' for the port side launcher. This asymmetric position was to compensate the unequal rotor downwash. The fuselage under the wing and the lower side of the wing included hooks and lugs for attachment of the manually operated crane for weapon installation in field conditions. A K-4V gun sight and control station from the Mi-4AV was sited in the nose of Mi-24A, with an A-12.7mm machine gun in an NUV-1A turret (later replaced by the improved NUV-1U variant introduced during serial production, sometimes called NDS-1U). This aiming station was transplanted fully from the Mi-4AV model and was operated manually by the use of bicycle grips.

The Mi-24A was also able to carry bombs of up to 250kg calibre on all underwing stations and up to 500kg on inner stations. Bombing was directed by the weapon systems operator using an OPB-1R bombing sight with long tube. The bombing capability was relatively unique as no other helicopter manufacturer in the world has adopted it as a standard operation procedure. Nevertheless, in the USSR it was a common practice. The weapon array was quite late in the production, boosted by a UPK-23-250 cannon pod with GSh-23L twin-barrel cannon (Soviet industry code 9A-681). This pod was originally designed by the Yakovlev design bureau for its V/STOL Yak-36 'Freehand' aircraft, as it lacked organic armament and pods were to be used as primary weapon. Its total weight of 218kg made it ideal in terms of weight to performance ratio. It contains 250 rounds of 23x115mm ammunition, and it can fire up to the 4 kilometres range against ground targets and 2 kilometres against aerial targets. However, when fired against armoured vehicles, the recommended range was below 1.5 kilometres so the rounds had sufficient penetration energy. Its theoretical rate of fire of 2,500 rounds per minute meant all the rounds could have been fired within six seconds. To prevent it, the burst was limited to twenty or fifty rounds. The Mi-24A could carry the pods under the inner hardpoints only, as the outer were not wired for them. Before installation, the electrical junction box on the rear wall of the cargo cabin had to be reconfigured. The pilot aimed the gun pod with the K-10T gunsight like the FFARs. It came too late to be widely used, with subsequent Hind models benefiting from this gun instead.

The Mi-24A helicopter was further equipped with advanced avionics of its time such as Vyer-AD short range navigation system; ARK-U2 UHF direction finder and ARK-15 automatic direction finder; DISS-015D drift and velocity sensor; SAU-V24 automatic control system; VUAP-1 autopilot; RV-5 radio altimeters; R-860-1 UHF radio (with very late models augmented by R-828 type), M-24 Karat HF radio and personal R-855U emergency beacons. The set of avionics was very modern when

Mi-24A prototype with its full array of weapons, consisting of an A-12.7 machine gun, four UB-32A-24 rocket blocks and 9M17M missiles on the launching rails. (*MVZ Mil*)

The same helicopter; note the ATGM guiding antenna under the nose. The camouflage pattern with typical 'shamrocks' became a kind of standard for Hinds. (*MVZ Mil*)

compared to the other helicopters then in production. The instrument panels in both cockpits were manufactured using the latest technologies of that time. For example, both panels were made by chemical milling with many lightweight materials used in the production. One of the major improvements incorporated during the production of Mi-24A was the relocation of the tail rotor. The original position on the starboard side with a pusher scheme was replaced by a port-side position with tractor scheme. This modification, which was applied to the Mi-8 as well (this is, together with the TV3-117 engines, the main feature distinguishing the Mi-8MT/Mi-17 from the Mi-8) and Mi-14, significantly increased the directional control. It so happened that with every single Hind operating, both variants were used—with port-side and starboard-side tail rotor. Such a mess for the crews! For that purposes the early ships were mostly transferred to training duties. The different distribution of the forces in the tail boom, and especially higher loads from the more efficient tail rotor, caused structural cracks of the tail boom in early service. This is why a modified variant with seven reinforcement ribs on the port-side of the aft fuselage was introduced in 1974. This modification, frequently connected with other improvements, such as the relocation of the IFF antenna from the canopy frame to the top of the oil filter cooler intake for better reception of signal, was later performed on Mi-24As during general overhauls. In some media this modification was associated with a change of

Serial Mi-24A photographed near Reztow firing range close to Berlin. This picture was used by US intelligence agencies to recognise details of the type. (*US DoD*)

designation to Mi-24F, but this name was never adopted, either by the production organisation or by the Mil Design Bureau.

One of the major problems that had been revealed was the dynamic system. The reliability and service life of the TV3-117 engines was problematic and the main rotor was causing a lot of problems as well. The first series' engine had a time-between-overhaul of just fifty hours, but this was later improved. Both engines were identical, differing only in the position of the exhaust pipe, and both had independent hydraulic control systems. To minimise the drop in performance in service on the early series of the engines, maintenance crews had pay special attention to proper adjustment of the engines. Several attempts were made to increase the output of the engines and the effectiveness of the main rotor. For example, special fairings were tested on the rotor blade tips, and engines were modified in various ways. All the modifications were made on one dedicated Mi-24 prototype first. It lacked the newer wings but carried a special air-data probe on the nose. Nevertheless, as stated above, the rotor profile was not ideal and in the event of both engines inoperative, for example, the helicopter was often unable to land in the autorotation regime. The final solution was the water-spraying system which splashed water into the compressor for a short-term slight increase in performance.

To protect the engine blades from attrition when operating in dusty areas, special mushroom-shaped filters called PZU were introduced as an add-on system. They worked on the ejection principle. Instead of sucking the air directly into the engine, it was sucked through a slot between the PZU and the intake inner wall, and there the vector of its movement was changed. Due to centrifugal forces, heavier particles (dirt) moved along the sides of the central tunnel of the intake duct and were carried into a multi-stage collector, while clean air continued to the inlet. The device could clean the air by up to 70 to 75 per cent and reduce erosion of the blades by one to two thirds. The PZU system was electrically heated, so could be used in winter. However, it further reduced the engine output by some 6 per cent when it was on, and by 3 per cent even when off by blocking the air.

When compared to the first Mi-24 model, both Mi-24A engines and critical systems were protected by armour installed on the outer side the cowlings. The cockpit was also protected by 4mm thick armament plates attached to the primary construction. It was thought to be able to stop the rounds up to 7.62mm calibre. To increase endurance, two fuel tanks could be installed in the cargo cabin with corresponding reduction of the available cargo space. Each tank had 850 litres of fuel. To enable their installation, the left door was slightly taller, measuring 1,115mm × 1,235mm compared with 1,085mm × 1,235mm for the right-hand door.

Mi-24A series production was launched in the Arsenyev plant at the end of 1970, and in 1971 the first production Mi-24A with the construction number (c/n 0200101) performed its maiden flight. Manufacturing the Mi-24A had not proved to be an easy task for the production facility as it had to adapt to many new technologies. In addition, this was the Arsenyev plant's first large-scale helicopter-production programme. During production, many service improvements were implemented. These resulted in a higher empty weight, with the original 7,762kg increased to 7,783kg from the 18. block, increasing again to 7,830kg from the 24th Production Block. Up to 1975 some 204 Mi-24A helicopters were completed for the Soviet army, and to 1977 a further thirty-four for export customers. The initial series of helicopters were delivered to the 760th Research Independent Aviation Regiment at Voronezh airbase, south of Moscow, where a conversion and advanced training centre was located. It was a detachment of the famous 344. centre for combat training and conversion of flight crews located at Torzhok, where the helicopters were relocated later. The instructors, all experienced with Mi-1, Mi-4 and even Ka-25, passed training on the V-24 and Mi-24 ships at the Mil Design Bureau and after return to the unit were responsible for elaboration of combat operation guidelines for the regular army regiments. They also elaborated on the training aids for further conversion courses as the Mi-24A was found quite different from the Mi-4 in handling characteristics and performance. The unit started regular operation in 1971. It is worth noting that this unit benefited from pilots and operators with huge experience from Soviet helicopter deployments in Vietnam and Cuba.

In the mid-1970s the Soviet air force rotary wing units were reorganised into the newly independent Soviet army aviation. The Mi-24s were gradually assigned to former independent transport helicopter regiments renamed to independent transport-combat helicopter regiments. Each helicopter regiment had two squadrons equipped with Mi-24s and one with Mi-8Ts, each having twenty ships or so. The first regular unit rearmed with Mi-24As became the 319th Independent Helicopter Regiment located at Chernigovka airbase, close to the production plant for easy problem solving. It was followed by the 55th Independent Helicopter Regiment located at Brody airbase, fully rearmed in 1972, and later by 172nd Independent Helicopter Regiment located at the Parchim air force base in East Germany, not far from the 'Iron Curtain' border. It became the first foreign deployment with a lot of attention from Western military experts. Some notes about usage of this variant in Czechoslovakia may be found, but these are incorrect. In reality, the Brody unit sent one helicopter to a small air fair in Czechoslovakia during local celebrations in early 1970s.

The Mi-24As were involved in many Soviet army military drills and the Torzhok unit demonstrated the type regularly to the foreign delegations. During the Shield-79 large-scale military exercise a very interesting but unplanned demonstration occurred in front of delegation members from the Warsaw Pact and other countries. One of the Mi-24A crews got behind schedule and arrived over the target area too late for its attack, when the artillery shells were already hitting the area. The crew, quickly realising its error, decided to fly low and fast out of the area but was hit by the fragments of one of the shells. The engine puffed out a thick black smoke, but the helicopter continued to fly and landed safely at the rearming point. The impression of the attack chopper could not have been better.

With Soviet army aviation the Mi-24A remained in frontline service until 1978, when the Mi-24D model (mentioned below) was available in sufficient quantity so the Mi-24As were transferred to a training role. However, it is documented that one Soviet Mi-24A was shot down in July 1980 in Afghanistan. Several Mi-24As were retained in military museums in Russia and other CIS countries such as Ukraine, where one ship was even repainted into Ukrainian national colours, although it never served with those.

A flight line of the Chernigovka-based regiment—the grassy airfields were typical for early operation. Note the Mi-8T helicopters. They were operated alongside Mi-24As. (*MVZ Mil*)

Above: Another picture taken in East Germany where the Soviet air force deployed dozens of Mi-24As. There, the type was revealed. (*US DoD*)

Below: An early Mi-24A with starboard side tail rotor is flying over later ships with the rotor on the portside. Such a mess to have both configurations in the same unit! (*MVZ Mil*)

Above: An Mi-24A is taking off for a training sortie with loaded UB-32A-24 rocket blocks. If empty, the barrels would be illuminated by the passing light. (*US DoD*)

Below: A late Mi-24A showing that parts were frequently swapped between ships—the tail boom pattern does not match the fuselage. (*MVZ Mil*)

Shortly after the introduction of the first Mi-24As into service, it became obvious that the common training system involving the transition from the Mi-8 to the Mi-24 was not ideal due to the many differences in performance and handling between the types. Particularly for pilots, the transition to the Mi-24A proved difficult, as they had just a few hours in the front cockpit, with no useable dual controls (operational Mi-24As had only basic 'emergency' dual controls), and then flew their first solo with

Above: A fully serial Mi-24A of the Soviet air force. The helicopters were regularly flying with rocket pods no matter if loaded or not. (*MVZ Mil*)

Below: A pair of Mi-24As flying over the desert area somewhere in the southern USSR. The ships are from late batches as they wear the codes on the tail boom and not the fuselage. (*ITAR-TASS*)

the instructor sitting in the front cockpit or cargo cabin and giving voice commands and recommendations only. The instructor had no flight instruments on the board and was unable to correct errors of the student by other than visual means. When a new generation of pilots with limited experience on Mi-4s and Mi-8s went to combat regiments, the in-unit training became too complicated and lengthy. Therefore, a directive to prepare a dedicated training variant of the Mi-24 was issued to Mil Design Bureau. The first prototype was a conversion of an operational Mi-24A performed by the Mil's prototype facility. It was given the designation Mi-24U with the internal code of Izdeliye 244 (Hind C in NATO code). This helicopter lacked the nose NUV-1 turret with A-12.7 machine gun, its sighting system, and the ATGM system. Those were not needed for the training role. The type also lacked the capability to carry the FAB-500 bombs unusable for training purposes. Instead, a full set of flight controls and indicators was installed with a small instrument panel in front of the pilot. With significantly lower weight after the deletion of the guided weapon systems and machine gun, the helicopter became recognised as the best performing member of the family. The instructor sat in the former WSO's station with excellent visibility out of the cockpit. The Mi-24U served largely for pilot training, with WSOs having just a few hours on the type before passing their full weapons training on a simulator, and later on a standard Mi-24A.

The first few examples assigned to the Soviet army were modified from regular Mi-24As during major inspections as a solution to enable the rapid delivery of the first machines. Usually each regiment operated two Mi-24Us for training purposes. After the first aircraft were fielded, production of brand-new Mi-24Us proceeded at the Arsenyev plant, with the first completed in late 1973. In total approximately twenty-five helicopters for the domestic operator were finished. Curiously, although the type was never intended for export, two Mi-24Us were delivered to Libya and a single unit was built for Ethiopia. With Soviet army aviation the Mi-24U remained in an active role until 1982, when the last ships were replaced by newer models. Those helicopters did not usually even pass an overhaul in service and were withdrawn from use after reaching less than 1,500 flight hours.

In 1975, Libya became the first export customer, receiving an initial batch of six Mi-24As. To expedite delivery, these helicopters were diverted from production batches originally intended for the Soviet army. This order, opening the Hind's export career, was a direct result of the visit of Libyan prime minister in Moscow in 1974, during which he signed several weapons' deals. Libyan leader Gaddafi, with his dream of unified Arab countries and facing strong opposition from the USA and France in the region, accepted Soviet proposals for new armament, although Gaddafi was strongly anti-communist and just a few years earlier had called the USSR an 'imperialist, atheist state'. However, both countries were getting closer and in 1974 the first group of Libyan pilots arrived at the Mil Design Bureau in Moscow, where the type rating on the Mi-24A, using the older Mi-24 ships, started.

The Libyan pilots came from the Al Watiya Air Base and had experience with Bell 47 and Alouette III, some of them just finished the helicopter training course. The training in the USSR became difficult, because all pilots had previously been trained in the British-style scheme and spoke English; the air traffic control in Libya, and even manuals for the choppers, were in English only. In Russia, of course, it was different, and translators played a role in the training while the documentation was being translated into English in parallel with the course. Later, Libya used the USSR training facilities in the Soviet city of Frunze (now Bishkek, the capital of Kyrgyzstan) for regular training well into mid-1980s. Some other foreign pilots recalled that during their training in the late 1970s Libyans became incredibly popular in the Frunze area as they were spending all their petrodollars in local bars and heavily supported everyone in the area, from grocery store cashiers to taxi drivers. They enjoyed the Soviet life and became drunk every second night or so. Not all of them were allowed to fly solo and not all of them returned with Hind type rating. Before delivery of the first six helicopters, they were downgraded to the so called 'B' standard with simplified IFF system, as well as limited modes of the ATGM system. Such export standard later became a typical solution for customers outside of Warsaw Pact countries.

All helicopters were ferried in a disassembled condition in wooden crates on a merchant ship to Tripoli, where they were assembled by Soviet technicians and then flown to Al Watiya Air Base, which became the home base for the initial period of service. In 1976 following six Mi-24A helicopters and two Mi-24U were delivered and a brand-new unit, the 1324th Helicopter Squadron at the Abd el Nasser Air Base south of Tobruk became the new operational airbase. Hinds came just in time to take part in the clashes with Chad in the Aouzou Strip south of the country, a piece of land formally belonging to Chad but claimed to be under control of Libya. Gaddafi used that strip as an advanced zone for Libyan raids into Chad.

In 1978, with increasing opposition to Gaddafi's plan by united Chad leaders, also supported internationally, Libya dramatically increased its involvement in the combat operation, yet still unofficially. After some political pressure peace accords were signed with Chad accepting that all French forces in the country should leave, which was another long-term goal of Gaddafi. The French army left Chad but later came back as a part of operation Tacaud to support the falling Chadian regime. In 1983 the Libyan forces entered Chad when supporting one of the local pro-Libyan factions, and a full-scale invasion began, using Aouzou Strip as a launch zone for many attack missions. This time the invasion included complete close air support, including Mi-24As and later Mi-25s, described below. Hinds were operated from the Ouadi Doum airbase which worked as refuelling and rearming point. Helicopters were used mainly for urban attacks where the S-5 rockets proved to be very effective against typical African buildings made of mudbricks. The fast advancement of Libyan troops with a lot of pressure from French-speaking African countries led to the French president agreeing to support Chad with military intervention within Operation Manta. French forces drew a 'red line' around 16. parallel and neither side was willing to cross it to avoid escalating the original regional conflict. In September 1984 this situation finally led to a mutual withdrawal of French and Libyan forces from Chad signed. While France respected the agreement, Libyan troops remained in the country till 1987. This chapter of the war is then described below with the Mi-25 model. The Mi-24As were used in combat until full retrieval of the Libyan forces from Chad while the Mi-24Us were used for in-country training of new pilots. No reports were available of the Mi-24A and Mi-24U fleet from the late 1980s until 2021. At least six Mi-24As and one Mi-24U with PZU filters were discovered on the photos from Al Watiya Air Base hangars. All helicopters were covered with dust and without weapons, and usually even engines were stored in two hangars and open air.

In 1975 (some sources say much later) Algeria became the second export customer of the Mi-24A with twelve ships delivered. All were brand-new and were assigned from the production planned originally for the Soviet army aviation, but not ordered due to the switch to the later Mi-24D model. Very little is known about the service of the model in North Africa. At least three helicopters were deployed in the border zone with Western Sahara when the clashes between the local Polisario Front, backed by Algeria and Morocco, and Mauritania-backed units started. The Mi-24As, shortly after delivery, were used for controlling the area around the provincial city of Tinduf, then the far west settlement of Algeria. Helicopters were used to patrol the surroundings of the city where the Polisario members were retreating for rest and regrouping. Although there were some plans for deployment abroad, the helicopters were never used outside Algerian territory and only fired their unguided missiles and machine gun as a warning when pushing back an opponent approaching the border zone. Later, the helicopters were used for border patrolling activities and eventually were supported by the newer models described below. In the early 1990s a limited number of Algerian Mi-24As were equipped with Western-origin dust filter boxes, also used widely on other ships in the country. The Mi-24As were withdrawn from use around 2004. Although no Mi-24As are displayed in the country, one ship is kept as a gatekeeper at the airbase close to the city of Biskra in the north of the country. A second is displayed at the South African Air Force Aviation Museum at Swartkop, repainted in Russian camouflage and is likely the very best-preserved early Hind in the world.

Ethiopia became the last customer to acquire newly built Mi-24As, with all following customers receiving second-hand ships. These specific helicopters marked the type's first combat deployment in 1978 during the Ogaden War against Somalia. Ethiopia received ten Mi-24As finished in 1977, followed by a single training Mi-24U model in the same year. Those helicopters were the last models produced alongside with the Mi-24D model described below. Some sources, especially in Russia, say over forty Mi-24As were later transferred to Ethiopia from the Soviet army aviation surpluses, but it seems unlikely and probably only eighteen ships were transferred. The Mi-24As came just in time, because in 1977 the situation in the border region with Somalia in eastern Ethiopia became very tense. When the USA turned down all requests for delivery of weapons to Ethiopia, the Addis Ababa government asked Moscow for help, expelled all US forces from its territory and in a peace attempt agreed with the plan to create a common state of Ethiopia, Djibouti and Somalia into the socialist federation, of which Moscow dreamed. Cuban revolutionary and leader Fidel Castro arranged a meeting of the three countries' delegations in the port of Aden.

At the meeting Somalia's leader, General Siad Barré, described the Ethiopian control of the Ogaden region as occupation. The diplomatic talks failed entirely, with the Somali delegation returning home. The Somali rebels, united under the Western Somali Liberation Front, had already been conducting guerilla operations in the Ogaden region and increased their activity, supported by the full-scale invasion of the Somali national army in July 1977. The Somalian army, comprising of a massive combination of armoured vehicles, tanks and heavy armed units, progressed very quickly.

By a twist of fate, both countries relied on Soviet defence materiel and so Moscow attempted to mediate a ceasefire, but failed. Later the USSR decided to interrupt the Somalian support and provided Ethiopia with heavy artillery, tanks, vehicles and other materiel, while Cuban mercenaries sent by Castro and East German army officials helped to operate some of the sophisticated weapons. The support came just in time and the Mi-24As, flown by a mix of Soviet, Cuban and Ethiopian pilots, significantly helped to change the course of the war in early 1978. The Ethiopian counterattack, led by Soviet general Vasily Petrov, started with the insertion of airborne regiments and a carefully planned ground offensive including artillery shelling and fast jet attacks deep in the battlefield. The role of the Mi-24As, augmented by eighteen more helicopters quickly delivered from the USSR, was to provide air cover to the advancing ground troops and destroy enemy armoured vehicles and strongholds. The intensive counterattack continued for two months with varying intensity, always with aerial support of the Mi-24As. Hinds, firing the A-12.7mm machine gun, S-5 FFAR rockets and FAB-100 and FAB-250 free-fall bombs, were literally unpunished in the area and the retreating Somali crews were devastated by the repeated air raids of the helicopters, some of which flew fifteen combat sorties per day. The Soviet commanders refined the combat tactics, relying on the advanced refuelling and rearmament points. Although there were no real armoured targets and very few ATGMs were fired, the Mi-24 showed its combat potential.

General Petrov became the commander in chief of the Soviet army in 1980 and was one of the strongest proponents of the Mi-24's further development. It is worth noting that some of the Ethiopian Mi-24As were equipped with the PZU filters because the frequent landing outside of the bases when deploying special forces damaged the engines. Although Ethiopia won the Ogaden war, another conflict was about to start in the northern provinces, known today as the Eritrean War of Independence. Hinds were heavily engaged in the conflict and also the Ethiopian air force suffered its first combat losses there when, in 1984, several Mi-24As were destroyed by mortar shells at the Asmara airport, today Eritrea's capital and back then still an Ethiopian base. Several more Hinds were shot down when the Soviet support of Ethiopia dropped in late 1980s and the Eritrean rebels got international support. Several Mi-24A airframes were long-term stored in the open air at the Debre Zeit, the main airbase of the Ethiopian air force, a few having the original Soviet fuselage codes partially exposed. After two decades of abandonment they were eventually scrapped, and one ship was used as an instructional airframe. Two Mi-24As and one Mi-24U were overhauled locally by the contracted Danubian Aircraft Company of Hungary in 1999 and 2000. The Mi-24U suffered hydraulics failure during one of the test flights and the crew had to perform an emergency landing. Although the helicopter was later repaired, photographs of the emergency landing in the bush appeared in the press, thereby confirming the type's operational status. The last Mi-24A flight is documented in 2008.

Alongside the below mentioned models, six Mi-24As and one Mi-24U model were transferred to Afghanistan in 1979, where they belonged to the 373rd Mixed Air Regiment located at Kabul airport. They became operational in 1980 and with more newer models delivered a new 377th Independent Helicopter Battalion was created at

Ethiopian Mi-24As at Debre Zeit air base, captured a decade before. They are in non-airworthy condition. Note the missing ATGM rails, PZU filters and the original Soviet fuselage codes partially exposed. (*Jan Drdák*)

Kabul airport, equipped only with Hinds. It later provided support with its helicopter detachments at Jalalabad and Kandahar. The equipment of the helicopter was downgraded to the export standard with the IFF removed but UPK-23-250 cannon pods were provided with the ships. Helicopters were initially operated by the Soviet crews and when the Afghan pilots were finally trained, usually mixed crews performed the missions. Hinds were used primarily for patrolling and protective missions around the Kabul airport especially when transport aircraft were taking off and landing. They shoot unguided rockets and machine gun to supress the enemy should it be found in the proximity of the airport. The operational tempo of the Mi-24A and Mi-24U was very low, namely due to low performance of the type in the mountains. After all, used helicopters delivered for the 'final stage of flight career' were provided and the demanding, dusty and high-altitude environment (Kabul airport is 1,791 metres (5,877 feet) above mean sea level) took the toll.

In May 1979 the first loss occurred when the engines of an Mi-24As surged in flight due to attrition caused by sand abrasion. The helicopter crashed and after the accident investigation the ships, together with the Mi-24U,were used primarily for training and were equipped with PZU dust filters. Another Mi-24A was shot down by rifle fire in July 1979, and another was destroyed in February 1980 when the pilot was hit. Mi-24As, although originally intended for at least eight years of operation, were grounded in 1983 and were parked, protected with canopy and rotor blades' canvases, at Kabul airport. The Mi-24U became later an exhibit at the Kabul-based military museum; the Mi-24As were harvested for spares and eventually scrapped.

The sole Mi-24U was 'rearmed' with non-original cannon and became an exhibit of the OMAR museum in Kabul even with Shturm missiles under the end wing pylons.

In 1978, in total three Mi-24A helicopters were transferred from the active Soviet army aviation inventory to Vietnam, followed by three more in 1979 and by six ships and one Mi-24U in 1980 (older sources mentioned as delivery year 1984, but it was proven to be incorrect recently when photos from 1978 with Vietnamese Mi-24As appeared). These were demanded by Vietnam to increase the combat capability of the army as the country was under constant guerilla warfare-style attacks from the neighbouring Khmer Rouge-led Kampuchea (now Cambodia). Although previously an ally, Kampuchea was afraid of potential dominance in the region by Vietnam. Both countries held some negotiations, but the border war was in full swing. The training of Vietnamese crews took place directly in the country with Soviet instructors providing tuition. By the end of 1978, leaders in Vietnam decided to end the Khmer Rouge-dominated government era.

On 25 December, over 150.000 Vietnamese troops invaded Kampuchea and gained control over the entire country within two weeks, ending Pol Pot's regime which was responsible for the genocide of almost a quarter of the Kampuchean population. As the first Mi-24As were available in the country, they were used during the large offensive. Curiously, they were used mainly against the Kampuchean navy, and

Afghan Mi-24U in the Kabul military museum shortly after removal from active service. Note the PZU filters on the engine intakes. (*Author's collection*)

several ships were badly damaged by rocket fire. Hinds were also heavily engaged in the later conflicts with Khmer Rouge militia as it fled to jungles of eastern Thailand from where they were attacking the regular Vietnam army units. Surprisingly enough, the Mi-24As were delivered with a very limited stock of the S-5 unguided rockets and Vietnam asked Moscow for urgent deliveries of the armament but received no response. It became a big problem as there were no targets for anti-tank missiles, and rockets were the main weapon used when attacking the camps of Khmer Rouge militia. For the A-12.7, which was using the same rounds as other types of weapons, the problem did not arise. So the ex-South Vietnamese technicians, of which some were trained by the Americans as armament specialists for UH-1 an AH-1, checked the wiring of the Mi-24A and realised it used the same voltage of electrical signals for firing, and even similar logic as the UH-1s. US-made M261 19-tubes rocket launchers and signal boxes were harvested from stored Huey helicopters. The M261 pod, as with all American armaments, used a different spacing of the attachment lugs of the hardpoints and so a provisional adapter was needed. Sometime in 1979 the Mi-24A was for the first time tested in the air with the M261 pods and American 2.75-inch rockets, of which thousands were available. The accuracy of the rockets aimed by the pilot using the original Soviet gunsight proved to be sufficient for combat, although the light missiles were affected by the main rotor downwash during some manoeuvres. Several pictures capturing M261 pods with M229 warheads are in the Hanoi-based aviation museum, as well as pictures showing low formation flight of three Mi-24As over the Kampuchean jungle.

A Vietnamese pilot leaning on the ATGM launch rail of an Mi-24A operated by his country. This is one of the ex-Soviet ships. (*Dũng Nguyen's collection*)

Detail of the Vietnamese Mi-24A nose with A-12.7 machine gun. The ship is a gate guard but with all weapon guidance systems included. It is in non-original colours. (*Pavel Pánek*)

The Hind raids became extremely effective and the air force was using tactics developed by Americans. An-2 biplanes illuminated the area with flare bombs and Mi-24s then attacked the enemy at night with unguided rockets. Some sources say over 500 combat sorties per year were flown on average in the early 1980s. Since 1984 seven Mi-24As were permanently stored at the Tân Sơn Nhất airport in the Ho Chi Minh city, from where they were flying to the border zone. This airport became the major operational base then, where Mi-24As were subordinated to 304th Squadron of the 916th Regiment. On the other hand, the jungle war showed the lack of true night deployment capability. When no illumination was provided by other aerial means, the combat flight ceased due to difficulties in flying the ship low over the mountainous jungle tree cover. The Mi-24s were operated until 2007 at least, with the Mi-24U being the last operational type used for training purpose. Four to six Mi-24s were pictured with rotor blades removed, parked under canvases at the Tân Sơn Nhất airport few years later. Vietnam never purchased a newer variant and became the sole operator of the Mi-24A, not progressing further. At least four Mi-24As are displayed in museums in Hanoi, Ho Chi Minh city, Bien Hoa and Da Nang.

In 1970 the first 9A-624 machine gun became available for integration purposes. Hence, a modified Mi-24B model with internal code Izdeliye 241 was finally revealed, also with the 9M17P missiles. The 9A-624 cannon significantly increased firing power as the rate of fire was as high as 5,000 rounds per minute. The 9A-624 machine gun was designed by the Tula-based design bureau specifically for use on the Mi-24. As the main engineer was named P. G. Yakustchev, with B. A. Borzov as his deputy, the gun is sometimes referred to as YakB-12.7 (in this case, the first three letters of the design leader's name were selected instead of only one. Usually 'Ya' is represented by a single character in the Russian alphabet, and YaB would sound like a rude word in the Russian language). Borzov became the chief engineer after the death of Yakustchev in 1973. Unlike Western equivalents, the Soviet 'Gatling gun' combined electrical and mechanical power, not just electrical. In 1970 the first three sets were delivered to Mil EDB for prototype installation into the USPU-24 turret. During the first ground tests it was discovered that it had to be constructed from different materials as the original barrels were only able to withstand 400 shots out of the 8,000 planned. After several design changes the machine gun underwent environmental tolerance tests in 1973 and 1974 in hot, dusty and cold conditions.

In June 1973, an approval for production was granted. Although the 9A-624 was an excellent gun, it was very sensitive to dust and prone to overheating and therefore the maximum burst rate was limited for intercooling of the barrels. Later, in 1988, a modified YakBYu-12.7 model was introduced with a maximum burst rate of 750 rounds instead of the original 470. The 'Yu' letters in the name are derived from the B. D. Yuritschev, the chief designer of the modification. In the Mi-24B the 9A-624 was for the first time operated by the KPS-53AV guidance station. It was electrically powered and was able to compensate for the helicopter's movements. The USPU-24 turret allowed 60° movement in azimuth and +20/-60° in elevation. The new ATGMs with the above mentioned guidance kit in the meantime helped to increase the firing accuracy to some 60 per cent.

The Mi-24B prototype during take-off with a full array of weapons. Minus the ATGMs, it features the final Hind weapon configuration. (*MVZ Mil*)

In 1971, the first Mi-24B was completed and entered state trials. It had a massive wire-supported boom on the front frame of the canopy with multiple measurement sensors, while the probes of the Pitot-static system were relocated on the port-side of the canopy frame. Later, a second prototype joined the effort. The flight and weapon tests started in 1971 and continued for another eighteen months until 1973, led by the Mil Design Bureau with support of the Flight Research Institute and Air Force Research Institute. The Mi-24B also included improved TV3-117 engines with better performance. Although all the systems proved to be fully compliant with technical requirements, the Mi-24B was not cleared for production and less than ten Mi-24Bs were built from unfinished Mi-24A airframes for testing and training purposes. Because the army already demanded a more radical nose redesign based on the initial operational experience with the Mi-24A, no more Mi-24Bs were required. Since the Mi-24B never reached full-scale production, it ended the 'veranda-style' Hind lineage. The existing ships were widely used during testing of systems for the Mi-24D and Mi-24V models described below, such as the DUAS-V air data probe, etc. The only survivor is the Mi-24B mock-up marked with serial number 241-0202-12 stored at the Moscow Aviation Institute. Curiously, it is equipped with a single barrel machine gun as various guns were tested in the turret. Its number indicates it might be converted from the last Arsenyev-built Mi-24 ship.

Mi-24B prototype in the Moscow Aviation Institute with non-original machine gun and testing air data boom braced by three ropes. (*Daniel Vuković*)

3

First Tandem Hind

It Is Almost Right

In parallel with Mi-24A serial production, Mil EDB worked on a new variant, which was about to reflect all the comments of the state committee from previous operation and testing. It would be named Mi-24V and it was to bring the Hind to its final design configuration—with different cockpit arrangement, a machine gun with a high rate of fire and Shturm ATGM missiles. In June 1972, two Mi-24 pre-production examples were equipped with the new front fuselage section. Modification was not easy as it required a complete change of all installations. It was intended to be armed with new-generation 9M114 Shturm-V missiles. However, the design and testing of those weapons was still not finalised, therefore a decision to launch production of an 'intermediate' variant, Mi-24D (internal designation Izdeliye 246, Hind D NATO code), with the weapons system from the Mi-24B but with the Mi-24V cockpit, was accepted. The D letter is fifth character in the Russian alphabet following the G, which was omitted due to its typical use for civilian versions (*grazhndanskyi* means 'civilian' in Russian). Going by the sequence, Izdeliye 246 was in the pipeline following even the then non-existent cannon-equipped variant.

The experience gained during Mi-24A operation with regular units clearly showed that the cockpit layout was problematic. Primarily the visibility from the pilot's seat was very bad, with many 'blind spots' and angles where the pilot was unable to see the area around the helicopter. The front-sector view was quite acceptable during high-speed level flight when the helicopter flew in slight nose-down position, but it was totally unacceptable when the helicopter hovered, or was about to land or take off with nose-up position. The combat tactics required rapid deceleration as a standard approach manoeuvre, allowing a fast stop and landing for troops disembarkation, which is normally achieved by tilting the helicopter backwards and changing the vector of the lift passing through the main rotor during rapid descent. Unfortunately, in that position the Mi-24A pilot saw the sky and nothing else. The position of the pilot in the rear cockpit, where he sat offset to the central axis, caused no downward visibility in the frontal area and almost none in the right sector. The pilot could only partially control the ground clearance from the left window blister which was close to the seat. Not much view to look out from an 11-tonne chopper with large dimensions.

It was even worse when the additional armour was installed as it almost completely prevented downwards visibility. The additional armour plates were installed into the lower segment of the sliding window blister exactly into the area which served for ground position check. When firing, the cabin was frequently filled with smoke from the nose machine gun, and it obstructed even the pilot's visibility. Last but not least, during night landings the reflections of the lamps in the front cockpit dazzled the pilot. But it was not only the pilot who had cause to complain. The WSO had his workspace stuffed with various guidance systems, with one for each weapon type. Their operation was not very comfortable due to very unnatural position of the body and obstruction by all the elements. For example, for guiding the ATGMs the WSO had to lean to the starboard of the ship, frequently after loosening his shoulder harness, to just reach the visor. It was one of the reasons why the shoulder harness was barely used and only belts were typically fastened. The absolute worst was operation of the OPB-1R bomb sight, which was physically impossible to use for tall operators. At the same time, the fact that the crew could all be injured by a single hit had to be taken into consideration. Also, test pilots complained about the typical summer 'greenhouse effect', overheating the cockpit. When flying in southern areas of the USSR, the cabin temperature frequently exceeded 50°C and the fans or air vents did not help to cool it down. When the ship was left parked in the sun, the temperature in the cabin rose to some 70°C or more, even if the entry doors were left open. Flying the Hind in hot areas was no fun at all.

The obvious solution was to equip the helicopter with an entirely new design of canopy. In total, eight cockpit configurations were considered and some were made in the form of wooden mock-ups for physical visibility tests. After detailed evaluation one was selected that featured separate, tandem cockpits for pilot and WSO. The idea was to give to both crew members an independent cabin with much better visibility and protection. The layout of the cockpits was tested on several ground rigs before being finalised. The final variant was very well received by test pilots during mock up testing. Both crew members had newly independent glazing of the cockpit with large bulletproof windshields, which later proved very reliable in many combats. Entry into the cockpit was made easier through the provision of a separate door for each crew member, also allowing easy disembarkation in the event of an emergency. The front windshield panel was made of 42mm thick multi-layer glass. The area of both cockpit stations was almost three times bigger when compared to the original glass of the Mi-24A. It allowed the pilot and WSO to be well protected from rifle fire hitting the ship from the front hemisphere. The later combat deployment in Africa or Afghanistan showed that it could not be penetrated, even by a hit of 30mm shell. Seeking intelligence on Soviet hardware in 1980s Afghanistan, the CIA compensated Mujahedeen fighters for capturing Mi-24 helicopters and subsequently testing their armour protection by conducting documented live-fire tests on the ships from various directions. The front windshield, despite multiple hits from 12.7mm, 23mm and even 30mm calibre weapons, never failed. On the sides of the cockpit additional panels made of 4mm thick steel plates were screwed on the skin of the helicopter. The lower segment of the pilot's cabin door was armoured as well and was therefore augmented by a telescopic strut. All in all, with reduced total weight the protection of the crew rose dramatically. The side windows were made of curved Plexiglass and remained unarmoured, as Soviet design focused the aircraft's protection primarily on the frontal sector.

One of the design requirements was to install the aiming and guidance equipment in a way that allowed easy operation without too crowded an arrangement in the cockpit. The decision was made to install part of the system outside of the cabin, mainly under the floor of the front cockpit. Because the Shturm missiles were still not released for serial production and its development faced many technical issues, the 9P145M Phalanga-PV ATGM system with Raduga-F guidance set and 9M17P missiles was selected. This system was an upgraded variant of the one installed on the Mi-24A. For example, the 9M17P missile included several improvements such as new generation 9Kh419 lighting spots for easier detection of the missile in flight, and the minimum firing range was reduced to 600 metres from the original 950 metres. With this system the kill-probability ratio increased to 80 per cent. Four missiles were installed on 2P-32M launching rails under wing end pylons. The axes of those launchers were converging to the longitudinal axis of the helicopter as was the case with the Mi-24A. The optics of the Raduga system was installed under the nose on the starboard side. It was equipped with pneumatically operated doors, which shielded the optics from insects and dirt when not in use. The zoom ratio worked with a wide

Detail of the Mi-24D stepped cockpits with car-style doors of the rear pilot's cockpit and the new guidance sensors and machine gun in the nose. (*Author*)

Above: Detail of the optics of the Raduga-F guidance system. The protective doors were opened before firing. The doors prevented the glass from getting dirty. (*Author*)

Right: Rarely visible detail of the 9M17P ATGM guidance antenna array. The whole housing could rotate 60° of the centreline. (*Author*)

field of view with 3.3x zoom, and a narrow field of view with 10x zoom. Under the port-side nose an antenna for the guidance of the missiles was installed in a rotatable housing. It could track targets moving 60° left and right relative to the longitudinal axis, which dramatically helped to increase the firing accuracy and allowed the helicopter to manoeuvre after missile launch, although only in a horizontal direction. The antenna was under a fibreglass cover, and included a coding block for pairing with the missiles of the helicopter. The majority of the guidance system's electronics were installed under the cockpit floor, leaving only the guidance controls in it. The WSO finally had space to move.

Another new feature of the Mi-24D model was the nose-mounted USPU-24 turret for the 12.7mm calibre 9A-624 machine gun. It was able to rotate the gun 60° to either side in azimuth and -40°/+20° in elevation. The USPU turret was coupled with a KPS-53AV stabilised gunsight in the cockpit, making automatic corrections for the helicopter's movement. Its movements were pretty fast and the WSO could even track flying enemy helicopters, even if the Hind itself was not manoeuvring evasively due to its moment of inertia. The right side of the lower front fuselage was taken by a hinged ammunition box. The total count for the ammunition stored in the ammo box and in the route to the machine gun was 1,470 rounds. The ammo box included a folded lever for opening, allowing it to be fully opened in a moment by experienced crew. On the nose several control windows were integrated for the ammunition belt check in case of jamming. The gun was installed in a turret with an ammunition belt wound around its upper part, which helped to relieve the potential belt pressure and tension when the gun moved. Initially, a spent-shell collector was installed under the gun, but it was rarely used; the middle section cover was typically removed due to typical overheating of the gun when the covers were in position. The KPS-53AV stabilised gunsight was used primarily for the gun operation as well as for bomb-dropping when in fixed position. By a combination of those functions the obsolete OPB-1R bombsight was removed from the cockpit entirely. The gunsight housed its own PAU-457-2M camera gun for photos of the aiming accuracy and target confirmation. Since the gunsight moved in all directions it became the second gun camera, as another one of S-13 type was used for forward-firing weapons. The S-13 camera gun, originally installed on the left inner-wing pylon, was removed to the end-left pylon because in the previous position it frequently became affected by rocket smoke leading to poor results. The Mi-24D weapon array was further extended by the capability to carry more bombs with the MBD2-67U multiple ejector racks, which were introduced for all underwing pylons, each capable of carrying four 100kg bombs of any previously mentioned type. Because of the brand new guidance optics system and antenna under the nose, the front undercarriage leg had to be extended for better clearance on the ground. Unlike the Mi-24A, the Mi-24D model stands on the ground with a 3° 32′ angle-of-attack. The front wheel bay was now covered not by doors, but a simple aerodynamic fairing on the oleo strut only, leaving the wheel partly exposed when retracted. The new cockpit also dramatically reduced the internal cabin space, which resulted in lower performance requirements for the filtration system. Finally, the better distribution of the cooling air helped to reduce the internal temperature and even in hot climate the cabins were cooled down easily.

Above: Detail of the 9A-624 four-barrel machine gun. The inner section of the cover was used seldomly as it reduced the cooling effect. (*Author*)

Below: Mi-24D wing with full weapon array—two UB-32A-24 unguided rockets blocks and four 9M17P anti-tank missiles. Note the gun camera on the top of the end pylon. (*Author*)

This is how the Mi-24D was proposed to the state trials. It were the test pilots S. V. Petrov, M. V. Razomazov and L. Z. Tatarchuk. who were responsible for the model verification and state trials. The state examination proved the model to be far better from the pilot's perspective, with a consistent view from the cockpit during all stages of flight. The WSO had much better working conditions, which contributed to the higher firing accuracy. With this Mi-24D standard established and proven, the order for series production was granted in 1973. For the first time the order was granted not solely to the Arsenyev plant (which was in any case heavily occupied by the manufacture of previously ordered Mi-24As) but also for Rostov on Don-based Rostvertol plant, at that time manufacturing Mi-6 and Mi-10 helicopters.

The first five Rostov-built helicopters were completed in 1973, with the Arsenyev plant turning out its first machines a little later. Originally, both plants manufactured helicopters for the domestic operator, with Rostov being selected as the main export production line for Mi-24D and every following Hind model. This decision came from the high level of interest in the Mi-24 model expressed by several potential export customers. After all, the Mi-24D eliminated the majority of the complaints of its early users and the USSR finally had its 'devil's chariot' for spreading the communistic ideology through superior firepower. After a programme of testing, the Mi-24D model was formally accepted for service within the Soviet army on 29 March 1976. This decision actually came the year after the aircraft's real entrance into the service, but this was usual Soviet practice. A very limited number of early production helicopters had been built with the tail rotor on the starboard side due to a lengthy reshuffle of production jigs, but this was soon changed to the port side. During production the model evolved significantly.

The first helicopters were equipped with modernised TV3-117 2. series engines with a 300-hour period between overhauls, while later also versions offering 500 hours, 750 hours (3rd Serie) and even 1,000 hours in the newest export models were available. The majority of engines was upgraded to a higher standard during periodical overhauls. In addition to the improvement to the engines, PZU devices for dust protection, originally developed while the Mi-24A was in service, were introduced on the type as a later standard feature. This was important for the Mi-24 as the dust posed considerable risk of damage to the engines occurring during lift-off in dusty areas, to the extent that a directive was issued to pour water on the ground around the helicopter before running the engines up. Of course, such a procedure was not ideal for the battle zone. Some avionics improvements were introduced such as the new R-863 VHF/UFH radio (instead of R-806 Pero-I type), R-828 Evcalypt UHF and Karat M-24 HF radio (later replaced by Yadro-1A), MS-61 radio recorder.

Since the late 1970s there have been several testbeds used for the verification of various modifications for the Mi-24 family. For example, two Mi-24Ds were used for performance tests of the new countermeasures system, one Mi-24D was used for trials of TV3-117V engines described below, another Mi-24D for tests of new tail rotor blades, and another Mi-24D used for weapon systems testing. In total, some 625 helicopters were manufactured between 1975 and 1981, with fifty-one built in Rostov and 148 in Arsenyev for the Soviet army, and 423 in Rostov between 1978 and 1985, for export customers. The numbers make it obvious that the Soviet army preferred

The very first Mi-24D prototype with the starboard side tail rotor. Note the additional air data boom on the front and behind the cockpit. (*MVZ Mil*)

the later Mi-24V model for its own forces, regarding the Mi-24D as the main export variant. The European export operators received a practically identical standard, only with a slightly downgraded Phalanga-P missile system. Non-European customers received the more downgraded Mi-25 export standard.

When the Mi-24D model entered service, the need for a dedicated training model resurfaced. The Mi-24U's handling characteristics differed significantly in many aspects from those of the Mi-24D, and the first trained crews suffered from some 'bad habits' being carried over from training. Hence, a new model, the Mi-24DU with internal code Izdeliye 249, was launched based on the Mi-24D design. The new cockpit arrangement allowed for an excellent view from both cockpits. The pilot was expected to sit in the rear cockpit, while the instructor was sitting in front in the position of WSO.

Above: One of the later Mi-24D prototypes already with the portside tail rotor and gun camera relocated above the wing endplate. (*MVZ Mil*)

Below: Detail of the weapon systems operator's cockpit of the Mi-24D with the KPS-53AV guidance system in the middle. The GPS receiver on the top was added in the late 1990s. (*Author*)

Above: Pilot's instrument board in the Mi-24D with simple PKV gunsight. It was ready to absorb a more sophisticated gunsight not available at that time. (*Author*)

Below: Cargo cabin of the Mi-24D with clearly visible armouring plate on the wall and folded weapon pintle mount. Only one bench is installed. (*Author*)

Originally, two variants were under consideration. The first required the full ATGM system to be deleted, while the second retained all weapons but the cannon. In the end the latter variant prevailed as it allowed the installation of an instrument panel for the instructor in front of him instead of having all instruments out of his direct line of sight on the right side (where normally the guidance system for the ATGM would be located). Replacing the USPU-24 system with 9A-624 machine gun allowed the KPS-53AV gunsight station to be dispensed with, giving way to a panel displaying all essential flight instruments. In addition, a full set of controls, excluding single engine control levers, could be installed in the cockpit due to the space that had been freed up. On the left side a special panel controlling the simulation of failures was installed. The first two prototypes were basically modified production Mi-24Ds lacking machine guns and ATGMs.

The first prototype passed state trials in late 1976 and was accepted into service. However, all production Mi-24DUs were equipped with the Phalanga-PV ATGM system because it allowed practice on the type, and also the weapon engagement missions. The first machines were completed in 1977, and the latest completed for the export air force in 1991. In total, approximately 107 helicopters were delivered, including an export modification referred to as Mi-24DU for Warsaw Pact countries and Mi-25U for countries outside of Europe.

In the Soviet air force, the Mi-24Ds gradually replaced the Mi-24As with the above mentioned units, and several more were rearmed. Due to a change of command the rotary wing section was moved from the air force to the army command with typical organisation of 'independent' units assigned to provide fire support to ground units under the same command. A typical unit was the independent helicopter regiment OVP (*Otdelnyi Vertoletnyi Polk*) consisting of three squadrons, two with Mi-24s and one with Mi-8s, each with twenty helicopters. Should the squadron be separated,

The first prototype of the Mi-24DU training model lacked the ATGM system entirely because the guided weapons training was expected to be passed on standard Mi-24Ds. (*MVZ Mil*)

it was called OVE (*Otdelnaya Vertoletnayia Eskadrilya*). The units under army command were structured as OVPBU/OVEBU (*Otdelnyi Vertoletnyi Polk/Otdelnaya Vertoletnayia Eskadrilya Boyevogo Oopravlenyia*) and those were equipped with all-Hind squadrons or, in case of regiments, a mix of Hinds and armed Mi-8TVs squadrons. The smallest unit was the OVO (*Otdelnyi Vertoletnyi Otryiad*) with usually three ships only.

The organisation changed dramatically over time with the majority of helicopters being located in European parts of the USSR and a few in Far East and southern border areas. The Mi-24Ds were primarily assigned to European units while Mi-24As were sent to Far East for the rest of their service life. Next to the ships assigned to the units located on the territory of the Russian republic of the USSR, many Hinds were deployed in other Soviet republics. Unlike the deployment of Hinds in Europe these were typically located in areas where there was an internal security problem of the USSR. This is why on the territory of Azerbaijan republic of the USSR the 362nd OSAE Mixed Aviation Squadron (*Otdelnaya Smeshanaya Aviatsionnaya Eskadrilya*) was located at Kirovobad airbase, 381st OVE at Nakhchivan airbase, and 386th OVE at Sangachal airbase, 65th OTBVP Independent Transport-Attack Helicopter Regiment (*Otdelnyi Transportno-Boyevoy Vertoletnyi Polk*) in the neighbouring Armenian republic of the USSR, or 66th OVP at Chirchik airbase in the Uzbek republic of the USSR. The Mi-24DUs were concentrated at the Syzran higher aviation college, where the majority of the Soviet Hind pilots passed their training, as well as at the 784th Helicopter Training Regiment located at the Frunze and Kant airbases in the Kyrgyz Republic of the USSR. The larger regiments were operating individual Mi-24DUs only.

The Soviet army aviation was located not only on the territory of the USSR, but also in the countries of the Warsaw Pact. The densest location of units was in East Germany, with several independent regiments and squadrons equipped with Mi-24s—exactly in the direction of expected main confrontation with NATO. In East Germany, in the north region, the 9th OVEBU and 336th OVEBU at the Neuruppin base, and 172nd OBVP at Parchim base were equipped with Mi-24Ds after phasing out the Mi-24As. In the Central region it was 337th OBVP and 296th OVEBU at Mahlwinkel airbase, 113th OVPBU at Oranienburg airbase, and finally 178th OVP and 440th OVP at Stendal airbase (this unit was armed with Mi-24D, the very last one in 1991, when all remaining squadrons and regiments already operated newer models). In the south region, it was the 6th OVEBU at Dresden-Hellerau, 139th OVE at Jüteborg, and in the south-west region the 327th OVE at Allstedt airbase, and 298th OVEBU at Erfurt airbase, 241st OVE at Hassleben airbase, 312nd OVEBU at Merseburg airbase, 311st OVE and 345th OVE at Schlottheim airbase, 338th OVP at Nohra airbase. In Czechoslovakia, rather newer Hinds were located with the Mi-24D documented only with the 238th OVP and 490th OVP at Sliač airbase in Slovakia. In Poland the 55th OVP was located at the Bagicz airbase.

All in all, Soviet Air force rotary wing aviation had, in Europe, over 180 Mi-24As and Mi-24Ds. A truly credible formation which was more than doubled when newer Mi-24Vs and Mi-24Ps became available. The majority of the Mi-24DU helicopters were serving in the Soviet air force later passing to Russia, Belarus, Ukraine and Kyrgyzstan. Many Arab and African countries were using Soviet facilities for training due to the high cost of the training model. In 1989 when the Soviet army pulled out of Afghanistan, and in 1990 when the withdrawal of Soviet forces from Europe began, Hinds were deployed to new units. For example, in Kazakh republic of the USSR, 486th OVP was formed from the 241st OVE, 311st OVE and 345th OVE originally located at East German airbases and in the Belarussian Republic of the USSR the 50th OSAP returning from Afghanistan was, with its 3rd Helicopter Squadron, moved to Mary airbase, and in 1996 it turned into 286th OVE at the Lipki airbase near the capital of Minsk, as did the 181st OVP, which moved to Pruzhany airbase. In the USSR several overhaul facilities were selected for Hind overhauls which were scheduled to be passed every five years with the initial series of helicopters. Facilities at Konotop and Lugansk in Ukraine were major overhaul facilities.

A formation take-off of the Soviet air force Mi-24Ds. Note the ships lack the DUAS-V air data boom tabs. All are in pre-final configuration without a fully functional weapon system. (*ITAR-TASS*)

Above: A fleet of early Soviet air force Mi-24Ds getting ready for a night flight. The closest ship wears the badge of a perfectly maintained helicopter under the WSO's cockpit. (*ITAR-TASS*)

Below: Another very early Mi-24D shot, again without DUAS-V sensor and PZU filters, which were not available with very early series. (*ITAR-TASS*)

Above: A formation of early Soviet Mi-24Ds in flight. Theoretically, only three ships were needed to destroy six enemy tanks. (*ITAR-TASS*)

Below: A picture of serial Soviet Mi-24DU from the Syzran aviation college. Note the ZSh-5 flight helmets originally designed for fighter pilots. (*ITAR-TASS*)

Another picture of two serial Soviet Mi-24Dus from the Syzran aviation college. The USSR was operating absolute majority of produced ships. (*ITAR-TASS*)

The Soviet air force formed 50th OSAP (Independent Mixed Aviation Regiment (*Otdelnyi Smeshanyi Aviatsionyi Polk*) in 1980, and it was subordinated to the 40th Army—a major unit of the Soviet contingent in Afghanistan. Its inventory included Mi-8MTs and Mi-24Ds. It was initially based at Kunduz airport, where it landed in January 1980 and two days later first combat sorties of two Mi-24Ds were performed. At that moment the almost decade-long engagement of Hinds in Afghanistan started. In late May, the unit moved to Kabul airport. A year later the unit was rearmed with more powerful Mi-24Vs and Mi-24Ds performed over 1,200 combat flights. The first ship was lost in combat in February 1980 after the crew was hit by heavy calibre gunfire and the ship crashed. Two months later, two helicopters performed emergency landings after being hit by rifle fire behind enemy lines. After landing, the crew destroyed the helicopters with hand grenades and burned them down, and the same scenario was repeated a few days later when another helicopter struck the mountains at 3,000 metres and fell and rolled over. In May 1980, one helicopter from the Soviet contingent was hit by the DShK 12.7mm calibre gun and crashed, and another was downed by RPG explosion near one engine with crash from 3,000 metres altitude as the ship was unable to continue in flight with only one engine. In total, eight ships were lost within few months and a few more in 1981 and 1982, when they were fully replaced by more powerful Mi-24Vs.

In 1976 it was decided by the Warsaw Pact executive committee that the Mi-24D, and later Mi-24V, should become a standardised 'eastern tank buster'. With the concept of buffer zone in the satellite countries Moscow demanded that Czechoslovakia, Poland, East Germany and Hungary buy the type in substantial quantities so their armies might act as a first-line barrier in case of a NATO tank attack, or to form the spear of the Warsaw Pact should it attack first. To start training in all mentioned countries in the shortest time, each country received four ships in 1978. In sequence, the East German helicopters were produced in February and March, Hungarian in March, Czechoslovak ones in May and June, and Polish ships in September 1978. They were somehow in a series as the East German ships were given serial codes B4001 to B4004, Hungarian ships K2005 to K2008, Czechoslovak ships M34009 to M34012, and finally, Polish ships A1013 to A1016, with the last two digits clearly showing the production sequence from 1 to 16. The crews from all countries typically formed from the Mi-4 and Mi-8 pilots, were sound in their knowledge from flying on the Mi-8T turboshaft type before they were sent to USSR. North of the Soviet city of Frunze was located a training unit mentioned above in relation to foreign Mi-24A training, which later also operated Mi-24DUs and Mi-24Ds, mostly without PZU filters. It was providing full training to the foreign crews using Soviet air force fleet. The training started with academia and was purely in the Russian language. On grounds of secrecy, no handbooks were passed to the pilots in training and they had to remember all the information and write it down manually every day. This is how the first manuals for operation were created in each country. In the summer period the temperature rose to almost 40°C, which showed the Hind performance limits on an airfield located some 900 metres above mean sea level. Typically, an experienced pilot passed thirteen flights before he flew solo. Some pilots later recalled that other pilots from Libya, Mongolia and Algeria were passing the training at the same time.

It became the East German air force LSK NVA (Luftstreitkräfte der Nationalen Volksarmee) who received the very first export Mi-24Ds in July 1978. All were flown by Soviet crews from USSR to Soviet bases in Legnica in Poland and then to Basepohl airbase near Brandenburg, home of helicopter wing HG-54 (Hubschraubergeschwader). To obscure the exact number of the ships in operation, they were given tail codes 403, 406, 407 and 412. Training started when Soviet instructors arrived later that year.

Czechoslovak army received the first ships ferry-flown from Rostov to Minsk in today's Belarussia, and then to Prostějov on 24 August 1978. They landed at the base of the 51st Helicopter Regiment (Vrtulníkový Pluk), previously using Mi-4s and Mi-8s and being the only purely helicopter unit of the country. All ships were flown by Soviet crews and curiously all were wearing Soviet red stars without white line on the fuselages.

The arrival happened completely under clandestine conditions and helicopters were parked separately, surrounded by masking nets disallowing to any spy seeing them. Yellow lines were sprayed on the ground and only selected personnel directly involved in Hind operation were authorised to pass it. All ships were given serial numbers derived from production codes, so they were labelled 4009 to 4012. Although two Czechoslovak pilots passed instructor rating in Frunze, the command of the army air force was concerned to start training without a Soviet air force instructor. He arrived in October, so the real start of the training was postponed to then. The standard operation commenced in November 1978. Hungarian Mi-24Ds arrived the same day, as did the Czechoslovak ships, on 24 August 1978 to the Szentkirályszabadja-based 87th Regiment of Transport Helicopter (Szállítóhelikopter Ezred) located near the city of Veszprem, north of Balaton Lake. The Hungarian sources say the delivery was delayed by two months and the crews, returned from Frunze, had to fly the Mi-8Ts for a while to keep currency. The Soviet instructors were even flying with the Hungarian army aviation.

Poland received her first four Mi-24Ds on 20 September 1978 and all were given tail codes 13 to 16, later during service changed to 013 to 016. Due to the delay in crew training, the regular operation started on 1 January 1979, and all helicopters were assigned to the 37th Transport Helicopter Regiment (Pułk Śmigłowców Transportowych) at the Leźnica Wielka airbase. The beginning of 1979 meant the Warsaw Pact entered a new era, with five countries operating the Hind. Bulgaria became the sixth operator and sent the first crews to the USSR for training in December 1978. The first four helicopters landed in Bulgaria on 17 July 1979. They wore serial codes U5065 to U 5068, but in their new home got the fuselage codes 101 to 104. All were assigned to 44th Helicopter Aviation Regiment (Vertoleten Aviatsionen Polk) at the Krumovo airbase. Romania decided not to purchase the type as the plans for arming the Puma helicopters built under licence prevailed, and Albania never found a budget for the type.

In 1979 the deliveries continued with four more helicopters handed over to LSK NVA and twelve more to Bulgaria. In total, East Germany bought forty-two Mi-24Ds, Czechoslovakia twenty-eight Mi-24Ds and two more Mi-24DUs, Hungary thirty Mi-24Ds, Poland sixteen Mi-24Ds, and finally Bulgaria, thirty-eight Mi-24Ds. Since the late production of Mi-24Ds overlapped with the Mi-24V model mentioned below, they shared some features in the last production batches. Helicopters bought in 1985 by Hungary, Poland and Bulgaria are sometimes unofficially referred to as Mi-24D+ or Mi-24D plus. They were equipped with the new warning system, infra-red jammer, flare dispensers attached to the tail-boom beam without metal strips, and TV3-117V engines with increased shaft power for hot and high conditions, capable of exhaust gas-cooler installation. On the other hand, some non-European Mi-25s finished the same year were completed to the 'old' standard. Although the Warsaw Pact Hinds were expected to be the main anti-tank means of the Warsaw Pact, they were actually never used in real combat during the pact existence. It was the other operators who deployed the ships in combat. For the first time they were widely deployed during the Shield 79 large exercise involving practically all Warsaw Pact Countries. The Mi-24Ds were of key importance because until they arrived, the destruction of the enemy tanks was a task for the ground troops and in a limited way, for fast jets. Hinds entirely changed the strategy with their dedicated anti-tank and special combat troops insertion role. For all the European operators it became the very first rotary wing model able to cope with enemy armoured vehicles. It also came with other new features and when training flights in the simulated NBC were practiced for example, due to hermitization the Mi-24 crews did not wear oxygen masks, which made flying very easy. Initially, the helicopters were assigned to transport helicopter regiments, but soon special attack squadrons emerged.

The East German Mi-24Ds were short lived with the original operator. The HG-54 wing operated the type together with the Mi-8TVK assault-transport type. The latter one, although with higher weapon load, lacked many features and capabilities of Hind and proved the ship was overloaded. The increased number of Hinds in service, with four more delivered in 1979, eighteen in 1981, six in 1982 and ten in 1983, led to reorganisation of the unit into Attack Helicopter Wing KHG-57 (Kampfhubschraubergeschwader-57) and another unit, KHG-67, was created and later sent to Cottbus airbase when it familiarised with the Mi-24Ds delivered in 1982. Each wing had two squadrons of attack helicopters, one with Mi-8TVKs and one with Mi-24Ds. The VEB facility at Dresden was tasked with type overhauls.

The German army was always extremely pedantic, and it refused to take over some of the helicopters because they did not pass the entry tests. It was a typical problem of the Soviet serial production where processes such as levelling of the airframe were done just for reference, and when the parameters were 'close' to the tolerance limits the ship was still released for service. A little crooked is still good! But not so for German officers, who dogmatically insisted on the tolerance limits being met. The Hind squadrons' participation in several military exercises showed that organisation under the LSK (air force) was problematic and both wings were subordinated to ground forces command LaSK (Landstreitkräfte), which was in reality the major user of the anti-tank capability. Two years later the wings were renamed KHG-5 for KHG-57 and KHG-3 for KHG-67 respectively. In 1980 one helicopter was lost when the ship entered the '*podkhvat*' regime during energic manoeuvring. This occurs when the pilot initiates a steep climb following a dive, when the main rotor, tilting back, may hit the tail boom. Another helicopter was badly damaged in an accident two years later. The airframe was later reused as an instructional airframe and now rests at Berlin-Gatow Millitary History Museum. The ship was given the new code 5211, the only four-digit code of all East German Hinds. Since the ATGM Phalanga-PV system became obsolete, a plan to obtain one Mi-24V for evaluation was laid down in the mid-1980s. The East German industry was considering developing a specific missile from the Konkurs type, which was produced under licence there and was technically close to the Shturm type; however, those planes never materialised. The Mi-24Ds were also tested with illumination rockets and other equipment.

When the Iron Curtain fell, the Hind wings were still in operation; originally they were even placed on alert to protect the falling regime, but were never used. The East German government stopped any further orders of the type and accepted only twelve Mi-24Ps as described below. After German reunification the wings were reorganised to new helicopter units 70 (Heersfliegertruppe, ex-KHG-3) and 80 (KHG-5). The WTD-61 test squadron (Wehrtechnische Dienststelle-61) in Bavaria was given two Mi-24Ds and one Mi-24P for evaluation tests. Mechanics applied the Luftwaffe insignia on all helicopters and the new fuselage codes of 96+xx style, with the 96 code reserved for Hinds. The last flight under the NVA command happened on 25 December 1990. The WTD-61 crews used the type for evaluation and flew several dozen flight hours aimed at mapping the performance and tactical capabilities of the type. There were also some rare tests not related to the type itself; for example, the only Mi-24D was equipped with Hawk missile seeker instead of a machine gun.

WTD-61 helicopters were recoded to 98+xx style. One Mi-24D was supplied to the US-led OPTEC programme (Operational Test & Evaluation Command) based at Alexandria, Virginia, with the Mi-24P described below. They were used for flight evaluation of countermeasures and tactics, and were flown frequently at Fort Rucker base in Alabama, Reese and Fort Bliss air force bases in Texas, and at the Nellis Air Force Base in Nevada. Formally, the aircraft belonged under 3rd Battalion of 210th Aviation Regiment at Biggs Airfield in Texas. After the below described Libyan Mi-25 and Iraqi Mi-25, it was another boost of the 'red air' rotorcraft capability and the US army was finally in a position to abandon attempts at using QS-55 helicopters based on the Sikorsky S-55, mimicking the Hind with its laminate fairings.

The flight evaluation helped to determine the tactical procedures and the German Hind flew over 300 hours. Some of the flight activity was, after 2001, dedicated to training of pilots supporting the US in the world war on terror. The ship was interestingly equipped with a laser scoring system and fake three-barrel cannon for the in-flight evaluation of the combat, as well as with the reflector on the barrels blinking when firing was initiated. In the cockpits all labels were in English, and US-origin radios and GPS receivers were added. This Hind is frequently identified as Mi-24V because of 9M114 Shturm ATGM launching tubes on the end pylons, but those were never enabled on the type. The helicopter was selected for overhaul in 2010, but it eventually never happened. In the meantime the German fleet, operated formally under the HFS 70 at Cottbus and HFS 80 at Basepohl (Heersfliegerstaffel) within the new

East German Mi-24D belonging to the KHG-57 regiment. Note the camouflage weathering caused by open-air parking. (*Thomas Girke*)

Two East German Mi-24Ds captured in low pass during army drills. Both ships have the original camouflage from OEM. (*MVZ Mil*)

Luftwaffe structure, was gradually grounded, with the last flight in 1993. Due to the German defence policy and actual obsolescence of the Mi-24D weapons system it was not recommended for further use as were all other types except MiG-29s. Eighteen Mi-24Ds were sold for 1 German mark each to Poland and a further fourteen to Hungary. Only a few Hinds remained in German museums.

The Czechoslovak 51. Helicopter Regiment swiftly launched a massive training programme for new crews, and the belief in the new model was almost unlimited. When the first ships landed at the base, all were equipped with PZU filters on the engine intakes and as the rated pilots returning from Frunze had previously flown Mi-24Ds without the filters, they had no clear idea how they worked, commenting: 'power reduction measures limiting the incredible power of the engines'. The first year of operation was focused on training and also a lot of demonstrations. During one of them in May 1979 a helicopter was almost lost. The pilots experienced for the very first time in a real operation the flight regime '*podkhvat*'. Only a quickly initiated left descending turn avoided a catastrophic result and luckily the pilot, trying to push the completely jammed controls—even asking the WSO to help—recalled a small notice from the manual and turned the ship left. During that stage of flight, the forward

Above: When Germany reunited, the Hind fleet passed to the Luftwaffe and helicopters were given new insignia and fuselage codes, like this Mi-24D. (*Thomas Girke*)

Below: The ex-German Mi-24D pictured around 2010 in Fort Bliss, Texas, where it ended its career as a 'red air' ship. Note the laser tracked on the cannon. (*Petr Kunetek*)

motion of the cyclic stick is practically impossible, and only lateral movements are possible. Some 30 metres above the ground the crew managed to recover some and landed shortly after, sweating and shaking from being close to death.

The demonstration had been organised for the Czechoslovak and some Soviet generals, who watched the demo and nodded their heads at how great a helicopter it was, and what energetic manoeuvres it could do, not realising they came very close to witnessing a crash. A minimum time of 6 seconds for transition from dive to climb was set as a rule then. From then on, pilots referred to the Mi-24 as the only helicopter able to kill itself during flight. Another accident happened a few weeks later, when the annunciators indicated zero oil pressure in the left engine. The crew, unfortunately, shut down the other engine, which was then prevented from starting by the automatic protection system and the captain chose to execute an emergency landing. During the descent, flames some 8 meters long were bursting out of the exhaust pipe and immediately as the helicopter hit the ground, the jammed engine shut off completely. It ran without oil for eight minutes, a very good value then for a Soviet helicopter. The engine was destroyed, but the helicopter was in a good condition and later flew again.

In October 1979 the first live ATGM firing occurred, and it immediately showed the effectiveness of the Hind. During a week-long exercise, crews of three Mi-24Ds destroyed all the practice targets the very first day, a feat which normally lasted for week at least. Since the single ATGM missile cost was exceeding the cost of a new Lada family car, only the most experienced WSOs who had trained for weeks in advance on a ground simulator were allowed to live fire. The initial exercise showed 100 per cent success rate and later the average of 0.9 kill ratio was regularly achieved, although in good 'peaceful' conditions with missile failures typically representing the remaining 0.1 ratio.

In the 1980s, the Czechoslovak Mi-24Ds were deployed abroad for the first time, in East Germany during the Brotherhood in Arms 80 exercise (Waffenbrüderschaft). In the 1980s four more Mi-24D arrived, followed by ten in 1981 and a further ten in 1982. The increased number of ships allowed for some to be sent to Plzeň-Bory airbase in the western corner of the country. Originally they were subordinated as detached to 4. Squadron of 51st Helicopter Regiment, but later a specific 11th Helicopter Regiment (11. Vrtulníkový Pluk) was established there. While the Prostějov-based helicopters were used mainly for drills with regular army units, the Plzeň-based unit became part of the country air defence system. Hinds were patrolling the western border, and hunts with US army Cobras and Kiowas became a regular joy. The deployment in the hilly and mountainous border region took its toll in 1985.

During one hunt of the US army AH-1F Cobra helicopter, the Mi-24D pilot tried to hold the lock in the area of small mountains with 1,300 metres elevation. The Cobra decelerated on the German side of the border and hovered, while the Mi-24D crew tried to do the same. Unfortunately, the combination of high weight, high elevation and hot weather resulted in insufficient power to hover, and the helicopter fell into the trees with serious injuries to all three crew members. The command centre sent another Mi-24D helicopter, which almost ended up the same way. The Mi-24D was underpowered for hovering in mountains and following this accident it was forbidden to reduce speed to below 100 km/h in such an environment. However, Hinds, and mainly the newer Mi-24V model, were used for border patrolling until the mid-1990s, as they were better able to cope with pursuit of helicopters or sports planes, usually lost in bad weather.

From 1984, the 51st Regiment also became involved in southern border control and it usually dealt with sports planes flying into the country from Austria. After several clashes and shooting down of intruders in the 1960s and '70s by the MiG-21s and L-29s, live firing was quite rare with the helicopters. The Czechoslovak Mi-24s also became intruders from time to time when the crew got lost and flew over foreign territory. In the 1980s the Czechoslovak army tested Mix-1 mining containers, which would dispense mines during a low pass directly over enemy tanks. However, the Mix device did not meet the required criteria and was abandoned after several live tests performed by one Mi-24D helicopter. Instead, Soviet RBK-250-275 cluster bombs with 159 sub-munitions each were selected.

In the 1980s, an LRM-122 block with four 122mm unguided rockets was tested on Mi-24D and Mi-24V models. Those rockets, being a derivate of the Grad ground-based system, did not see widespread adoption due to the high risk of the engines surging after firing. Czechoslovak Hinds also used CCP-100-70 and CCP-250-70 concrete practice bombs. In 1984, the massive Shield 84 exercise took place in Czechoslovakia with twenty-four Mi-24Ds involved, and others from the Soviet units. The domestic training capability was boosted in 1985 by delivery of two training Mi-24DU units, one assigned to each regiment. The Czechoslovak Mi-24Ds, when they had reached the time limit between overhauls, were serviced in Tököl, Hungary, like the Mi-8Ts were. Due to standardisation, they returned from the works in the same camouflage as Hungarian or Bulgarian ships. In the late 1990s the overhauls were mastered locally by LOK company, based in Prague.

During the operation helicopters were added with new features for self-defence, developed based on Soviet experience in Afghanistan. On the rear side of the fuselage the L-166-1VE Lipa infra-red xenon lamp jammer was installed, together with four ASO-2V flare dispensers attached by metal strips under the tail boom. The captain's cockpit had rearview mirrors added for better control of the area behind the helicopter. Those features were provided as a kit, and other Warsaw Pact countries updated helicopters in a similar way.

In 1991, Prostějov-based helicopters headed towards the West for the very first time and Mi-17 and Mi-24D landed at Payerne in Switzerland, where they performed the first Czechoslovak public display outside of the Eastern Europe. The organisers, not realising the Hind's power, assigned it a parking lot near light choppers, whose rotors started to turn from the Hind's downwash before it had even initiated its final descent, and the poor marshal waved like crazy to abort the landing. Hind then parked behind the lot. The Mi-24Ds were domestically demonstrated in group flights and became a very popular item on the agenda of annual air shows. Equipped with smoke generation devices made of unused UB-16-57 rocket blocks, actually seldomly used on Hind, they even performed smoke shows in the national colours.

In 1992 a political decision to split the Czechoslovak federation was taken and several Mi-24Ds were sent to the Slovak airbase at Prešov, where they tested the feasibility of the location of a new Slovak air force helicopter unit there. In total, eight

Mi-24Ds and single Mi-24DU were transferred to Slovakia to the newly created 4th Helicopter Regiment (Vrtuľníkový Pluk) at the Prešov airbase. The Mi-24Ds were assigned to 2nd Squadron. The airbase was far from perfect and the helicopters were frequently operated from the grass airfield, regardless of whether they got stuck in the mud after every rain. Since the newly created Slovak air force did not have enough of type-rated pilots, the ferry flights of helicopters dedicated to Slovakia were performed by mixed crews. It was somewhat upsetting for the Czech crews when the Slovak side demanded only airworthy and flyable helicopters, while in the Czech Republic many ships with various defects remained and airworthy ships were frequently used as a source of spare parts to make the Slovak ships flyable. The initial Slovak task was to stabilise a training system as the annual number of flight hours dropped below forty for all pilots. The unit was soon restructured to 4th Helicopter Wing (Vrtuľníkové Krídlo) and later to 34th Airbase (Letecká základňa).

Due to loss of ties to the Russian and Hungarian overhaul facilities, the Slovak state-owned company LOTN started an overhaul programme of the Mi-24, with some overhauls spanning more than two years. Slovakia, led by a pro-Russian government back then, was considering replacing the entire Mi-24 fleet, and even Ka-50 was displayed in the country as a potential candidate, while the country redeemed the Russian state debt by making deliveries of spare parts as well as new MiG-29s and Tu-154. In the mid-1990s less than half of the helicopters remained operational. Those which survived were upgraded due to legislation requiring even military helicopters to be able to fly in common 'civilian' airspace. Attention was paid to communication and navigation items, and in 2004 the first prototype, Mi-24D with code 0149, was updated with Trimble 2101 navigation, V/UHF radio AN/ARC-210, APX-100 transponder, ELT-200 emergency location transmitter, Czech Speel FDR-39HGM flight data recorder, new anti-collision flash lights, and a modification of the radar warning receiver (RWR) system, allowing the automatic firing of flares when a threat is indicated. At least four other Mi-24Ds were updated in this way, with the removal of ATGM launching rails rendered useless when the original missiles went out of production.

In 2001, another reorganisation passed and the 34th Airbase was renamed as 3rd Airbase. Because it became clear that the acquisition of new helicopters was out of discussion for budget reasons, the Mi-24Ds being stored long-term were cleared for overhauls at LOTN, which ended with a new paint scheme as a distinguishing factor. Next to the participation in various military exercises in 2005, the Mi-24 were called on duty to protect the meeting of US president George W. Bush and Russian Federation president Vladimir Putin in Bratislava. In 2006 the oldest of the helicopters reached the end of its service life, and an era of service withdrawal began. The operating unit was again reorganised to helicopter wing (Vrtuľníkové Krídlo), with all surviving Hinds serving under its helicopter squadron. In 2011 it was decided to phase out all Mi-24s due to the high cost of overhauls. Some Mi-24Ds were donated to local museums, some are used as gatekeepers.

After the fall of Iron Curtain and split of the Federation, the Czech Mi-24Ds remained in service and in 1995 were all assigned to former jet airbase in Přerov with both 51st and 11th helicopter regiments being disbanded and replaced by newly

Above: The very first Czechoslovak Mi-24D from the 51st Helicopter Regiment shortly after delivery, yet without its self-defence suite, which was installed later. (*VHÚ*)

Below: A formation of early Czechoslovak Mi-24Ds delivered in the second batch. Formation flights were particularly important for offensive tactics. (*Robert Kučera*)

The Mi-24D was slightly underpowered for operation in mountainous areas, a fact sadly documented by this wreck of Czechoslovak Mi-24D, which crashed while hunting a US Army AH-64A Apache in 1985. (*VHÚ*)

created 33rd Airbase. Several modernisation attempts were considered, including new weapons and sensors integration, but eventually the only decision made was to equip helicopters with additional altimeters measuring in feet (the original was in metres), GPS receivers and new transponders in order to allow at least some compatibility with NATO. Since the country operated the Mi-24Vs described below, and from 2003 it acquired brand new Mi-24Vs and Mi-35s, only very few of the old Mi-24D models passed one general overhaul at the LOK Prague facility before they were withdrawn from service. Some ships were grounded in the mid-1990s, and the last five ships flew in 2003. All were sold to arms dealers or museums and none of them flew again. Of all ships, the Mi-24D with fuselage code 4011 became particularly known for its white paint scheme with Tiger-themed details applied in 1994 to commemorate the twenty-year anniversary of the 51st Helicopter Regiment. During a mid-1990s air show, it was displayed with R-60 missiles mounted on the ATGM launching rails. Although added purely as a joke and lacking the launcher and wiring required to be fired, this configuration confused many observers and led some sources to mistakenly describe the R-60 as an integrated weapon system. The Mi-24D with code 0220 was refurbished as a collection item of the Prague-based aviation museum and is likely the best-preserved Mi-24D in the world.

Czechoslovakia became the sole Mi-24DU export operator in Europe and one ship passed to the Czech Republic. (*AVIS*)

Detail of the front Mi-24DU cockpit with an easily visible full set of controls. It had a standard instrument board with all essential flight instruments. (*Author*)

Bulgarian Mi-24Ds were operated under the 44th Regiment at Krumovo. Initial operation was complicated by the lack of some spare parts as the railway shipment included Mi-24A spares instead of Mi-24D—a result of a typo in the order. In 1981 the Mi-24Ds participated in the massive flyover of fourteen ships commemorating 1,300 years of Bulgaria, and a year later in the Shield 82 exercise that took place in Bulgaria, in which total of 500 military planes and helicopters participated. The final combat sortie involved twelve Mi-24Ds flying 50 metres above the terrain at speeds of 240 km/h. Bulgarian army aviation also practised amphibious operations of the type and supported its marine corps during annual exercises.

Due to heavy traffic at Krumovo airbase a separated 13th Attack Helicopter Regiment (*Vertoleten Polk Boyni Vertolety*) was founded at the Stara Zagora airbase. Due to perfect preparation some twenty-four ships were flown to a new destination within a day, and two hours after landing performed their first regular task there. Later, remaining ships were delivered there and 13 Regiment became the only operator of the type. Some instructors were flying more than 150 flight hours per year and the operation was extremely intensive with over 4,000 flight hours flown annually.

Although so intensive, only a few mishaps occurred, even though no simulator was purchased despite the regiment command constantly requesting it.

In 1985, one of the helicopters almost hit a power line during low-level flight. The incident was caused by the violent manoeuvrers of the captain trying to avoid crashing; all the main rotor blades were in a steep bank, which were shortened by 1 metre, but the helicopter landed at the base! Since Bulgaria was a popular vacation destination for the Soviet Union, some Soviet pilots returning from Afghanistan also visited it. Bulgarian general staff used this opportunity and systematically gathered combat experience from them for improving of their own procedures.

In 1984, the Mi-24s entered the air defence system and were tasked with interception of slow-flying targets. In 1989 one crew allegedly found an An-2 biplane defecting from Ukraine, but did not declare it as they saw no reason to shoot down a civilian plane not posing any threat. The plane eventually landed safely in Turkey. The first Bulgarian Hinds were serviced in the USSR and later in Hungary. In 1991, when the Warsaw Pact was dissolved, a decision to overhaul the helicopters locally was taken and the local company Terem performed those works with no official support from the OEM. After the Iron Curtain fell the helicopters were used less for budgetary reasons. They were put on standby due to the war in Yugoslavia, and in 1997 during riots in Albania. The commanding officer received an order to ready a few Mi-24Ds for potential evacuation of the Bulgarian embassy in Albanian's capital of Tirana; he asked for refuelling trucks on site and some extra weapons but was denied any support. Lack of funds caused a dramatic drop in the quantity of airworthy helicopters to seven only, and some others were being overhauled by Terem for an incredible eight years—longer than the time-between-overhaul interval itself. Unfortunately, in 1999 a massive hailstorm damaged six helicopters beyond repair.

In 2000, the surviving helicopters were relocated to Krumovo airbase, where 24th Helicopter Airbase (*Vertoletna Aviabaza*) was formed. It was gradually equipped with helicopters coming from overhaul but due to many difficulties typically only two to three helicopters of eighteen planned were available at any time. In 2004, Bulgaria launched an upgrade project for six Mi-24Ds alongside six newer Mi-24Vs. Avionics upgrade work was to comprise installation of an on-board processor integrated with a digital map, embedded GPS/INS navigation system, and multifunctional displays in both NVG-friendly cockpits as well as a control and display unit. New surveillance and aiming equipment on board the Mi-24 was to include a high-performance multi-sensor turret, as well as an advanced helmet-mounted display and targeting system and also a Western-standard navigational system, all-new self-protection suite, and new radios and weapons interfaces. Next to the Elbit company of Israel, which was later declared the winner, another consortium, ATL, comprising South African company ATE, Bulgarian companies Liconex and Terem, and French company Thales, attempted to win, and they even modernised one Bulgarian Mi-24 into an advanced model Sova Attack (described later) at their own cost. The prototype flew for the first time in February 2005 and was expected to become a benchmark for other European operators. Russia then interfered and called the Elbit-led programme illegal unless the Russian Design Bureau was involved. Although the contract was signed and a prototype was in the process of refurbishment, the project stalled as Russia denied any support or spares. A subsequent upgrade involving Russia failed as well, so the fleet of airworthy helicopters shrank and no upgrades happened.

In 2010, the desired number of Mi-24s in operation was further reduced to twelve, but even that was too much for the budget. The pilot training was cut to an absolute minimum, and live firings were rarely practised. In 2002 two helicopters escorted and protected the Mi-8P helicopter with Pope John Paul II on board, and five years later two ships guarded the capital of Sofia when US president George W. Bush visited. Following their withdrawal from the Bulgarian air force, six Mi-24Ds were delivered to the United States, intended for use as opposing forces in live, realistic training exercises. To accurately mimic the more modern Russian Mi-35M, at least two of these helicopters underwent extensive visual modifications. These included a black paint scheme, shortened wings, simulated twin-barrel cannons, mock ATGM launch tubes, and altered guidance sensors. Ultimately, however, their anticipated large-scale use as 'red air' aggressors was not realized. Two more were delivered to Burkina Faso where they flew for several years, and six were delivered to Mali. They had the ATGM system removed and used solely machine gun and rocket pods. At least two of them were destroyed on the ground when rebels attacked the Gao airbase where both choppers were stored in a hangar. The attack, followed by a French-led counteroffensive with mortar fire, caused significant damage to them. Five more at least were delivered to 'Cote d'Ivore. Six Mi-24Ds were kept as strategic reserve but their condition prevented them from further use.

Although apparently examples of the Mi-35M, these are actually ex-Bulgarian Mi-24Da helicopters, operated as 'red air' after some modifications by US company Vertol Systems. (*Vertol Systems Company*)

In 1980 the Hungarian 87th Regiment took delivery of a further sixteen ships, split between two squadrons, each operating ten ships in total. The lack of a dedicated training variant, which had been requested by the commanding officers but never purchased due to its higher price, was solved by the modification of five ships (fuselage numbers 006, 110, 118 and 581) by the replacing the KPS-53AV gunsight with a small instrument board. Those ships were allowed to use the machine gun only in fixed position, which was not a problem for a training model. In the early 1990s, Hinds were put on alert due to war in neighbouring Yugoslavia but they were not deployed in any live action. The fleet was to be augmented by the Mi-24Ds sold from Germany to Hungary, all of which were delivered via rail transport to the Szentkirályszabadja-based 87th Regiment. None of them became operational at that time and all were open-air stored after arrival. When the unit was disbanded, all the attack helicopters were newly subordinated to 87th Helicopter Squadron based at Szolnok airbase and the stored ships were removed to a permanent storage location, while only two Mi-24Ps were overhauled.

The ex-German Mi-24D fleet served as a source of spare parts for the original Hungarian ships, which remained operational under the newly created MH 86 Helicopter Regiment at Szolnok Airbase (Magyar Honvédség Helikopter Ezred). This unit lasted for three years only before being reorganised into 86th Helicopter Base (Helikopterdandár) and the Mi-24s were assigned to its Phoenix Attack Helicopter Battalion (Phoenix Harcihelikopter Zászlóalj). The helicopter with fuselage code 117 in eagle paint scheme became particularly popular. Originally Hungary had intended to deploy the helicopters into international peacekeeping missions, but this never materialised due to lack of budget, although some helicopters were equipped with American radios and navigational systems. The Mi-24D fleet was used extensively for flight operation, although no more than twelve ships were operational in the long term. They participated in various military exercises in the region, and alongside its regular duties were also used for a test flights for a local scientific institute, focusing on the detection of radiation pollution. A special pod under the wing was created for the ship and several flights were made.

In the past two decades, some ten Mi-24Ds have been sold to Ethiopia. The Hungarian Tököl-based Danubian helicopter overhaul company performed overhauls of Ethiopian Mi-24As and Mi-24U and other Mil helicopters, and had a plan to overhaul even the Hungarian ships prior to delivery. However, their destiny is yet to be confirmed, although the Mi-24A and Mi-24U overhauls are documented. Remaining Mi-24Ds were removed from service before 2012 and some are preserved on air force bases.

Initially, four Polish Mi-24s were operated under the 37th Transport Helicopter Regiment (Pułk Śmigłowców Transportowych) at the Leźnica Wielka airbase and were augmented in 1981 by four more. The training of the crews stared in January 1979 and in mid-year the unit achieved operational readiness with first participation in a military exercise. It was a moment when reorganisation of the armed forces took place and new units were selected for rearming with the Mi-24 model, the first being the 49th Regiment of the Ground Forces Aviation (Pułk Lotnictwa Wojsk Lądowych) at Pruszcz Gdański airbase. The unit was soon reorganised into 49th Attack Helicopter

Above: Very late production series of the Mi-24D, like this Hungarian ship, can be distinguished by the L-006 RWR antennas under the cabin and TV3-117V engines. (*Miklos Takács*)

Below: Unlike the previous picture, which shows an Mi-24D in original OEM camouflage, this shot shows a Hungarian Mi-24D with a later camouflage pattern. Note the underslung hook on the belly. (*Petr Štefl*)

Regiment (Pułk Śmigłowców Bojowych) in 1981 when the Mi-24D were introduced into the service under its 8th Attack Helicopter Squadron (Eskadra Śmigłowców Bojowych). The helicopters were soon boosted by six more ships delivered in 1984 and two more year later.

The unit was operating normally and was considered several times to be active in case of the anti-communist uprisings in the country. As with the majority of Warsaw Pact countries, the initial servicing of the fleet was done in USSR. When this was no longer an option, overhauls were introduced at the local WZL-1 (military works) company in the city of Łodż, which was preparing for this likelihood prior 1989. The Warsaw Pact repair capabilities worked both for renewal of the aircraft airworthiness and for maintaining the skilled workers and logistics system during peacetime. Should a war start, these capabilities allowed for rapid battle-damage management. Also, the calendar servicing limits, the most frequent reason for overhaul, would be lifted during war. This is why overhaul technology was an obligatory part of aircraft deliveries. The 49th Regiment operated the Mi-24D model, while the later established 56th Regiment in Innowrocław was selected to operate the newer Mi-24Vs. The latter unit introduced a small display team consisting of four ships and a fifth solo helicopter, and the shows became particularly popular. However, the team ceased to operate in 1998 and the idea of group flights was taken over by the 49th Regiment. The new team, later called Scorpions (Skorpiony), performed a large number of displays and demonstrated precise formations.

When Germany sold the Mi-24Ds to Poland, unlike those from Hungary these were scheduled for flight operation. After general overhaul at Łodż the first two ships were introduced into service in 1996, the final ships three years later. Of eighteen helicopters the two oldest models were used for spares and all remaining were overhauled, creating a second squadron at Pruszcz Gdański airbase. In the early 1990s a project for the integration of air-to-air 9M32ML Strela-2 missiles was approved by the defence ministry. Those missiles were familiar to the Polish industry due to their installation on some Mi-2 armed modifications. In 1991, one Mi-24D and one Mi-24V (designated Mi-24W in Poland due to the different alphabet) were equipped with the missiles. Several live test firings were made but with no introduction into service. In 1999 three Mi-24Ds were subordinated to 3rd Combat SAR Squadron as the country entered NATO and the capability was promised to the alliance. Those helicopters were replaced in 2011 by newer Mi-24Vs from Innowrocław.

In 1991, the 8th Attack Helicopter Squadron was renamed to 3rd Attack Helicopter Squadron. In 2004, a decision was taken to support the Polish military contingent in Iraq with helicopters, including six Mi-24Ds. One ship was from the original Polish deliveries, the remaining five were ex-German ships. The selection was made to prevent high economic loss should any of the ships be destroyed. The German ships were to participate in combat after all! Before shipment by sea, all passed maintenance at Łodż and were equipped with GPS navigation, new radios, L-166V-11E infrared jammers, ASO-2V flare dispensers and lighting compatible with Polish-made NVG goggles, while the ATGM rails were removed. In Iraq they were subordinated to an air assault group located at Al-Kut airbase southeast of Baghdad and Camp Echo. They were engaged in multiple combat missions with live engagement, during election period for example. Both the machine gun and unguided rockets were used against insurgents and the troops also used their machine guns firing out of windows. In July 2006, one helicopter almost crashed during take-off and in October another ship was shot down by machine gun, with the crew fighting on the crash site until combat SAR helicopters arrived. The helicopter was later retrieved to the base and returned to Poland. Because of the attrition, six more ships of the original Polish deliveries were shipped to Iraq. Following damage, one of the ships was stripped down and later destroyed by explosives by the infantry. In the meantime some early Mi-24Ds in Poland reached end of their service life and were withdrawn from service, effectively disbanding the second squadron at Pruszcz Gdański. In 2011 both regiments were formally disbanded and 1 Brigade of army aviation (Brygada Lotnictwa Wojsk Lądowych) was created instead with command of 49th Airbase at Pruszcz Gdański and 56th Airbase at Innowrocław. Both airbases had 1st Attack Squadron (Eskadra Szturmowa) which as equipped with a mix of Mi-24Ds and Mi-24Vs. In 2025 six Mi-24Ds were still operational with both squadrons.

In mid-1978, Iraq became the first non-European operator of the Mi-24D model. Buying out all the remaining production slots of that year with thirty-one ships acquired. They were yet marked as Mi-24D, although were downgraded in terms of avionics and weapon systems. In 1979 they were followed by seventeen Mi-25s, and

This Polish Mi-24D also belongs to the latest standard with features from the Mi-24V. Note the UB-32A-24 rocket block and FAB-100 bomb under the wing. (*Miłosz Rusiecki*)

Above: The very first delivered Polish Mi-24D, nicknamed 'frog' for its distinguished camouflage. Here, in hover, it is launching the 9M17P ATGM. (*Miłosz Rusiecki*)

Below: A Polish Mi-24D captured during a low-level flight over the Iraqi desert. The obsolete 9M17P ATGMs were removed from the ship to save weight. (*Bartek Bera's collection*)

A Polish formation of Mi-24Ds. All these ships belong to a display group 'Skorpiony', which performed a stunning helicopter ballet with 11-ton ships. (*Vertolet*)

in 1984 by eight more, totalling fifty-six ships assigned to 66 Squadron and later also 61 Squadron. They came just in time to be used in the long Iran-Iraq war which brought a lot of opportunities for deployment of the type. Although the war officially started on 20 September 1980, the first Hind loss occurred on 7 September when it was shot down by a F-14A Tomcat using the M61A1 Vulcan cannon, after the AIM-9P Sidewinder missile failed to lock the target against the hot desert background. Iraqi Mi-24s and Mi-25s were all painted with large flags on the front fuselage to be easily distinguished by ground troops in order to avoid friendly fire.

Hinds were located at El Tadji airbase with a detachment of two ships permanently stationed at Basrah International Airport close to the presidential palace. East German military advisors were in the country helping with elaboration of combat tactics for the Hind crews. Although armed with ATGMs, Hinds were primarily used as combat-transport types, inserting commandos into the combat zone and providing immediate close air support. Later, the tactics relied on hunter-killer teams composed of Mi-25s and SA-342L ships. From the beginning of the war with Iran they were engaged in dozens of combat flights and were relocated to airbases at Baiji, Fallujah, Mosul and Samarra, and gradually subordinated to new squadrons. In September 1980 another Hind was shot down by the ZSU-23-4 Shilka self-propelled anti-aircraft system when attacking the Iranian army convoy.

Hinds were used in dozens of combat sorties every year and next to destruction of armoured vehicles they were also escorting transport Mi-8Ts and Mi-17 when inserting the troops. During some of the attack missions nine to twelve helicopters were flying in groups of three and performed devastating attacks on Iranian positions. Some Iraqi WSOs fired over forty ATGMs per year, several times more than anybody else in the world. Next to the ATGMs and unguided rockets the Mi-24Ds and Mi-25 were using bombs and also special chemical bombs, especially late in the conflict. One of the helicopters was captured by Iranians during operation in 1982. The helicopter had to perform an emergency landing behind enemy lines in the battle zone, and yet before the Iraqi fighters were able to destroy it, Iranian air force experts managed to disassemble it and load it onto a truck. It was then carefully evaluated, including engine runs for mapping the infrared signature before it was eventually donated to the War Museum of Tehran.

During the war, much information about dozens Mi-25 air combats against AH-1J appeared with details of shot-downs on both sides, but the latest sources seem not to confirm such war engagement. Although there is evidence of Hinds pursuing the AH-1Js and vice versa, including cannon firing, no shootdown apparently occurred. Another story, repeated in practically all Hind books, describes the Iraqi Mi-25 hitting the F-4E with 9M17P anti-tank missile. After a lot of research this author can finally declare that this is likely to be an urban legend. It originally appeared in the *Baghdad Observer* news and was taken over by the Washington-based Foreign Broadcast Information Service agency. Some sources then claimed this secondary source as 'Western intelligence' and confirmed with it the legitimacy of the information, although the agency was nothing more than a commercial organisation compiling foreign media information. Also, technically it would be hard for the 9M17P missile to explode at the right moment due to its construction, which is aimed at armoured vehicles with contact-mode explosion being the only option. On the other hand, there is a documented case of one Hind crew noting an approaching F-4 and firing all S-5 missiles with the aim of repelling the fighter from the operational area. Some Iraqi sources mention nine Hinds in total being destroyed during the war; Iranian records double that number. It is likely that the Iraqi information is correct as the US intelligence from the pre-Desert Storm era declares thirty-six Hinds as operational and few more stored.

Hinds were used during Saddam Hussein's annexation of Kuwait as an aerial cover of the tank columns and were flying over the Kuwait City when Iraqi army reached it. Due to little resistance from the Kuwaiti army, Hinds retreated back to Iraqi bases shorty after the start of the operation. When the following Desert Storm operation started, Hinds were all back in Iraq. During the coalition raids they were supporting ground forces rather than fighting the tanks, and frequently flew low-level flights with special forces teams. When the teams were extracted, Hinds provided aerial cover.

During one of the missions, three Iraqi Hinds extracted special commandos into a location where US Special forces operated. The US team got into a fierce firefight, were ambushed by Iraqis and called for aerial support. No available attack assets were available in the area, so the AWACS commanded pair of F-15E Strike Eagles flying a combat air patrol mission focused on search and destruction of mobile Scud ballistic missile launchers. The WSO of one of the planes managed to find the area and saw in the LANTIRN targeting system the rotor of one of the Hinds. The helicopter was flying very low with short stops and landings and it was apparently resupplying the Iraqi troops on the ground. The Eagle crew selected GBU-10 Paveway II laser-guided bomb as their weapon of choice and started to lase the Hind. The helicopter lifted off when the bomb was released and the pilots believed it would miss them, though probably killing all the Iraqi soldiers around the target area. The bomb hit them; it passed through the rotor and cockpit, and while it was coming out of the bottom of the Hind it exploded, turning it into a spectacular fireball. The other F-15 crew were ready to hit the second helicopter but did not do so to avoid endangering the leading plane in the area. Curiously, it is still the only aerial victory of the F-15E Strike Eagle. The Mi-25 became the only Hind destroyed in air, with a few more destroyed on the ground. One Mi-25 was captured at Basra airbase after a forced landing, with the crew disappearing before the US forces secured the ship. It was fully armed with machine gun, S-5 rockets and 9M17P ATGMs. The US army captured the helicopter and transported it to the USA. Many crews of Iraqi jets defected to Iran, but it was not the case for Mi-25s as the helicopters were stationed too far from Iran and did not have the necessary endurance. After Desert Storm the number of Hinds in service dropped gradually as the newly independent Russia did not support the type and Iraq never arranged for any servicing. No Hinds were operational during the Iraqi Freedom operation in 2003.

As late as 1979, in negotiations with the USSR over further supplies of equipment, Vietnam pushed for the Kampuchea armed forces loyal to the Republic of Vietnam and fighting the Khmer Rouge militia to receive attack helicopters. Moscow, worried about the potential increase of Chinese influence in the region, eventually agreed. In 1979 the plan to produce four Mi-25s with an urgent requirement for delivery

Above: An Iraqi Mi-25 captured by the 82nd Airborne Division during Operation Desert Storm. Note the open hatch on the fuselage as the ATGM coding system was first removed. (*US DoD*)

Below: A detailed shot of the Iraqi Mi-25 armament—UB-32A-24 rocket blocks, 9M17P ATGMs and belt with 12.7mm rounds for the machine gun. (*US DoD*)

in the same year emerged. The reason for the rush was the ongoing Vietnamese offensive in Kampuchea. The helicopters were delivered at the end of the year and, as the Kampuchean army was virtually non-existent, their operation was handled by Vietnamese crews experienced with Mi-24As. All ships wore no national insignia. The newer Mi-25 version was preferred over the Mi-24A transferred from Soviet regiments because the view from the cabins was more suitable for night flights. The helicopters were mainly used to attack Khmer Rouge militia camps in the jungle. Many of the sorties were conducted at night when the militia were setting campfires and these could be seen from a great distance due to the smoke. T-41Ds usually flew into the area first and dropped illumination bombs, and then it was the turn of the Mi-25s. The most commonly used weapons were S-5 unguided rockets and the 9A624 machine gun as there were no targets for anti-tank missiles. Operations were conducted from field airfields and it was not until the late 1980s that the helicopters were stationed at an airfield in the capital Phnom Penh and rotated to Battambang airfield in the north-west of the country, from where the Khmers were being pursued as they tried to flee to Thailand and hide in the border jungle. During some offensives they were flying alongside with Vietnamese Mi-24A ships. One of the Mi-25 helicopters was lost due to crashing in service, the other three remained operational into the second-half of the 1990s.

In 1979 another customer joined the operators—Afghanistan. Under the Soviet directive its modest air force received seven Mi-25 helicopters. All were delivered to the 373rd Mixed Air Regiment located at Kabul airport equipped with Mi-24A and Mi-24U. Curiously enough, the anti-tank missiles were never delivered and crews did not even train in how to use them. For the majority of the time Mi-24Ds were used in the vicinity of Kabul and looked for rebels shelling the main airport. As with the Mi-24A, even the Mi-25 suffered from the high altitude of the base, meaning many flights had to be performed either early in the morning or later in the evening. In March 1980 one helicopter crashed during take-off as it was unable to stay airborne due to high temperature when the engine rpms dropped slightly due to the ingested sand. The majority of the helicopters were eventually damaged or destroyed during the war period and newer Mi-35s were preferred due to better performance.

In May 1985, a pair of Mi-25s of the local air force left Afghanistan and flew away, landing beyond the border of Pakistan near the city of Miran Shah. In many Western presses those are described as Mi-35s, but that newer model was delivered a year later. Pakistani military command initially believed they were Mi-8s, but after discovering that Mi-25s landed there, there was an immediate pair of Puma helicopters sent to the area. At the same time, the American side was informed and the CIA immediately sent its field experts for Hinds assessment. At the insistence of the Americans, who were afraid of over-the-border Soviet aerial attacks, both helicopters were flown to the city of Kalabagh by Pakistani Mi-8-rated crews, with undercarriages down throughout the flight and covered by Mirages IIIEP.

The opportunity to study the then latest Soviet attack helicopter was an intelligence dream. Both machines were flown the next day to the Mianwali base. The Pakistani government was asked by British intelligence, and even by the Chinese, for an opportunity to inspect the type. Curiously, even Soviet diplomacy tried to put

Rare picture of an Afghan Mi-25 in the early years of operation. The red roundel was used from 1978 to 1980 only. (*MVZ Mil*)

some pressure and asked for a detailed survey. Since the type formally belonged to the Afghanistan government, the Soviets were not allowed to demand anything. One helicopter was disassembled, and it is believed it was used for aggregate tests, while the second was flight-tested in Pakistan and its infrared signature, as well as electromagnetic spectra, were carefully evaluated. A mystery remains about the production plan of 1979, where twenty-four helicopters were produced based on an order from North Korea. Pyongyang apparently did not pay for them and so they might have ended up in another country. Some sources say they were split between Iraq, Algeria and Syria, but it is almost impossible to confirm.

Libya received its first thirteen Mi-25s in 1982, followed by thirteen more in 1983 and one in 1985 as attrition replacement. They were intended to replace the Mi-24A model, whose operation in the super-hot climate was full of troubles. Helicopters were delivered during the ongoing low-profile war activities in the Aouzou strip south of the country. When Libyan forces entered Chad in 1983 not all Mi-25s were delivered and Gaddafi urged their delivery for the offensive. Eventually the delivery schedule was accelerated.

As the first ships were available in September 1982, they were used for training of local crews and were soon engaged in the combat activities as the crews, having previous experience with the Mi-24As, had already passed type rating training. The major airbase for combat activities was at Ouadi Doum, and Hinds were used alongside piston-engine SF-260s and jet-engine L-39ZOs. All those relatively slow speed aircraft proved to be ideal for the attacks on the Chadian army units. Hinds were supporting the insertion of soldiers transported by Mi-8Ts. After the French forces drew a 'red line' which covered a large area of the previous combat activities, combat activity decreased. Although French forces really withdrew from the country and formally ended Operation Manta, Libyans remained in their original positions, although respected the 'red line' in attempt not to escalate the situation.

On 10 February 1986, Gaddafi launched another offensive, which was threatening the Chad capital of N'Djamena. Hinds were used for attacking the positions of Chadian units discovered by L-39ZOs. Also, the Libyan Tu-22A bombers attacked the airport in N'Djamena and the war was again in full swing. The Chadian government agreed with France on common repulsion of the Libyan army. During the high intensity clashes in the northern Chad Tibesti mountains, France supported the anti-Gaddafi rebels with drops of ammunition and fuel.

In January 1987, Chadian troops regained control of the Ennedi Plateau, largely because of the anti-tank Milan missiles from France, which proved to be extremely effective. Libya launched a counteroffensive and crossed the 'red line', with France reacting by bombing the Ouadi Doum airbase within the Operation Épervier and damaging several aircraft there. During the following battles Libyans lost their stronghold in Faya-Largeau, the first large-scale defeat of Gaddafi in the war; they were also unable to maintain control of several other locations. Subsequently, French forces declared the 'red line' was no more valid and their presence in the area increased, including the fortification of their positions. Libya sent from Ouadi Doum a Tu-22A bomber to hit the airport at Chadian capital and the crew. Flying low-level to stay hidden from radars, it hit precisely with three bombs but crashed on the return due to damage sustained from heavy fire over N'Djamena. In return, French forces attacked the Ouadi Doum airfield again. On 6 September, Chadian forces performed a surprise attack on the Maatan-as-Sarra airbase where twenty-two aircraft were reportedly destroyed, including one Mi-25. It was one of the moments that significantly contributed to ending the war.

In September 1987 a ceasefire was agreed between Libya and Chad, but some clashes of various intensity continued as not all Libyan units retreated. Hinds were retrieved back to Libyan bases, except aircraft left at Ouadi Doum. In total, at least four Mi-25s are reported to have been shot down during the clashes. The French army, supported by US intelligence agencies, informed its American counterpart about two Mi-25s remaining at the Ouadi Doum base. One was entirely intact, and the second was damaged by a nearby explosion. At that time the Mi-25 was still a relatively new piece of Soviet inventory and the Americans put together a plan to capture one of the ships for evaluation purposes. After agreement with France and Chad, who, during the war, both relied on US intelligence from electronic reconnaissance aircraft flying from Sudan, the plan was agreed. But both countries were very reserved in providing any support. Since the area was still not fully stabilised and Libyan attack was possible at any time, Americans put together plans for operation Mount Hope III. It expected to partially disassemble the Hind on site and then to transport it under the sling of MH-47D, operated by E Company of the 160th SOAR Special Regiment to a safe zone. In the US some flights with a mock weight were performed and US Intelligence provided as accurate as possible data for the Hind weight.

It was not the first attempt, as earlier the Americans had tried to capture one Hind after an emergency landing and then transport it by truck, but the plan failed. The order came on 21 May 1988, and on 31 May the first part of the US crew was at N'Djamena airport, followed two weeks later by a C-5 Galaxy strategic airlifter bringing to the area two MH-47Ds in a partially disassembled condition. Both helicopters were stripped of any unnecessary equipment, including sound insulation, to make them lighter. Two ships were selected in case one of them faced technical difficulties or enemy action. After the test flights both helicopters flew the 885 kilometre-long route to Ouadi Doum, both fitted with internal auxiliary fuel tanks. Both American choppers flew in loose formation so as not to be endangered by a single threat, and landed close to the selected Hind. The crew got out and pushed onto the apron the auxiliary fuel tanks. At the same time, an air force C-130 landed at the airport, bringing some tooling and mostly taking back the auxiliary fuel tanks and parts removed from the Hind, such as rotor blades, wings, armament—including machine gun and armour plates from the cabin. Americans were afraid of a potential bomb attack from Libya should Gaddafi be aware of the mission, so it all went on a tight schedule.

Mechanics disassembled the rotor blades and wings, using the metric tooling brought by the C-130. Two specially built belts with force distribution pads attached to the Chinook underslung-hook system were laid under the Hind and the Chinook crew hovered over it so the blades and wings could be attached to its two hooks. The belts and ropes were done in such a way to allow release from the Chinook without the Hind being damaged by falling carabiners and lugs. At first the crew did a hover to check the load stability. It was not twisting or rocking, so the Chinook headed to its first refuelling stop at Faya Largeau airport. Another C-130 with a fuel filling station landed there and awaited both choppers. First the Chinook had to lay down the Hind, unhook it and then land for refuelling. Unfortunately, the refuelling system had broken and the Chinook had to turn off its engines, although they had originally planned for hot refuelling. The crew decided to provisionally fix the refuelling, and although taking longer than expected it was eventually done. Another stop for the Chinook with its load but without auxiliary fuel tanks was Moussoro airfield, operated by French Foreign Legion forces. The local Chadians started to approach the landing site but were warned off by French soldiers with heavy armament, without a single shot being fired. The flight in the afternoon took place at 45°C and the worst position was that of the of load master, who was lying on his belly on the hot floor of the Chinook, controlling the precious cargo. When the helicopters arrived at N'Djamena airport, a sandstorm hit and both helicopters landed while totally engulfed by sand. After landing the crews stayed in the helicopters till the storm passed. The Hind was then loaded into the C-5 cargo aircraft and headed to US. Curiously, the C-5 coming for the MH-47s was delayed due to a hard landing and maintenance issues, so both Chinooks with crews stayed in Chad for few weeks extra. Gaddafi's forces did not react to the rapid extraction and the Hind was made airworthy at the Fort Rucker airbase in Alabama, where it was carefully evaluated including mapping of the electromagnetic and thermal radiation characteristics and performance limits. It was later handed over to the US army Threat Systems Management Office for cooperation exercises and displays.

An MH-47D of the US Army 160th SOAR regiment transporting the Libyan Mi-25 captured at Ouadi Doum airbase to a safe place in Chad. (*US DoD*)

Some sources say France took possession of another Mi-25 after a hard landing and the UK also got access to another, but those were inspected in Libya and none of them actually left the country, although they were partially disassembled. The Libyan Mi-25s were operated till 2007 or so, when the last one was grounded. At least four Mi-24Ds were discovered on the photos from Al Watiya Air Base hangars taken in 2021. All helicopters were stored in two hangars and in the open air, they are covered in dust and are without weapons, and usually even engines.

Syria was interested in the Mi-24 from the mid-1970s, when the Syrian delegation saw a demonstration near Moscow. When the Israeli army started to operate the AH-1 Cobra type, Syria pushed Moscow for approval and delivery of Hinds. Nevertheless, Damascus didn't approve the order of Mi-25s until 1980, and in the meantime bought French SA-342 Gazelle helicopters with HOT missiles. The first twelve Mi-25s were finished in late summer of 1981. Due to engagement in combat activities in Lebanon the crews' training was significantly delayed, and instead of Mi-8-rated crews, dragged into war activities, fresh pilot cadets were sent to USSR for training.

Although it is frequently stated in Hind monographs that the helicopters participated in 1982 operations, this is incorrect. In late 1982 the helicopters reached

Tartus port in wooden crates, where they were assembled by Soviet specialists and flown to Marh Ruayiil airbase where they belonged to the 64th Brigade and formed the 765th Attack Helicopter Squadron. Helicopters were initially used for training and although the Syrian press still refers to around ninety-three combat missions and fifty destroyed Israeli tanks, ships were only engaged in the war operations from 1983 when the initial Israeli offensive was already over. Yet before delivery, at the time of the Israeli offensive in Lebanon, additional ships were ordered, of which twenty-seven came in 1982, ten in 1984 and twelve a year later. With sixty-one helicopters with 765, 766 and 767 squadrons, Syria became the largest foreign operator of the type, with a strong Soviet presence in the country including plans for local technical sustainment. Some sources say the helicopters were later distributed to Blei and Almazza airbases and subordinated to 30th Helicopter Brigade.

Once delivered, Hinds presented significant attack power and they definitely had an impact on Israeli plans in Syria and increased the country security. Syria used Hinds in Lebanon and in 1989, by mistake, one crew attacked a Soviet ship believing it to be an Israeli one. After the USSR breakdown the support for Hinds ceased almost immediately, and after the war in Iraq the air force in general faced a time of serious neglect. Lack of funds and even organisation led to storage of many Hinds, with only ten ships operational in mid-1990. In the twenty-first century the Syrian maintenance crews have managed to keep fewer than a dozen ships airworthy, this is because stored Hinds with low usage have been cannibalised and used for parts. Low availability led to slow training and pilots were not allowed to fly at night or at low-level due to lack of experience. It finally changed in 2008 when Syria signed a deal with Russia to overhaul thirty-six helicopters—the only ones considered worthy of salvaging. Only twenty-four were eventually overhauled in Russia, of which the four last ships were detained due to loss of insurance for ferrying by the British broker. They were later delivered by alternative means and Russians also helped to train some Syrian crews. The remaining twelve ships were ready to be shipped to Russia, but such plans were interrupted by the uprisings in Syria in March 2011, followed by riots in Damascus and Aleppo, the country's two largest cities, eventually growing into a full-blown civil war.

Since June 2011, Hinds have been utilised in combat operations in the Idlib region, typically fighting with machine guns and unguided rockets. Later they were also deployed in the Homs area, both being places with fierce opposition. It is no secret now that the regime ordered pilots to target civilians, something that was refused by some crews when they were detained, arrested and tortured. Due to concerns of anti-aircraft fire, Hind crews were flying at altitudes of 1,500 metres or higher, and used free-fall bombs as a major weapon. The altitude, with little guidance and wind drift led to terrible accuracy and much collateral damage, but it was still more accurate compared to fast jets. High operational tempo and the growing air defence capability of the rebels led to a very high attrition and some further stored Hinds were provisionally refurbished to replace worn out or damaged ones. Because the stock of standard bombs was utilised, improvised barrel bombs made of explosives, nails and bearings were dropped later, as well as flammable liquids cannisters; RBK-250-275 cluster bombs were also used. The tactics were merciless: targets were selected at random, or based on lousy intelligence, and the effect on the civilian population was devastating. The combat activities later affected the majority of the country against various militant anti-Assad groups, including high-intensity clashes in the Darayya suburbs of Damascus. Just for reference, Hinds dropped no fewer than 564 bombs there over three weeks.

The high combat potential of the air force, and Hinds in particular, led the opposition to change tactics, and airbases became regular targets. At the airbase at Taftanaz, one Mi-25 was shelled and damaged both by the rebels and the governmental army trying to recapture the base. It was the third Hind delivered originally to Syria, showing that even the oldest ships became operational. Interestingly, it was armed with UPK-23-250 cannon pods and OFAB-100 bombs ready to scramble when it was hit. Due to the lack of suitable armament, any type of available bombs, including napalm canisters, were used during the offensives, as well as 9M17P ATGMs. During the clashes at least four ships were lost, one after being struck with a TOW anti-tank missile.

Surprisingly, Hinds were not used during the fall of the Assad regime. Instead, Hinds were captured by the rebels but not damaged, unlike many other types of aircraft inventory. It took till March 2025 before they were used in the Latakia province to fight remnants of pro-Assad forces. At Istamo airbase in Latakia at least four Hinds

A Syrian Mi-25 badly damaged after being shelled at the airport. Note the UPK-23-250 cannon pod and OFAB-100 bomb under the wing. (*SNN*)

were made operational again and a few more are supposed to be located at other bases. Some were targets of Israeli airstrikes, so the total count of airworthy ships does not exceed a dozen. Syria, along with Peru, is the last Mi-25 operator worldwide.

In the 1980s Algeria purchased a batch of twenty Mi-25s, supplementing the Mi-24As already in service. Since the situation on the western border was under control by then, they were all located at the Biskra airbase, where they belonged to the 421st and 441st combat helicopter squadrons (Escadron d'Hélicoptères de Combat). Helicopters were used for border patrolling and also for combating the Islamists groups in the southern territories of the country. Until 1990 they were maintained by Soviet teams in the country, and when the civil war broke out in 1992, Hinds had just gone through the initial round of overhauls and were directly engaged in scout and patrolling missions, usually using machine guns and unguided rockets. They were withdrawn from service in the late 1990s due to attrition and obsolete weapon systems, with at least one helicopter lost in accident during that time. Because Russia was unable to provide support, Ukrainian teams attempted to overhaul them. After inspection they were found to be in bad shape so instead, Ukraine offered delivery of second-hand Mi-24Vs, which were upgraded delivery with the help of the South African ATE company as mentioned below. Mi-25s were then open-stored and later scrapped, with one helicopter provided to ATE company for testing.

Cuba purchased only twelve Mi-25s in 1981, which were delivered at the beginning of the following year. They original plan was to station them at the Cienfuegos airbase, where the local Mi-8Ts were newly assigned to transport role only. Eventually, they were all assigned to 361st Combat Helicopter Squadron (Escuadrón de Helicópteros de Combate), located at the Santiago de Cuba airport. Hinds were purchased especially for the purpose of repelling the potential amphibious assault from the US side, but the fleet size was very modest and due to the expense of new generation fighter acquisitions, there were no plans to purchase any more Mi-25s. The initial crews were composed of pilots with experience from Ethiopia and Angola, as well as fresh pilots trained in the USSR. The helicopters were used until the late 1990s, when their service life was already expired and lack of funds led to their gradual withdrawal from use. In the late 1980s Cuba considered training the pilots of other Latin American countries, and even supporting various guerillas in the area, but the ships never flew outside of Cuban territory.

Another Latin American country, Nicaragua, ordered six Mi-25s in 1980, but accepted only one, with a dispute over payment for the others. It wasn't until 1984 that five more ships were finished and all were shipped, via Bulgarian freighter, to Nicaragua. The Sandinista government, heavily supported by Cuba, took over the control of the country in 1979 and tried to implement their socialist ideas. The opposition (the Contras) fought the Sandinista National Liberation Front in a guerilla-style war, hiding in the forests for protection. The government reacted by acquisition of the Mi-25, and at first the newly delivered ships were used for protection of the capital, Managua. Initially, the Cubans maintained the Mi-25s, and later even piloted them before the local crews were trained. All helicopters were located at the single operational base built as new at Santa Rosa (sometimes called Punta Huete), north of the capital, Managua. Hinds proved quite effective, so in 1984 they were first used against Contras. All Mi-25 helicopters were directly engaged in jungle warfare with guerillas, armed with a machine gun, S-5 rockets, UPK-23-250 cannon pods, free-fall bombs and even anti-tank guided weapons. They inserted troops, provided aerial cover and performed scout missions. The combat raids were extremely efficient with dozens of targets destroyed, forcing the guerillas to split into small groups. The 250kg FAB-250 bombs became particularly popular, dropped in ultra-low-level flight they gave the rebels no time to hide. Hinds were frequently deployed in the border zone with Costa Rica and Honduras as many Contras units sought protection there.

Combined operations with Mi-17-1Vs and Mi-17s used for transport proved to be the best tactic. Nicaragua even tried the Mi-8TVK heavily armed model, but it was abandoned in favour of more manoeuvrable Hinds. Successful deployment was followed by an order of six more ships. Since production had already switched to Mi-24V, six Mi-24Ds from Soviet stock were refurbished, equipped with EVU exhaust gas coolers, IR jammer and flare dispensers, and delivered to Nicaragua. The Mi-25 fleet was used intensively in 1986 during several offensives, when Contras lost a large proportion of the villages taken over in the previous years. In one case the Hind was damaged in the air by a Honduran F-86 fighter supporting the Contras in the border zone. It was the first, but definitely not the last, clash of the Mi-25 with Honduran fighters. The threat connected with the delivery of Mi-25 is clearly described in recently disclosed CIA materials; the US administration had agreed that Red Eye portable air defence missiles were to be provided by the CIA, including training of

Nicaraguan Mi-25s taxiing before take-off. Note the ships were using both flare dispensers and IR jammers due to the MANPADS threat. (*CIA*)

the Contras. Use of those changed the course of combat operations, with two Hinds together and three Mi-17-1Vs shot down in 1987, one Hind being destroyed near Cano Negro following an ambush when it was lured to approach the area because of thick smoke from burning tyres. After that, the operation of Hinds was dramatically reduced. In December 1988, when the Sandinista regime began to fall, the pilot of one Mi-25, with fuselage code 355, defected to Honduras to request political asylum.

The helicopter was intercepted at the borderline by two Honduran F-5E fighters and followed to landing at the Toncontin military airport. Although the press later referred to the solo decision of the pilot, it became apparent he had been paid by the CIA who had proposed $1 million to any defecting Hind crew. When the ceasefire was signed in 1990, the helicopter was returned to Nicaragua. One Mi-24D is still displayed at the Managua airport. Of the remaining Hinds, seven were sold to Peru in 1992, as the country had no use of them during peacetime.

Angola received the first twelve Mi-25s in 1983, followed by twelve more a year later. No formal unit was created at the beginning of their deployment and the helicopters were operated from the base at the capital of Luanda and Lubango. All ships were provided by the USSR as a support in the Angolan civil war against the UNITA guerilla. Hinds were used in a typical hunt for guerilla units hiding in the forest with machine guns and unguided rocket attacks. They were piloted and serviced by a mix of Angolan, Cuban, East German and Soviet crews. For the combat operation rotations, four Mi-25s were deployed at the Menongue airport, where transport Mi-8Ts and Mi-17s were also stationed. When inserting troops, Hinds covered the transport helicopters and cleared the landing zone with aerial cover during the disembarkation of troops. Once equipped with Hinds, the offensive of the Angolan government became efficient, and the UNITA guerillas had to seek help abroad. Subsequently, they received a large delivery of portable anti-aircraft systems of various origin from the US.

The UNITA leader Jonas Savimbi also called for help in South Africa and asked for South African air force aerial cover, mostly against Mi-25s posing a major threat. Initially, the South Africans, who were deeply involved in the war, were against it as there was no experience in aerial combat of the particular style, and there were logistical difficulties caused by the distance between South Africa and Angola; all this, along with concerns about the involvement of MiG-21s and MiG-23s of the Angolan air force, prevented such a deployment. However, later it practised some mock-fights of its Impala Mk.2 jets against Oryx helicopters and some combat fundamentals were verified. The deployment was approved in mid-1985. Three Impalas were selected for the operation, with a fourth being ready for covering the downed pilots should any jet be lost. It has recently been discovered that some of its pilots scored aerial victories with Impala Mk.2 jet aircraft equipped with two Defa 552 30mm cannons.

During the first attack in mid-September 1985, jets were alerted to scramble when a mixed fleet of Mi-8Ts, Mi-17s and Mi-25s was spotted heading to the combat zone. The jets approached the helicopter group from behind and the leading plane fired the rounds, which hit the Hind. The Cuban crew in the helicopter was not aware of what had caused the hit and tried to maintain level flight. In the meantime, the Impala pilot got ready for a second attack and hit the starboard engine, with the helicopter bursting into the flames and crashing into the forest. Two days later, two more Mi-25s were shot down in the very same manner. Unfortunately for the Hind crews, although the Angolan or Cuban pilots were trained in the USSR, including combat tactics, they were making a lot of mistakes in the tactical deployment. For example, they flew the same routes over clearly visible navigational reference points such as rivers or roads, flew only in a good visibility conditions and were greatly predictable in the deployment. Typically, they were flying 900 to 1,800 metres above the terrain to avoid rifle fire. When the MiGs were not present, Impalas had a chance. Some South African records indicate no less than six Mi-25s were shot down and it became the sole type attacked. South African air strikes forced the Angolan air force to cease operating helicopters in large groups. Consequently, subsequent missions were conducted strictly by pairs of Mi-25s, targeting UNITA positions. At least ten ships were shot down by Strela and Redeye MANPADS systems, and by the ZSU-23-4 Shilka self-propelled anti-aircraft system captured from the governmental forces inventory. Later, the surviving Mi-25s were stored when the war ended in 1990.

In 1984 Mozambique bought five Mi-25s and one Mi-25U, followed by two more Mi-25s the following year. The country wanted the attack model after experience in the Rhodesian Bush War, and especially after atrocities during the civil war which started in 1977. The Soviet Union heavily supported Mozambique and provided it weapons on loan so it could fight the anti-socialist rebels. Hinds were used for direct combat engagement and at least two helicopters were shot down. At its peak, almost 1,000 Soviet military advisors were present in the country, including Hind crews, but they were not encouraged to participate in combat. Hinds were located at Quelimane airfield, from where they performed raids. Poor training of the pilots caused low effectiveness of combat flights and MiG-17s were later preferred for attacks. After the withdrawal of Soviet military advisors, the Hind fleet was soon grounded and at least four are still stored at Maputo airbase.

India became a Hind operator in 1983 when it bought seven Mi-25 ships, followed a year later by one more. Those were scheduled for testing as India feared Pakistan may have access to new models of AH-1 Cobras due to its support of CIA at the time of war in Afghanistan. Helicopters were delivered to India, and crews were trained locally as the Asian country was long-term operator of other Mil helicopters. All ships were subordinated to the 125th Helicopter Unit 'The Gladiators', at Panthankot airbase close to the Pakistan border. The location was selected due to the low elevation of the airport at just 330 metres above sea level. Instead of domestic use in 1986, Hinds were getting ready for deployment to Sri Lanka as a part of the Indian Peace Keeping Force trying to help to the neighbouring country end the civil war by disarming all the militias in the area. The only guerillas not willing to end the war was the militant movement Liberation Tigers of Tamil Eelam, which was then targeted by the Sri Lankan army supported by an Indian contingent. The Indian involvement was delicate one, because there was a Tamil minority in India and so the approval to deploy attack helicopters was a lengthy process. Hinds from Helicopter unit were deployed in the area at the Palali airbase to provide aerial cover for the Indian troops. Soon the crews were engaged in direct combat with the rebels and were attacking supply vehicles in the jungle and on the sea and camps most frequently with S-5

An Indian Mi-24D in all-grey camouflage, applied in the mid-1990s, is being towed on a trailer during a military parade with its pilot standing by. (*Indian MoD*)

rockets, bombs and machine gun. Later, the Hinds were performing close air support in various areas prior to the advancement of ground troops.

Although the Hind crews passed relatively short conversion training, they mastered the new weapon systems very efficiently and managed to prevent the Tamils from fast regrouping, which they were able to do at night only. The Tamils tried to obtain MANPADS systems and eventually procured the 9K32 Strela system, but never used it. The Indian contingent clearly stated that should any ship be shot down by MANPADS, the air force would unleash its full combat capability. During three years of operation with over 900 combat flights, no helicopter was lost and all eventually returned to India. Helicopters were further used and the last of them were withdrawn from service around 2008 due to the availability of newer Mi-35s.

Peru purchased ten Mi-25s and one Mi-25U in 1983, and two more Mi-25s and one Mi-25U in 1985, with the first pilots' training course starting in Frunze, USSR, in late 1982. The South American country, having experience with the recent Paquisha war with Ecuador and combat activities on its home territory against the Sendero Luminoso and other Maoist guerilla groups, originally wanted to buy US AH-1 Cobra helicopters, but Washington clearly denied such a request. As a reaction, Peru asked for twenty-four helicopters from the USSR, but for budget reasons the quantity later dropped to fourteen only. Hinds were assigned to the air force (FAP—Fuerza Aérea del Perú), although the army aviation was also interested in the type. Hinds were considered to be the perfect tool, being able both to repel enemy infantry and to provide troop insertion capability.

All helicopters were stationed at the Vitor airbase south of the country and assigned to the EHC.211 unit (Escuadrón de Helicópteros de Combate) located there. Almost immediately after delivery the FAP launched training of domestic crews to reach the full operational capability with the new type. During the late 1980s, the Maoist guerillas became the major opponent of the type with dozens of jungle engagements. Due to high elevation profile of the country, some ships were later flying without the ATGM rails as there were no targets for those missiles anyway. From the beginning, the Mi-25s became the most powerful asset in the air force inventory.

Peruvian Hinds became notable for the large shark's mouth painted on the nose of all ships. In 1992, seven Mi-25s were purchased from Nicaragua as the country had no use for them after the ceasefire was signed. They were transported by ship to Peru, where two of them were found to be in such a poor shape that they were eventually used for spare parts. They had just been introduced into the service when the so-called Cenepa war with Ecuador erupted. Six Hinds were stationed at El Pato airbase close to Ecuadorian border, where they flew before the war during navigational exercises. Three ships were flown to a forward operational base for attack sorties and the remaining three were kept at El Pato as a reserve. In the combat clashes, Hinds were

Peruvian Mi-24Ds are the oldest Hinds in operation. Note this ship carries a B-8V20 rocket block from the Mi-24V, but lacks ATGMs. (*MinDef*)

A group flight of Peruvian Mi-24Ds with an Mi-24DU in the back. Almost all Peruvian ships featured a shark-mouth. (*MinDef*)

engaged extensively with dozens of MANPADS shots detected, and at least one ship shot down in February 1992. The short war ended up in a ceasefire. When the Maoist groups and Ecuador were no problem anymore, a new enemy emerged—drug cartels. Hinds were, and still are, used for combating the cartel camps. Mi-25s are still in use, including two ex-Nicaraguan ships, and have passed multiple overhauls. In 2012, for example, the Russian industry extended their service life. They belong to the Air Group 2 and its aviation squadron 211 (Escuadrón Aéreo). The Russian overhaul company installed new communication and navigation equipment on some helicopters and even changed their wiring so they can carry large 80mm unguided S-8 rockets in B-8V20 blocks described below. Peru, together with Syria, is the last operator of the Mi-25 worldwide.

4

Spiral Missile

Finally with the Right Gear

At the end of 1972, after more than five years, the Shturm-V anti-tank guided missile system finally began its state trials. The whole system was coded 9K-113, while the missile was named 9M114. Its design work started in 1967, and it took until 1970 for the missile to be fired from a helicopter—an Mi-8 based testbed—for the first time.

In February 1972, the 9K-113 system was installed on an Mi-24A testbed with the intention of verifying the mechanical installation and influence on other systems. In the summer of 1973 two Mi-24D helicopters were modified with the new ATGM system in order to perform the in-flight live firing tests. This helicopter modification received the designation Mi-24V with Izdeliye 242 being the internal code and Hind E the NATO code. Both prototypes, sometimes referred to as Mi-24PTRK, were intended for testing of the new 9M114 ATGMs, carried on RP-2-149TK launching devices attached to the ends of the wings, new Raduga-Sh sighting and guidance system (internal designation 9S-475), and also some new avionics features such as an ASP-17V gunsight in the rear cockpit, derived from the same device developed for Sukhoi Su-17 fighter-bomber. The first of the Mi-24PTRK prototypes made its maiden flight on 23 September 1973. The first one was still carrying the original Mi-24D guidance kid, while the second prototype, which commenced trials in November that year, was very close in configuration to the serial production state.

The new ASP-17 gunsight was used by pilots during aiming of FFAR rockets and 9A-624 firing, when the gun was in a neutral position. Such a device significantly increased firing accuracy as it included a simple ballistic computer allowing for compensation of the ship manoeuvres. The Raduga-Sh system introduced for the first time a new antenna under the port-side of the nose, which was not on a moveable turret because its emitter was in a gimbal covered by a dielectric fairing. Guidance kit total weight of 224kg was comparable with the previous Raduga-F model.

The gimbal-installed antenna allowed the helicopter to manoeuvre after the launch and take evasive manoeuvres and the test flights verified the missile could be launched during high-speed flight exceeding 300 km/h. The guidance optics were covered by dual protective doors. The first was used during flight and opened before target search. The second one was opened before missile launch and helped to prevent the optics from becoming obscured by insects and dust during low level flight. The WSO could select between a semi-automatic guidance mode and fully manual. The Raduga-Sh system allowed 9° angle of view during target search and 2° during missile guiding, with better zoom ratio.

The guiding radio signal was encrypted and proved to be very tolerant to enemy jamming. Originally, only the 9M114 model with high explosive anti-tank warhead was available, but in the 1980s, based on experience in Afghanistan, a 9M114F type with thermobaric warhead became available. The latter was used particularly against lightly armoured targets, buildings and bunkers. With the 9M114 ATGM system the kill-probability ratio rose to 92 per cent. Shturm missiles reached the end of their range in under 15 seconds, and some 4 kilometres within 10 seconds, which made any protection manoeuvres of the target very difficult. The number of ATGMs carried was increased during the production period. The first Mi-24V blocks were able to carry just four missiles, while some three years after the start of production, provision was made to carry RP-2-149TK launchers on the outer-wing pylons, and the total number of ATGMs increased to eight. In 1986 a new APU-8/4-U wing carrier for eight missiles each was tested, with total capacity of sixteen missiles per helicopter, but it was not adopted for series production and this modification was only implemented on the Mi-35M model.

Likely the very first Mi-24PTRK prototype, yet with Raduga-F guidance kit. There are 9M114 Shturm ATGMs on four pylons in total. Note the missing DUAS sensor. (*MVZ Mil*)

Above: A later prototype of the Mi-24PTRK model with the 9M114 ATGMs and new guidance antenna under the nose. The helicopter is missing the PZU filters. (*MVZ Mil*)

Below: Detail of the Raduga-Sh sight with double doors. The inner transparent doors were opened only after the target was acquired. (*Author*)

Above: Detail of the 9M114 system guiding antenna in a swivel mount. It was the reason why the Mi-24V could manoeuvre while guiding the ATGM. (*Author*)

Below: Detail of the Mi-24V wing with a total of four 9M114 ATGM launching tubes and a UPK-23-250 cannon pod. The Mi-24V doubled the quantity of ATGMs to be carried. (*Author*)

Mi-24V pilot's cockpit with the ASP-17V gunsight in the middle and the L-006 RWR control box above. Note the rearview mirrors retrofitted after experience gained in Afghanistan. (*Author*)

The tests took more than a year, and in November 1975 the type was approved for series production at both the Arsenyev and Rostov plants. The first helicopters were finished the following year for the Soviet army. The domestic operator was granted the highest priority, and for almost ten years, the Rostov plant delivered the older Mi-24D/Mi-25 model to foreign customers. With the 9M114 missiles the Mi-24V finally became a really credible attack type. During series production the Mi-24V saw many other improvements. In particular, the TV3-117 3rd series engines were replaced by the TV3-117V 'hot and high' variant, although in fact, those engines were not available neither for prototypes nor for the first produced helicopters. The original engine would lose some 10 per cent of its output at an outer temperature of 30°C, with another 10 per cent loss with every additional 10°C.

The TV3-117V model was derived from several experimental variants and even from models designed for Kamov helicopters. It allowed operation with no performance losses up to +35°C and featured electronic regulation. It also allowed the introduction of special exhaust gas coolers, designated EVU. These boxes attached to the TV3-117V engines and mixed the hot gases from the engine with the rotor downwash for reduction of temperature. This device was again developed as a result of Afghan experience. During flights in a very hot climate, or at maximum take-off weight, some control and stability difficulties occurred. In order to increase the helicopter's stability and control, the tail rotor blades were replaced on later Mi-24Vs by a newer type with a wider chord. This modification came from the similar experience with the Mi-8/8MT type. Other improvements were made in the radio and navigation systems.

Production Mi-24Vs were equipped with new R-863 VHF/UHF radio and Yadro-1A HF radio, new SRO-1P IFF (internal code Izdeliye 62-01) working both with the original Khrom-2M identification system and the new and more modern Parol-2D variant. Also with later ships, the S-13 gun camera installed on the left-wing end was replaced by a new type SSh-45-1-100-0C, installed inside the pilot's cockpit attached to the ASP-17 gunsight. This camera allowed not only confirmation of any target hit, but also recorded the aiming process with much better effectiveness during mission reviews.

Many improvements were driven by operational experience. For example, on the port-side of the fuselage an additional FPP-7 landing light was installed in order to increase the safety of night landings. Based on combat experience, the hydraulics system included more valves in order to prevent the helicopter from complete loss of hydraulic pressure in the event of weapons damage to the system, and the linkage to the tail rotor was installed with rods and cables spaced widely etc. One of the improvements affected the fuel system. The internal tanks were newly protected by a polyurethane foam covering internal side of the tanks. This helped to increase the resistance against fire, but reduced the internal volume of the fuel by some 5 per cent. The Mi-24V was also equipped with the provision to carry up to four PTB-450 external fuel tanks with 475 litres of fuel each. The main change appeared in the area of defence system.

The Mi-24V was the first model initially equipped with four ASO-2V-02 flare dispensers under the tail boom, later increased to six, which were relocated to the aft fuselage behind the wings. Originally, the dispensers were mounted in aerodynamic fairings, but the latest produced models had the dispensers uncovered. Aft of the main rotor an L-166V-11E Infra-red jammer (known also as SOEP-1V Lipa) was installed during production. This device was equipped with a very powerful xenon lamp emitting an IR pulse signal which flashed erratically. By rotation of the emitting unit in the housing it covered 360°, and the erratically disappearing and reappearing signal confused the IR-sensors of heat-seeking missiles which were theoretically unable to recognise the helicopter as a target. The original Sirena-3M radar homing and warning system was replaced by the new SPO-15 Beryoza (known also as L-006), with 'horns' under the cockpits, and later behind the rear cockpit, and antennae on the trailing edge of the keel for rear hemisphere coverage. All those improvements were later retrospectively introduced on the very last Mi-24D models as well.

Combat experience showed that the original Hind models were lacking sufficiently powerful unguided ammunition. The S-5 rocket had limited accuracy, relatively short range and low penetration capability, as it was not able to keep up with the increasing protection of armoured vehicles. That is why the larger S-8 type of 80mm calibre was created, using practically identical fuses and a similar composition with a larger rocket engine and an enlarged warhead. The spring-loaded stabilising fins were replaced by piston-driven ones for better reliability. For helicopter-based applications, the B-8V20 block with twenty rockets was developed. It became a perfect fit for the Mi-24V.

Although the number of rockets carried was reduced, the firepower and accuracy increased significantly. If the original S-5 weighed around 5kg, the S-8 weighed over 11kg. Even though the rocket engine is enlarged, its burning time is only 0.69 seconds, but it gives the rocket a higher initial velocity and therefore energy. For example, the anti-armour version of the S-8K can penetrate up to 220mm of rolled homogeneous armour. The versions of the rockets are identical to the S-5 type, in addition, there are, for example, the S-8B types (or BM with a rocket engine with an extended burning time), designed for penetrating fortified buildings and capable of penetrating up to 80cm of reinforced concrete; and the thermobaric S-8D/DM, which forms an ignition mixture and then, after its initiation, a detonation wave with a force equivalent to 6kg of TNT. Tests on polygons have shown that, for example, a salvo of twenty S-8s has the same effect at the target as ninety-six S-5 missiles. In other words, one B-8V20 block on the Mi-24V had the same combat value as three UB-32A-24 blocks on the Mi-24D.

In the course of production, various subversions of the S-8 missiles were created, which usually differed in the propulsion system (for example, the version with the 'M' suffix, meaning longer range) or the combined initiation and propulsion system. Later, a scaled-up variant of the S-8, designated S-13 with 122mm calibre, was adopted. This missile became ideal for attacking bunkers, aircraft shelters and runways. A B-13L block could carry five rockets but came too close to the collapse of the USSR to be introduced widely. The latest unguided type was the S-24, which became the most powerful serially integrated weapon of all Hinds. This was a 240mm unguided rocket, fired from the PU-12-40U launcher attached to the underwing pylons. It was carried by Su-7, Su-17 and Su-25 aircraft, with which it had proved very successful. However, it was used seldomly because its massive smoke trail always put the engines in risk of surge should the pilot fly into the smoke trail during manoeuvring.

Another extension to the array of weapons was accomplished by adding the GUV (9A-669) universal helicopter gondolas developed especially for the Mi-24 model. They were offered in the GUV-1 variant with one 9A-624 12.7mm Gatling gun and 750 rounds, and two 9A-622 7.62mm Gatling guns with 1,800 rounds each, or the GUV-2 modification with a single 9A-800 (internal code A-17A Plamya) 30mm grenade launcher and 300 VOG-17A high explosive grenades. Although the gun version was very effective, GUV gondolas were not popular in Afghanistan. The weight of the fully armed system exceeded 450kg and therefore significantly limited the helicopter's performance. However, in less hot climates they became very useful and the 'bullet rain' was highly effective against infantry. The GUV gondolas were delivered to only a limited number of export customers. One of the last pieces of new armament introduced on the Mi-24V was the KMGU-1 cluster bomb container, able to drop various kinds of sub-munition. For the Mi-24Vs, new PTB-450 fuel tanks for all underwing pylons were also introduced, increasing the Hind's ferry range. They allowed the cargo cabin to still be used, which was with the Mi-24D occupied by the tanks, should those be installed. The new variety of weapons and stores resulted in the installation of new junction box on the rear wall of the cargo cabin, where the crew could select the appropriate configuration of stores by re-switching the harness cables.

From 1976, Mi-24Vs were being delivered to the Soviet air force units, replacing the Mi-24D model. The sequence of armament of the units is not known due to the strict secrecy of it. It is only known that six regiments permanently stationed on the territory of the USSR were expected to be equipped with Mi-24Vs, of which each had roughly forty ships in two squadrons. This meant the quantity of the ships on the Soviet territory matched the quantity in the European countries where the Soviet army operated.

The Mi-24V model became particularly popular with airbases in Europe, where it gradually replaced the Mi-24Ds. The majority of the above-mentioned were stationed in East Germany, and even the Soviet presence was increased with newly rearmed units, partly due to an increase in the forces' capability, and partly due to reorganisations. Under the Central region the 113th OVEBU at Oranienburg was established in 1987 and in 1990, 41st OVEBU at Werneuchen with 487th OVP at the same base a year later.

In the north region, 439th OVP at Parchim was established in 1987, and in the south region 345th OVE and 486th OVP at Jüteborg were established in 1989 and 1991. Finally, in the south-west region, 225th OVE at Altstadt and 485th OVPBU at Merseburg were activated. The Soviet troops remained in Germany well after the collapse of the USSR and the withdrawal took several years, with the last unit being the 337th OBVP at Mahlwinkel airbase, which left the country officially on 16 May 1994 with one helicopter crashing at a refuelling stop-over at Oranienburg. Next to the German troops the Mi-24V was also widely deployed at the Central group of forces in Czechoslovakia. On its territory were the 231st OVE at Milovice Mladá airbase, 199th OVE and 230th OVE at Mimoň Hradčany, 232nd and 313rd OVE at Olomouc Neředín and finally 246th OVE, 238th OVP and 490th OVP at Sliač airbase.

In 1987, a huge reorganisation took place with the 230th, 231st, 232nd, 246th and 313rd OVEs being subordinated to the 490th OVP at Sliač, but retaining its helicopters on the original airbases. As in Germany, the Soviet helicopters were actively participating in military exercises on its own dedicated test ranges as well as on the Czechoslovak ones with several accidents and crashes. When the forces started to retreat back to the USSR, the Sliač base became a stopover for all forces. Due to the extreme political push of the Czechoslovak government, remembering the 1968 occupation, the first units pulled off in 1990.

In Poland, the Soviet air force had a much more modest presence due to having no direct border with NATO countries, unlike the two previous states. Mi-24V helicopters are documented with 55th OVP at the Bagicz airbase, with a detachment at Brzeg airbase, 79th OVE at Borne Sulinowo airbase and 314th OVE at Legnica having its detachment also at the Szprotawa airbase. In Hungary, neighbouring only with neutral Austria and socialistic states, only one unidentified helicopter regiment located at Kalocsa airbase is known to date, with withdrawal back to USSR in 1990, with Mezőkövesd airbase being used as back-up for military exercises.

Above: Early Soviet Mi-24V during salvo firing of S-5 rockets from UB-32A-24 blocks. Note the dispersed trajectory of the rockets. (*MVZ Mil*)

Below: Early Russian Mi-24V captured at Werneuchen airbase in Germany. Note the helicopter still uses the Mi-24D-style engine exhausts but features late-style ASO-2V flare dispensers. (*Thomas Girke*)

Above: A pair of Russian Mi-24Vs captured over Mahlwinkel airbase in Germany. Note the tail codes were repainted during reassignment to a new regiment. (*Thomas Girke*)

Below: An early Russian Mi-24V is taxiing at the Werneuchen airbase in Germany. Note the spent cases collector on the machine gun—a very atypical feature, rarely seen. (*Thomas Girke*)

shelters, causing rocks to fall, or destroying even armoured vehicles. Along with 100kg bombs they were the most frequently used weapon, because although bombs of 250kg and 500kg were also used, they were too heavy and limited the flight performance. Later, the much more powerful S-13 and S-24 rockets were used as well, although crews did not like them due to the risk of engine surge when fired. Because the aiming system proved to be troublesome in mountainous flying with frequent position changes, many crews were drawing white lines on the front windshield and relied on their own experience instead.

Late in the conflict the KMGU-1 cluster ammunition containers became particularly popular for mining the mujaheddins' paths. The ATGMs were used for high priority or heavily protected targets. The need to guide the missile during the whole flight was not popular because evasive Hind manoeuvres after fire were a typical protection procedure. On the other hand, the 9M114 type particularly showed extremely high accuracy in combat, and more than 8,000 missiles were fired during the combat activities. In 1987 some of the Mi-24Vs at Kandahar airbase were equipped with APU-60-1 launching rails for R-60 air-to-air missiles as a protection measure for helicopters operating close to Pakistani territory with the risk of engagement with their F-16s.

During combat operations, many protection features were tested. The crews were instead recommended to wear bulletproof vests and titanium-made helmets weighting 2kg. The crew seats were armoured with special headrest of the pilot seat. The statistics showed that almost 40 per cent of the bullets hitting the cabin penetrated the cabin of the weapon systems operator, while only 20 per cent penetrated the pilot's cabin. Next to the machine gun and cannon bullets, RPGs became a major issue. Mujaheddins used the high explosive anti-tank warhead with the fuse armed for self-destruction after a defined time. Even if the grenade did not hit the helicopter kinetically, the shrapnel after explosion caused significant damage. However, the ballistic protection of the Mi-24V was not improved beyond what is stated above. Another problem occurred when the mujaheddins started to operate MANPADS systems.

The UK-made Blowpipe and Javelin were of low effectiveness, with likely only two Hinds destroyed by the former type and three with the latter. Its in-flight guidance required a steady hand and an experienced operator—something not available when a Hind was under direct attack. All changed when FIM-92 Stingers were delivered to the country. The self-guidance capability and high sensitivity-seeker literally changed the war. The American CIA had a chance to measure the IR radiation of Mi-25s defecting to Pakistan and the sensor was fine-tuned to match the radiation pattern of the helicopter. In the field, it took only 10 seconds to get the weapon ready for launch and fire, with no need to guide the missile manually. No wonder the title 'Hero of the USSR' was proposed to any Soviet soldier able to capture an intact missile—eight were eventually captured by Spetsnaz, although none of its soldiers were decorated.

First Mi-8MT was shot down in September 1986 and Soviets got proof of the type two months later when they searched the area where the first Mi-24V was downed, with five launchers discovered on site. When the Stingers became available to dispersed mujaheddin units in 1986, they soon became the major cause of losses. Immediate measures were taken with new tactical procedures requiring flares to be launched during attack. Soon, the ASO-2 flare cartridges became a standard fit on all Hinds, with number increased from four to six on each ship. After the Stinger was evaluated by Soviet experts, the L-166V-1E IR jammers were introduced and several types of exhaust gas coolers called EVU were tested.

Although the Afghan war is sometimes nicknamed the 'Stinger war', of eighty-nine hits on the Mi-24s only eighteen ships were actually downed by the type, in a few cases by two missiles at a time. In several cases the Hind was hit by a Stinger but managed to land. In general, the Mi-24Vs showed incredible battle damage tolerance. For example in April 1987, one FAB-250 bomb exploded immediately when released from the hardpoint and the crew managed to perform an emergency landing, although the ship was badly damaged with the pilot not making it out in time from the burning ship. Of the 333 lost helicopters, some 127 were of Mi-24 type. Some crew members even reached 1,250 combat sorties in Afghanistan, and the majority of the crews exceeded 300. Although Afghanistan is frequently mentioned as the only area where Soviet Hinds were engaged in combat, in September 1990 the Soviet army attacked the Armenian guerilla positions in the Nagorno Karabakh region with Hinds, and remained in the area till very late 1991.

The Afghan experience gave the Mil Design Bureau many ideas for further developments of the type, and the Rostov plant serial design office also contributed. In 1981, the Rostov production plant modified an Mi-24V into the Mi-24TETCh-24

Late Soviet Mi-24V in Kabul, Afghanistan. The sign on the machine gun says the ship is armed—with two UB-32A-24 rocket pods and machine gun rounds only, due to airbase elevation. (*MMHP*)

Detail of the EVU exhaust gas cooler on the Czech Mi-24V. It could be installed on late Mi-24Vs and Mi-24P or Mi-24VPs only. (*Author*)

Left: Detail of the L-166V-11E IR jammer on the Czech Mi-24V. When not in use, it was protected by a metal cover. Note the plastic tiles on the fuselage of this RAM-coated ship. (*Author*)

Below: A later variant of the ASO-2V dispensers on a late Mi-24V, with three cartridges on each side of the tail boom. (*Author*)

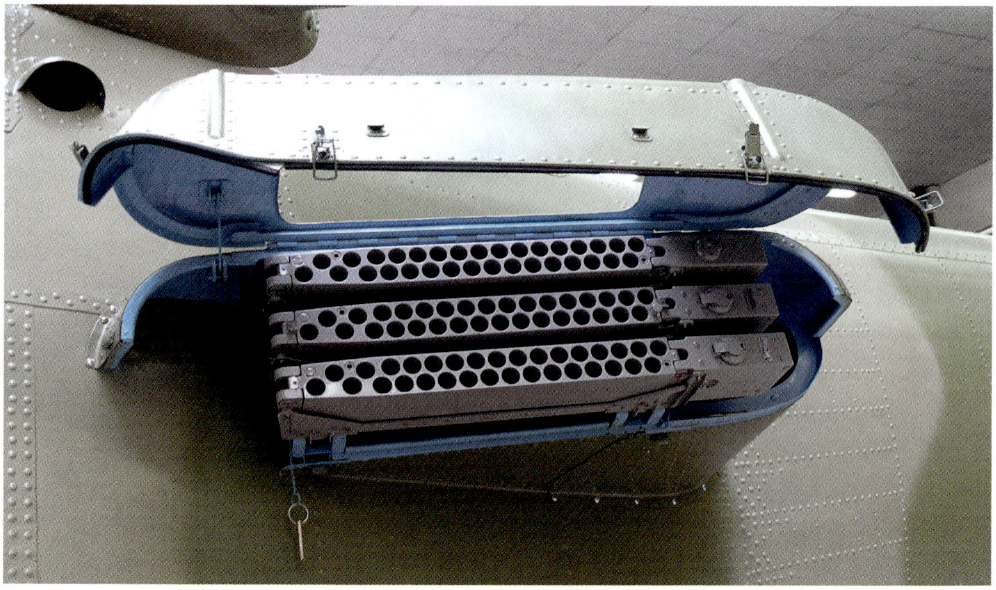

model, intended for in-field repairs of grounded Mi-24s, the analogue of the Mi-8TETCh-8 variant, which had been serving experimentally since 1977. The new modification was a flying service station with special equipment on board, both in the cargo cabin and under the wing pylons. Under the wings, there was even a provision to carry large components necessary for repair such as rotor blade sections etc. The crew consisted of pilot, WSO and two mechanics. As it was expected that the helicopter would fly in the combat zone, and was evidently an answer to the Afghan deployment experience, it was armed with the 9A-624 gun and B-8V20 FFAR blocks. In spite of tests going ahead, the helicopter was not adopted for production.

Based on the bitter Afghan experience, where transport Mi-8MTs were favoured by many crews, Mil EDB worked on various modifications to improve the battle effectiveness of the Mi-24. Many of the modifications mentioned above, such as EVU exhaust gas coolers, TV3-117V engines and defence suite, were driven by such a need. One frequent complaint of the crews was the lack of rear protection. When flying with the Mi-8/8MT, a crewmember manning a gun mounted at the rear door could cover the area behind the helicopter when it moved out from the attack area, but the Mi-24 offered no rear protection at all, and the side-door gunners were unable to see much of the rear hemisphere. Analysis of data from the field revealed that more than a half of combat hits came from the rear hemisphere, so a plan to install a rear mounted machine gun was approved.

A gun turret was installed in the area behind the cargo cabin where radio equipment was located, and which allowed some space for the modification. Initially, a USPU-24 station was considered, but this would require remote aiming and no sufficiently lightweight technology was available to enable this. Therefore, a hand-operated NSVT-12.7 Utyos machine gun was selected. The gunner sat in a capsule, aiming the gun manually. During take-off and landing there was not enough clearance for the gunner, so he was expected to sit inside the fuselage behind the cargo cabin. Before reaching the combat zone, he entered the capsule, with his legs in rubber hoses, left completely unprotected from the rifle fire. The gun had ammo boxes on each side with 300 rounds total. Evidently it was a desperate solution intending to provide little assistance.

In the summer of 1985, one Mi-24V prototype was modified and tested with the designation Mi-24VD. The impact of the installation on the aircraft's centre of gravity was excessive, however, and the expected firing accuracy and field of view of the gunner were inadequate. Also the safety of the gunner was compromised, as during a hard landing he would be extremely vulnerable—and to make matters worse, could not wear a parachute. Instead, rear-view mirrors were installed on serial Mi-24Vs for better rear-hemisphere awareness. Another Afghanistan-driven update was tested in the late 1980s. This was an Mi-24V modified with new flat cockpit-window panels inside the Plexiglass bubbles. Such a decision was made in order to improve the protection of the crews from the sides.

When flying in the Afghan valleys crews were frequently sniped at from mountain positions, and a hit through the side Plexiglas, which offered no protection against gunfire, could easily result in serious injury or death. One helicopter was modified, but the impact on weight and balance was so excessive that it was not even flight-tested as

Above: Detail of the Mi-24VD experimental model with a NSVT-12.7 machine gun for rear hemisphere protection. (*MVZ Mil*)

Below: Detail of the Mi-24VD tail gunner's position—it was an extremely risky position in case of a crash or an emergency landing. (*MVZ Mil*)

the ground crews complained about difficult movement in the cockpit, which was like working in a greenhouse. In any event, the visibility was evaluated as poor. Instead, the following Mi-28 model was favoured as a solution, having been designed with the benefit of combat experience from the beginning. Mi-24 crews were instead issued with a new generation of flak vests.

As a solution aimed at bringing the Soviet army better night capability, two projects related to optical and thermal imaging systems integration were introduced and tested in late 1980. In the first case, one Mi-24V was equipped with Merkuryi V24 optical and thermal viewer attached in a special container on the left outer pylon. The Merkuryi device was derived from the imager developed for the V-80 prototypes (in production known as Ka-50). This modification gained the designation Mi-24N. There was a dedicated CRT in the WSO cockpit for viewing the system pictures. However, flight testing showed the fixed image system to be poor. Instead, another system, the TP SPO-V Satrap, was installed on another Mi-24V in the USPU-24 station with the 9A-624 gun being removed. This position allowed better searching of the target area. The modification was given the name Mi-24VT. Tests were performed in late 1989, but with the withdrawal of Soviet forces from Afghanistan, the programme was stopped as the problem no longer needed an urgent solution, and instead the Mi-28 model was expected to address it in the long term.

Afghanistan worked well as an operational testing range for many new types of weapons. One such modification was the test firing of unguided S-25 air-to-ground rockets from O-25 launchers installed under the inner wing pylons. This rocket had a launch weight of some 480kg, and represents the most powerful unguided weapon ever fired from an Mi-24. In spite of generally good performance and huge impact effect, it was not adopted for wider service for numerous reasons. At first, the extensive rocket plume seriously damaged the helicopter's exterior, including cockpit glazing, and launching forces exceeded the design limits of the wing. Later, the air-to-ground Kh-25 missile was also tested. The nose of the missile included laser guidance, with ground forces expected to mark the target. The test launches of this missile resulted in critical wing cracks because of excessive forces during missile engine starts, and the testing was stopped.

Another series of tests, which involved two Mi-24Vs, evaluated multiple launchers under the inner wing pylons each for seven 9M41 illumination rockets. Those were requested by the army aviation service, as the standard SAB-100-90 illumination bombs required the helicopter to fly over the territory designated for lighting, while the rocket could be fired at the distance of some 2 to 3 kilometres. In Afghanistan, FOTAB flash light bombs, thermobaric ODAB bombs and DAB smoke laying bombs were also tested without being accepted for regular use. However, the ODAB bombs were revealed to be a powerful weapon in the mountains of Afghanistan, capable of triggering destructive rockslides above enemy positions. As well as Afghanistan-driven upgrades, several other schemes were intended to generally improve the Mi-24's capabilities.

For self-defence, several air-to-air rockets were tested, such as the R-73 or R-60. Both were flight tested, with the latter type being fired from an adapted APU-60-1V launcher. The R-60 was adopted in 1989 and a very limited number of Mi-24Ps and Mi-24VPs were equipped with wiring in the external pair of wing pylons. Missiles were attached on special launchers by two under each wing. However, those missiles had the infra-red seeker fixed with no movement for a better field of view. Several current modernisation programmes include integration of 9M39 missiles, which were also tested in 1989. The Mi-24 model helped the Mil Design Bureau with development and flight verification of several components for the later Mi-28 model. For example, one Mi-24V was equipped in the late 1980s with an 'X' shaped tail rotor consisting of two blades offset by some 60°. Although this rotor was designed specifically for the Mi-28 model, it was later adopted for some Mi-24 modernisation programmes as well. Two Mi-28-programme testbeds should also be mentioned. They are referred to as Mi-24PrPNK-28, and both were equipped with a special housing on the nose resembling the Mi-28 nose shape for testing of the Mi-28 navigation, piloting and avionics suite. After end of their career they were grounded at the Mil test range, where they remained.

The first Mi-24V export customer was Czechoslovakia in 1985 with ten ships delivered in late December, followed by Hungary with ten as well. In Czechoslovakia Mi-24Vs were assigned to the 11th Helicopter Regiment at Plzeň, where they were primarily used for support of Western military districts, as well as for border patrolling in the mountainous terrain due to the higher power margin. Flights along the border were tense, resulting in monthly incidents where Czechoslovak Mi-24s actively pursued US Army Cobras and Kiowas, or Bundeswehr Alouette IIs and Bö-105 PAH-1s. In 1987 ten more were delivered, with another eight in 1988 and the final three in 1989. Some sources say in total thirty-two ships were ordered and one crashed before hand-over, so only thirty-one were actually delivered. Several Hind monographs record that the further deliveries were put on hold due to the Velvet revolution, but this is inaccurate. Actually, the last ships arrived to Plzeň in March 1989, several months before the revolution, and the country was getting ready for the acquisition of the newer Mi-28 model instead of further Mi-24s, although it did not happen due to a change in the geopolitical situation.

In this new era the role of the Hinds changed. Because of their ability to carry four external fuel tanks for a longer range without obstructing the cargo cabin, their lower flight log and better performance, in 1990 they became a feature of aerial displays and visited many Western countries with their spectacular show. The 11th Helicopter Regiment even created a Hind display team called Box flying with four ships which demonstrated their art domestically and abroad. When, in 1992, the Federation started to split, ten Mi-24Vs were sent to newly created Slovakia and the rest remained at Plzeň for a while before the whole Hind fleet was unified under the newly created 33rd Helicopter Airbase; from there they formed the 331st Attack Helicopter Squadron (Letka Bitevních Vrtulníků) and 332nd Attack Helicopter Squadron, both equipped with the Hind and both merged into the former in 2001. The Mi-24V fleet then became a major part of the used fleet. Several modernisation attempts were considered, including new weapons and sensors integration, but eventually the only decision taken was to equip helicopters with additional altimeters measuring in feet (the original was in metric), GPS receivers and new transponders in order to allow at least some compatibility with NATO.

Of the Czech Mi-24Vs, the ship with fuselage code 0705 became particularly popular because of its tiger-themed paint scheme. The 331st Helicopter Squadron of the 33rd Airbase was accepted as a member of the NATO Tiger Association, and from 2001 was the first in Eastern Europe to have full membership. The unit was later restructured to 23rd Airbase at Přerov with 231st Attack Helicopter Squadron, eventually moving to Náměšt and Oslavou airport in 2008 where it sits to this day. In 2002 the Czech Republic reached an agreement with Russia to delete its state debt from the USSR-era, partially by providing military hardware. Consequently, the country received seven Mi-24Vs. They had different serial numbers from the previous deliveries except one which followed the sequence of previous ships. All were delivered on board An-124 cargo planes from Rostov and were introduced into the service of the Czech air force. They were purchased during a time when large modernisation of all Mi-24Vs was under consideration, together with other new NATO countries such as Poland, Hungary and Slovakia.

While the older Mi-24Vs were scheduled to be modernised, the newly delivered ships were intended for training and standard operation. For many reasons all of the Central European upgrade projects failed, and the Czech army decided to utilise the Russian debt for further acquisition of ten more Hinds. Those were delivered and called Mi-35s, because they featured NVG compatible cockpits, more powerful TV3-117VMA engines and new hydraulics boosters. All were delivered in 2005 and 2006, being the last Hinds delivered to a NATO country. Seventeen new ships allowed the country to donate six Mi-24Vs, together with six Mi-17s, to Afghanistan under the NATO SHAPE-led programme. All helicopters were overhauled and partially modernised by the LOM PRAHA state enterprise. The upgrade included TV3-117VMA engines installation, new KT-73 transponder, COM 1/2 AT-160 and Dayton Granger 17760 radios. Those aircraft became the best equipped helicopters of the Afghani fleet and were all flying from Kabul and later Kandahar.

Together with the helicopters the 22nd Airbase at Náměšť nad Oslavou participated in the operation mentoring and liaison teams supporting the Afghani army air corps. Some seven Mi-24Vs were sold to state-owned company and later were allegedly delivered to Libya via the United Arab Emirates. During the service of Czech Hinds several modernisation projects were again considered, but no large one was realised. The most interesting Czech upgrade appeared in 2002, when an experimental radar absorbing (RAM) and infra-red (IR)-absorbing four tone camouflage was applied on Mi-24V coded 0837. The camouflage was made of plastic tiles sticked to the surface. This project, manged by the Air Force Research Institute was a part of an experimental task focused on reducing the helicopter's radar and IR signature. The helicopter was completely stripped of paint and repainted. Later, a special set of measurement flights was performed, but with only limited results. Therefore this unique RAM upgrade did not become standard, and the helicopter was, after reaching the end of its service life, transferred to the University of Defence at Vyškov, where it is still used as an instructional airframe today.

A Czech-made PL-20 Plamen 20mm twin-barrel cannon was tested on Mi-24V code 0703, installed on the inner wing pylons. Later, other helicopters were used in testing this installation. This cannon was developed for the Aero L-159 ALCA light attack aircraft, with modification for helicopter use in the area of helicopter-pod interface and shell release after firing. Its advantage is using the NATO standard ammunition. In spite of satisfactory test results and type approval being granted, it has not been adopted for regular service. Some of the Mi-24V and Mi-35 helicopters were later modified for the Search and Rescue (SAR) role within the Czech national SAR system and were given an ADF device with control box in the place of the original map indicator. All Czech Mi-24Vs passed all general overhauls in the country at LOM PRAHA company, with the last ship overhauled in 2022. As the 231st Attack Helicopter Regiment became the first Eastern European member of the prestigious NATO Tiger Association, several helicopters were over the time painted in Tiger and other special schemes, starting with Mi-24V 0705 (two various full-scale tiger camouflages), 7353 (an all-black tiger), 3361 (tiger on the front fuselage), 3366 (alien tiger), 3369 (tiger with Second World War B-24 Liberator theme) and 3370 (camouflage similar to certain Second World War B-24 Liberators) with many others wearing tiger details.

Mi-24Vs with 9M114s on the outer pylons modified for the smoke generation took part in aerial displays. There were plans for Hinds to be used in service beyond 2030, but this has not happened. Seven of the Mi-35s have been delivered in several batches to Ukraine since 2022 as a support for the war with Russia, and all were engaged in direct combat with at least two ships shot down. All were flown by ferry flight to Poland. The remaining two Mi-35s and Mi-24Vs stayed in the country and were stored. Ten Slovak Mi-24Vs followed the history of the above-mentioned Mi-24Ds at the Prešov airbase, including the upgrade of elected ships. They were also used for the border patrolling but with decreasing tendency over the time. The majority of the helicopters, which were overhauled locally by LOTN company, were grounded between 2006 and 2009, two remaining ships in 2011. Such a decision was economical and since none of the ship reached 2,000 flight hours, five of them were sold to arms dealers for further use. Three were overhauled and delivered to Senegal, and two to Cameroon by the Polish WZL-1 overhaul plant.

The Senegalese helicopters were updated with a new navigation and communication system and NVG-compatible lighting derived from domestic Polish projects. The NVG position lights and anti-collision beacon are identical to those used on Polish air force helicopters. The communication and navigation system was added by Garmin VHF/GPS device with new antenna visible on the tail boom. The Cameroon Hinds were just overhauled without any significant upgrade.

Hungary became the second Mi-24V operator with ten helicopters delivered in 1985. A further twenty ships were planned to be procured, but the plan stalled due to lack of funds. Even in Hungary the Mi-24Vs followed the career of the Mi-24D model described above with the service under the 87th Regiment and later MH 86 Helicopter Regiment at Szolnok airbase. Of the Hungarian helicopters, the machine with fuselage code 713 was modified in service into a training variant, with the removal of the KPS-53AV gunsight and its replacement with a small instrument board. In 2001, one Mi-24V collided mid-air with Mi-24D, resulting in a tragic fall of the former killing the two crew members on board. Hungarian crews were engaged in the training and operational mentoring of Afghani Hind crews in Kabul.

During the military exercise Load Diffuser 2008, female pilot Éva 'Vivi' Horváth was piloting an Mi-24V and was able to keep a firm 'target lock' on the F-15 Eagle in the gunsight while the US Air National Guard pilot was completely unaware of the threat. This particular Hind then carried two symbols of the F-15 under the canopy.

Above: Czech Mi-24V with non-standard armament—the Czech PL-20 Plamen cannon pod, firing 20mm NATO standardised rounds. (*ZVI*)

Below: An ex-Czech Mi-24V in Afghan army air corps colours during a pre-flight check. Note the large HF rail antenna on the tail boom. (*Author*)

Above: Likely the sole Mi-24V with RAM coating—a Czech ship with 'plastic-like' tiles covering the surface for the reduction of RCS. (*Author*)

Below: A Hungarian Mi-24V in a very special eagle-themed paint scheme, fitted with EVU exhaust gad coolers not used during regular operation. (*Author*)

In February 2026 the Hungarian air force ceased operation of the type and withdrew it from service. One Hungarian Mi-24V with fuselage code 716 was painted as an Eagle, and another one with number 714 as a Hind during service, both becoming best known ships of the type.

In Bulgaria the Mi-24V model never became dominant because in 1986 only six ships were delivered. Some sources say seven, but this is incorrect as one ship was renumbered in service for administrative reasons. All Mi-24Vs were operated under the 13th Attack Helicopter Regiment and later the 24th Helicopter Airbase as mentioned, with the Mi-24Ds. They were overhauled, with the first ship being finished in 2001 and the last some eight years later. They were the most used Bulgarian Hinds deployed in the majority of the military exercises. Because of the lack of funds all were in a non-airworthy condition in 2010, with restoration in 2013 and later. Although there was always a shortage of helicopters, crews managed to relaunch weapon drills. Two helicopters are believed still to be in the active inventory and serving with minimum upgrades in terms of GPS navigation and transponder.

Poland received its sixteen Mi-24Vs in 1986. Due to the Polish alphabet, they are sometimes called Mi-24W (the Polish alphabet does not use the 'V' letter). They were all subordinated to 56th Attack Helicopter Regiment (Pułk Śmigłowców Bojowych) at the Innowrocław airbase. On delivery of the last ships, two units, one with Mi-24Ds and second with Mi-24Vs, became operational with the 56th Regiment and its 3rd Attack Helicopter Squadron (Eskadra Śmigłowców Bojowych) operating the newest model. In 1987 the squadron declared combat readiness and it participated in large Klon 87 military exercise.

In June 1987, first helicopter was lost during a night flight when the pilot lost directional control and crashed. The investigation showed it was caused by a manufacturing error, although the Soviet side rejected the warranty and blamed it on servicing. Polish general staff decided to replace the lost ship and in December 1990 ordered one more Mi-24V, which came in May 1991, being the last Hind delivered to a European ex-Warsaw Pact country. This is why this sole ship has 956 tail code while all the previous ones start with 7. After delivery a damaged engine was discovered and the collapsing USSR showed no interest in remedying the issue.

The fall of the Iron Curtain meant the Hinds were no more used for attack sorties and the Innowrocław Regiment decided to show the type in a formation flight of four ships with the fifth as a solo helicopter acting when the team regrouped. For the solo ship role the helicopter number 741 was designed, so high visibility orange strips were added to its paint scheme. The team's first display took place at Ławica airport in August 1991. It performed its spectacular show for seven years before it ceased to exist due to crew rotation. When the Mi-24Vs reached its time between overhaul in the mid-1990s, a decision was taken to overhaul them locally and all were gradually overhauled by the WZL-1 plant at the city of Łodz, with first ship overhauled in spring 1994.

Of all ships, the Mi-24V with fuselage code 731 is worthy of particular mention. It crash-landed in July 1997 when transporting a wounded technician to hospital, but it rolled over during landing and was damaged. The ship was eventually repaired using parts of the Mi-24D and was nicknamed Mi-24WuDe. It was the sole Polish Mi-24V not able to carry auxiliary fuel tanks because of the Mi-24D wings. Originally, two modernisation projects for the attack role and combat SAR missions were evaluated and presented under the name Mi-24 Pluszcz (sometimes referred to as Mi-24PL, with PL said to stand for Poland) as a Polish contribution to European attempts to modernise Hinds. These local upgrades were the most advanced in Europe, driven by the fact that Poland was Europe's major operator of Mi-24.

In 2002, four Visegrad countries, the Czech Republic, Hungary, Poland and Slovakia, agreed on a common modernisation approach for all their Mi-24s. In 2000, during MSPO Kielce Defence Exhibition, the Polish state-owned WZL-1 overhaul plant presented a project for a deep upgrade in partnership with BAE Systems. It included the live display of the standard Mi-24V with fuselage code 739 with a FLIR Sfim Strix turret attached provisionally to the nose. This device, being one of the most sensitive in the world, was fitted to the Eurocopter Tiger model. Alongside the helicopter, a single barrel GIAT THL-20 20-mm gun was displayed as a prospective option for up-gunning the helicopter, and Euromissile HOT 3 ATGMs were displayed as a proposed main anti-tank missile. In some media this helicopter gained the unofficial designations Mi-24WZL-1 and Mi-24PL.

In 2001, an improved variant, developed in partnership with IAI Aerospace, was presented at the MSPO exhibition. It featured the TM197B 20mm Gatling machine gun, Israeli NT-D ATGMs, Grom-L air-to-air missiles and local THL-5NV NVGs. However, despite an ambitious presentation, this project was never realised and the common modernisation plans among the Czech Republic, Slovakia and Hungary failed. During the same industry show, BAE Systems presented a mock-up of an Mi-24 nose as part of a planned upgrade programme.

Between August 2008 and 2014, Polish armed forces operated a contingent called Independent Air Group in Afghanistan. It was using four Mi-24Vs and seven Mi-17-1Vs at a time. Before being deployed, the helicopters passed overhauls at Łodz and were equipped with NVG compatible lights, VOR/TACAN/ILS/MKR and GPS XL-155 navigation aids, new Radmor RRC-9500, Harris RF5H-80MP and Rhode & Schwarz MR600R radios with frequency hopping and encryption, KT-01V Adros IF Jammer, ITWL S2-3a flight data recording system and other systems, as well as more powerful TV3-117VMA-SBM1V engines (referred to in Poland as TW3-117WMA-SBM1W), which significantly improved power output in hot and high conditions. From the original manufacturer, several sets of EVU exhaust gas coolers were purchased. As the first aircraft Mi-24V with fuselage code 730 was finished in 2006 and displayed publicly one year later. It was anticipated that this upgrade would be applied to the majority of remaining Hinds as well. The helicopters upgraded in this way saw action in the Afghan deployment and proved themselves well.

In addition to the programme above, a contract with the Danish Terma Company was signed in around 2012 to equip fifteen Mi-24s and seven Mi-17s with self-defence pods. On Mi-24s those were expected to be attached to the outer wing end pylons. The pod included Cassidian AN/AAR-60 UV sensors, and flare dispensers. One pod, with two sensors and two dispensers, was attached to each wing. Although this effectively replaced and surpassed the original ASO-2V dispensing system, the latter was retained. One Mi-24W, with fuselage code 727, worked as ground test platform with 729 ship serving for flight testing. Both were equipped with the pods and even now may be distinguished by additional bracing on the end pylons and extra screws on the outer side of the pylons. However, the contract was later cancelled because the supplier faced technical difficulties and was unable to deliver and install all of the sets by the end of 2012, as specified in the contract. The very strict time limit was a result of plans to deploy those helicopters to Afghanistan. Although this was an add-on system not requiring deep integration into the fuselage, this variant became the very first Hind really protected against IR seeking missiles.

Over the years, fifteen ships rotated in Afghanistan, always delivered on board an An-124. Originally the fleet was assembled and operated from Bagram but soon moved to its final destination at Ghazni. Polish crews developed specific tactics when one helicopter was flying armed with UPK-23-250 cannon pods and the other with UB-32A-24 rocket pods. Helicopters were engaged in support of ground forces and were flying very extensively with a total of three ships lost during the service, either after pilot error or due to enemy action. After the Afghan deployment only thirteen ships remained in service.

In 2011, the regiment was formally disbanded and 1st Brigade of army aviation (Brygada Lotnictwa Wojsk Lądowych) was created instead, with the subordinated 49th Airbase at Pruszcz Gdański and 56th Airbase at Innowrocław. Both airbases are having 1st Attack Squadron (Eskadra Szturmowa), which was equipped with a mix of Mi-24Ds and Mi-24Vs. Since 2010, no live ATGM firings occurred, and the helicopters were proposed for deep upgrade several times. Around 2013, plans led by the Warsaw Air Force Institute of Technology (ITWL) to upgrade the helicopters with some items derived from the W-3 Głuszec attack helicopter were introduced, which some media predicted would receive the Mi-24PL designation. Major changes included a ZSA flight management system, allowing the crew a full pre-flight preparation and post-flight debriefing. Both cockpits were expected to be modified with selected CMC Cockpit 4000 items such as MFDs and a head-up display (HUD) for the pilot. In order to boost the target-detection capability the helicopters were to be equipped with the Rafael Toplite FLIR coupled with Spike-ER ATGM laser guided missiles. As a domestic feature, Grom air-to-air missiles could be integrated on the end pylons.

At the time, the Polish air force planned to operate the type for the following decade at least, but no orders were placed and only a mock-up of the front cockpit had been presented. In 2019 the very last Polish upgrade was presented at MSPO exhibition in Kielce. Already under the influence of a rearmament programme searching for a Hind replacement, one Mi-24D was upgraded with fully digital avionics derived from last W-3PL Głuszec helicopters, including MFDs, HUD and its up-front control panel and helmet-mounted display, NSC1 Orion. Mock-ups of missile, laser and radar warning-system sensors were presented on the ship as well. The armament was proposed to include domestic 70mm NLPR-70 rockets with a 15-tube WW-15 launcher, or French-made 68mm rockets as well as long range ATGMs Spike ER2 or Spike LR from Israel, but built locally. For air defence the AAGM Piorun, a type later well used in the Ukrainian conflict, was presented as an option. The 9A-624 gun was proposed to be replaced by domestic WLKM machine gun of the same calibre. The electro-optical gimbal Toplite MHD from Israel was to be integrated as well. The upgrade was proposed as a 'plan B' in case there was a delay in the Hind replacement. When the AH-64E order was announced, the project was postponed.

Above: A pair of Polish Mi-24Vs, also known as Mi-24Ws, flying over Afghanistan with IR jammers and armed ASO-2V flare dispensers visible. (*Bartek Bera*)

Below: A modernised Polish Mi-24V displayed at the MSPO Kielce 2000 Fair with Sfim Strix FLIR and HOT ATGMs. (*Andrzej Kiński*)

Detail of the wing with two 9M114 ATGMs, four HOT 3 ATGMs and UPK-23-250 machine gun pod. Note the provisional HOT 3 ATGM attachment is missing wiring. (*Andrzej Kiński*)

Right: Another modernised Polish Mi-24V displayed during MSPO Kielce 2001 with the new TM197B 20mm Gatling cannon visible. (*Andrzej Kiński*)

Below: Polish Mi-24V with self-defence pods installed on the end plates of the wing. This upgrade was tested on serial ships but not used. (*Terma*)

Above: Latest Polish upgrade with Rafael Toplite FLIR coupled with Spike-ER ATGM laser guided missiles. On the end pylons are Grom air-to-air missiles. (*Miroslav Gyűrösi*)

Below: Details of the 70mm rocket launcher, Spike-ER ATGMs and Grom air-to-air missiles under the wing of this Polish Mi-24V. (*Miroslav Gyűrösi*)

Mongolia became first non-European operator of the Mi-24V model. This Asian country, which in 1986 received twelve ships, was practically under USSR military control with over 30,000 Soviet soldiers in its territory using Mongolia as a buffer zone against potential attack from China. The Mi-24s were assigned to the Unit 337 located at Nalayh airport, south-east of the capital of Ulaanbaatar. Although the Mongolian air force has always been modest in size, it generated pilots to be type-rated in the USSR for the Hind and after their return mixed-crews with Soviet pilots were flown only seldomly. Mi-24Vs were planned to be used for border patrol and ground forces support. Under the new president, Batmönkh, the country restored its relationship with China and since the late 1980s it loosened its ties with the USSR, who eventually withdraw from the country during the domestic political changes, and to normalise relationship with China. The withdrawal also meant the Soviet technical and military advisors gradually left the country.

The helicopters, still almost new at that time, were flown for few months only and were eventually all stored open-air at the base with none of them reaching more then 500 flight hours. After the 1990 revolution in Mongolia the air force practically ceased to exist. The helicopters remained on site for several years and in 2010 the country sought overhaul options, which were performed in Ukraine in 2014 at the Konotop plant. Ukraine attempted to purchase these helicopters following the outbreak of the war in eastern Ukraine, although it appears the transaction did not take place. Surprisingly, one ship following the Mongolian series was delivered to Sudan as a downgraded export Mi-35 model, with no information on its destiny.

Afghanistan received sixteen Mi-35s in 1986, followed by nine in 1987, five in 1988 and finally eighteen in 1990. The new model quickly replaced the underpowered Mi-25s. Surprisingly, the last deliveries continued as a part of the agreement on withdrawal of the Soviet forces and were provided to the Kabul regime to fight the mujaheddins on its own. There were further deliveries of Mi-35s planned but all the support was put on halt by the Russian president Boris Yeltsin in early 1990s. During Soviet intervention the helicopters were gradually distributed to the 377th Helicopter Regiment at Kabul, 379th Independent Helicopter Battalion at Kandahar, 375th Independent Helicopter Battalion at Mazar-e-Sharif and 376th Independent Helicopter Battalion at Herat. All units were flown with at least mixed Afghan-Soviet, if not entirely Soviet, crews till 1989. The operation was, however, plagued by sabotage and low availability of even brand-new helicopters, as well as by the low skill level of the pilots.

Hinds were used for several offensives as a support of the Soviet army, but the plan to burden the Afghan air force with its own combat operations failed entirely. Instead, defections started to be a huge problem, with multiple Mi-35s fleeing. In total at least three helicopters were seized by Pakistani air force (two in July 1989) with some of them even flown in the new country for testing purposes, at least five were captured by mujaheddins and two crashed in the attempt to defect. In reality, the Afghani Mi-35 force posed a limited real threat and assumed its role only after the Soviet troops withdrew from Afghanistan. Their major role was not only direct combat engagement, but also convoy or transport helicopters protection. When the Soviets pulled out of the country, mujaheddins attacked many cities, including Jalalabad, where two Mi-35s were permanently redirected from Kabul for aerial cover. Four crews there were flying daily and destroyed dozens of fortified posts of Taliban militia shelling the city. One of the helicopters was shot down by Stinger missile.

Later with major cities falling under Taliban control Hinds were concentrated at Kabul airport and Bagram. Some of them were used as a source for spare parts, as the transport Mi-8MTs were given priority. In 1992 Mazar-e-Sharif fell to militia led by General Abdul Rashid Dostum, and with the capture of the city the airbase was newly controlled by the Junbish militia led by General Dostum. When in 1997 a military parade was held at Mazar-e-Sharif one of the Junbish forces presented its inventory, including Mi-25. Although General Dostum was active against Soviet troops during the occupation, after its withdrawal he did not join the Taliban and kept a relatively peaceful part of Northern Afghanistan under its control. Another large city, Bagram, was conquered in late 1996 by Talibs with at least three Mi-35s and one Mi-25 captured at the airfield, all grounded due to technical issues. The airworthy ships were flown to forward areal posts near the Panjshir Valley where also a huge stock of armament and support equipment were transferred from Bagram.

In the Panjshir Valley helicopters were operated by militia led by Ahmad Shah Massoud, another former anti-Soviet militant leader called 'Lion of Panjshir' for his brave actions against the Soviet army. He controlled significant part of Northern Afghanistan and also did not join Taliban after 1989. He was historically supported by UK intelligence and also the CIA and had an opportunity to use his background in Tajikistan. He even led a small unit of aircraft technicians backed by the CIA and other agencies who put together helicopters returning from missions in Afghanistan. They were prioritising the transport Mi-8MTs but had few Mi-35s in the inventory as well, including two ships which defected to Massoud-controlled territory in 1989 with their crews calling for asylum and were captured and few ships flown from Kabul.

Hinds were repeatedly used to repulse Taliban forces from their regular attempts to seize Massoud-controlled areas. In Kabul the government armed forces were active even after the fall of the original post-Soviet regime, but were constantly engaged in clashes with various mujaheddin factions until a hardline Taliban faction conquered the city in September 1996. At Kabul airport four Mi-35s were seized, all in non-airworthy condition, as well as two Mi-25s and one Mi-24U at the military museum. All in all, a total of five militias including the Taliban claimed to operate the Mi-25s and Mi-35s after the withdrawal of Soviet troops.

When the Taliban gained control of Kabul, it enlisted the Mi-35s in its inventory and at least two helicopters were filmed during a victory parade flyover in 2001, both with restored paint and Taliban flag on the tail booms. The anti-Taliban militias in the north grouped into a northern alliance and were opposing the new regime with direct involvement in low intensity clashes well into 2001 when the US-led attacks on the country started. During the initial phase of war in Afghanistan Mi-35s of Talib militia fractions became a regular target for coalition fighters and at least two were destroyed during air raids on the airports. Later it was primarily Massoud's helicopters which were sent to Russia for overhaul when the renewed Afghan National Army Air Corps was being established under the command of Operation Enduring Freedom. And those four original Afghan Mi-35s became the backbone of the newly established air force. Remaining helicopters were gradually grounded or destroyed. Later, six ex-Czech Mi-24Vs were delivered as well, all operated by the helicopter wing from Kabul airport together with at least two ex-Russian Mi-24Ps (of which one was originally stationed at East Germany) and four ex-Indian Mi-35s delivered in 2015 and 2016, and four more delivered in 2019 from Belorussia but paid for by India.

In 2010, a US air force pilot from 438th Air Expeditionary Wing became the first American crew member to fly the Hind in live combat. It happened during mentoring of Afghani crew on tactics when the ship, delivered as surplus from the Czech Republic, engaged in combat with Taliban forces on the ground. Later, numerous American pilots, usually from other than governmental entities, flew the Hinds in Afghanistan. After the Taliban took over the control of the country in 2021, at least three Mi-24Vs and Mi-35s were captured at Kabul airbase and are subordinated to the rotary wing squadron. The Taliban therefore became the very last operator of the Hind to date.

Angola purchased twelve Mi-35s in 1987 and twelve more a year later. They were ordered as war attrition, replacing the downed Mi-25s, and soon became major operated type. The Angolan civil war became a high-intensity proxy war of East versus West, with the Angolan government supported by the USSR and socialistic bloc. Moscow even provided a loan equivalent to $1 billion, while the USA supported the opposition UNITA forces with money and weapons, including Stinger shoulder-launched missiles. Helicopters were assigned to the 22nd Combat Helicopter Regiment (Regimento Aéreo de Helicópteros de Combate) at the Huambo airbase, where two squadrons were formed—3rd with Mi-25s and 4th with Mi-35s.

In August 1987, a battle of Cuito Cuanavale started, the largest conflict on the African continent since the Second World War, which eventually ended up with defeat of government forces, despite them being backed by newly delivered and immediately deployed Mi-35s. Hinds role was purely support of the ground forces offensive and

Two Afghan Mi-35s destroyed by mujaheddin. Note the windshields were still not penetrated, although heavily tested. (*US Library of Congress collection*)

although the governmental forces controlled the airspace, the ground forces were outnumbered by the opponent. At least two helicopters were shot down within two months, both with portable MANPADS systems, and two crashed due to a fault in navigation. After the ceasefire the majority of the helicopters were kept operational under the helicopter regiment, and in the twenty-first century they were all concentrated under the helicopter regiment (Regimento Aéreo de Helicópteros) at the Luanda airbase. It is now the sole type operator within the Angolan air force, which also operated Mi-24Vs provided later from Ukraine, and Mi-24Ps from Russia. In 2006 the Russian 280th OVP, a unit with vast experience from Afghanistan, started to operate in Angola as a mentoring team with direct engagement in low-intensity combat operations with rebels.

In 1987 Mozambique bought twelve Mi-35s, but unlike previously delivered Mi-25s these helicopters were primarily destined for protection purposes. The local armed forces realised the risk of sudden attacks of the rebels and Hinds were an ideal tool to supress the enemy. The fleet was operated primarily from the Nacala airbase but a few ships were deployed to multiple places. When the civil war came to an end in 1992 Hinds were used for a decade until the last one was grounded due to lack of maintenance. Mozambique became one of the African nations which was unable to secure servicing due to lack of funds. Currently the helicopters are declared as withdrawn from service.

In 1987 Ethiopia took delivery of ten Mi-35s and wanted to use them in the civil war, but they came shortly before the leading Derg military junta started some reorganisation attempts in order to become a more civilianised political entity. They were involved in the massacre in Hausein and surrounding cities and proved to be a truly lethal tool against unarmed villagers. Subsequently, the USSR military advisors left the country, and Hinds were affected by lack of crews as many pilots left the service then. In 1991 the civil war ended with the creation of the independent country of Eritrea. Since the new government of Ethiopia did not provide any guarantees to its ethnical neutrality, a few days before the ceasefire several Ethiopian aircraft, including three Mi-24As and three Mi-35s, defected to Ambouli airbase in Djibouti. All helicopters were eventually returned to Ethiopia.

In the new regime, Hinds, operated in the so-called Tiger squadron, were soon engaged in war again when Eritrea launched an undeclared war on Ethiopia in 1998. All airworthy Mi-24s/35s were used for the combat activities and the government asked for support from Russian mercenaries. Also, the Hungarian company Danubian was involved in quick reinstatement of several Mi-24Aa and Mi-24U into airworthy condition at Debre Zeit air force base, where a major maintenance facility was located. One Mi-35 is reported to have been shot down in February 1999, with another one lost a year later. In 2021 two more Ethiopian Mi-35s were shot down in the country by the Tigray rebels when the crews attacked forest camps.

Libya purchased twelve Mi-35s in 1988 and had plans for delivery of additional 24s in 1990, but only the initial delivery materialised. With the withdrawal of Soviet Union advisors from Libya and due to the global ease of political tensions, no more orders came. Helicopters were delivered after the end of the hostilities with Chad and were used primarily for border patrolling missions. They belonged to the squadrons located at the Al Watiya Air Base and Sirte. Helicopters passed an overhaul in Ukraine in the new millennium and were, together with Algerian ships, the only African Hinds maintained in airworthy condition.

During the Arab Spring, a fight began between the internationally recognised Government of National Accord (GNA) in Tripoli, and rival Libyan National Army (LNA) of Marshal Khalifa Haftar. Both entities seized a certain number of Hinds. LNA helicopters were deployed on multiple airbases to support the anti-GNA operation. In February 2011 one Mi-35 was destroyed at the apron of the Benina airbase with two more Mi-35s captured by the rebels. One more Mi-24 or Mi-35 was shot down in March and two more in subsequent years, with one shot down by a Turkish-made missile in 2020 when the LNA crew was identified as Russians. One Mi-35 operated by the governmental air force crashed in Sumer 2013 during air display in front of the spectators. Both armed forces later maintained air force capability, with GNA concentrating Mi-35s at the Benghazi airbase. GNA was capturing the stored Hinds from various airbases and tried to fix them. During one such ground transport the Mi-35 on a trailer got stuck and was seriously damaged under bridge.

In 1989, South Yemen, the sole communist state in the Arab world, procured six Mi-35s in a form of support of Moscow in its clashes with its northern neighbour. It received Soviet support from 1972, as had North Yemen earlier; Soviet aircraft inventory was used by both sides of the conflict. Although South Yemen practised massive military exercises,

Libyan Mi-35s after overhaul at Aviakon Konotop facility in Ukraine. Each ship is armed with UB-32A-24 rocket blocks and two PTB-450 auxiliary fuel tanks. (*Aviakon*)

the ultra-short civil war and coup attempt in 1986 led to the destruction of the majority of the air force and defection of many pilots. This is why the Mi-35s were delivered to South Yemen, as a means of increasing its military capability. They were involved in low-intensity border clashes before the countries reunited. Although formally united, in reality the southern and northern factions were still in opposition, and in 1994 the Mi-35s were briefly used by the southern forces during another stage of civil war.

After the hot phase, Mi-35s were kept airworthy locally with dark colours hand sprayed over the original desert camouflage. An overhaul from overseas companies was sought, but they were eventually repaired by Russia after 2010, just in time to get involved in the conflict with the Houthis. What started as another round of local rebellion grew gradually into a full-scale civil war. Mi-35s were subordinated to 128th Squadron at the base at the capital of Sanaa and its detachment at Taizz airbase and were used for attack on the rebels' positions. During the conflict with the Houthis ships were also regularly operating from the airbases in Aden, Al Anad and Hodeidah. The operation was difficult as the crews faced threat not only when flying, but also when driving to the base with Houthi snipers targeting them. Later, when the government forces failed to keep control of the country, Mi-35s fell under the control of the Houthis, with pilots trained in Iran to fly the type. At least one Mi-35 was destroyed by Saudi air force in 2021 during resupply of the ground forces, and another one by the US Navy EA-18G Growler in February 2024. The destiny of remaining ships is unknown.

In 1989 another batch of twenty Mi-35s was delivered to India alongside four training ships. Since India insisted on unifying the equipment of attack and combat models, a new training variant was created and is unofficially called Mi-24VU or Mi-35U, with both names being unofficial. They were produced in a late 1980s standard with many improvements from the Mi-24V model, such as new TV3-117V engines for easy operation in the high altitude environment, EVU exhaust gas coolers, L-006 RWR system and 9M114 Shturm missiles as the anti-tank weapon. Although the army is the major Indian operator of helicopter, all Mi-35s were assigned to the air force. All Mi-35s were assigned to the 104th Helicopter Unit at the Suratgarh airbase, close to the border with Pakistan. Since the country was generally very satisfied with the type, especially when Soviet troops left Afghanistan and it became clear that Pakistan wouldn't be benefiting from the support of the US military as it had before, India agreed to procure an additional fifteen Mi-24Vs with a low number of flight hours from Kyrgyzstan. Those were delivered in 1995 and all were of late 1980s years of production. They were assigned to 125th Helicopter Unit at Panthankot airbase close to the Pakistan border, where they complemented and later replaced the Mi-25s.

Hinds were used in the Kargil war between India and Pakistan in 1999 but only in a limited way when protecting convoys reaching the disputed areas. The altitude performance of the Hind prevented it from reaching the area of conflict, which was 5,000 metres above sea level. Based on the experience with this war the air force expedited an upgrade project for its Hinds, selecting the Israeli Mission 24 modernisation programme for twenty-five Mi-24Vs and Mi-35s. The Mission 24 demonstrator, not yet linked with India, was displayed at the Le Bourget Air Show by the Tamam company, a division of Israeli Aircraft Industries (IAI).

The main purpose of this variant was to extend the helicopter's operation for night and adverse weather conditions and also to improve the weapon system. The prototype was later referred to as Mi-24VN and Mi-35O, both those designations being unofficial. The main difference apparent on the prototype was the FLIR ball turret on the starboard side of the fuselage, which integrated IR sensor, LLLTV sensor and laser range finder. This ball turret, known as HMOSP (Helicopter Multi-mission Optronic Stabilised Payload), was derived by Tamam from a device used on the Bell AH-1W. HMOSP allowed automatic tracking of a designated target. The front cockpit gained a dedicated CRT display, with joystick for sensors and weapons control in place of the KPS-53AV sighting station. Both crew members wore helmets with a display system relating to the FLIR. The WSO's helmet was coupled with the 9A-624 machine gun's movement and also with the HMOSP. All controls were modified close to HOCAS standard, again with using AH-1W grips. The avionics suite was supplemented by a Mil-Std-1553 data bus, digital mission computer and GPS navigation and digital map.

Both cockpits were newly NVG compatible. The original Russian weapons were retained, with the possibility of integrating 9M120 Ataka anti-tank missiles, supplemented by Rafael NT-D anti-tank guided missiles (later called Spike ER) and 70mm unguided rockets of various origin. As a part of the defence system, the engine exhaust pipes were reshaped in order to flow the exhaust gas directly into the rotor downwash for rapid cooling. An 'X' shaped tail rotor and IAI Elta laser and radar warning system sensors were offered as an option. Although IAI tried to persuade customers that the prototype displayed at Paris was capable of flight, this was not true. It had no engines and APU and its service ports were blanked off, indicating no functionality. The first and only customer who selected some features from this upgrade was the Indian air force. The project proceeded smoothly with only one exception—the integration of HMOSP with 9M114 Shturm missiles.

The firing accuracy, after removing the original Raduga system, was not good enough and Tamam had to contact the original missile manufacturer for help. The Russians supported the programme, despite its unofficial status, in addressing this. A total of twenty-five helicopters were upgraded, while the remaining few were maintained in their original configuration for training. They were seen publicly for the first time in 2003 during the Bangalore Aero India air show. The upgrade was designed to be modest and quickly available without affecting the flight control system, autopilot or powerplant system. The first upgraded Indian Mi-35 was test flown in 2001 and it was publicly unveiled two years later. The works were done locally at the 3rd Base Repair Depot at Chandigarh airbase with support of the Israeli industry. Alongside the upgrade the helicopters also passed general overhauls. During the operation some were further updated, receiving radar warning receivers for example.

Later, India became a generous supporter of the UN peacekeeping missions and its Hinds have flown 10,137 sorties with 10,890 flight hours in live missions in the white UN paint scheme. For those the upgraded Mission 24 Hinds were preferred, and helicopters were deployed in operation UNAMSIL in Sierra Leone, or MONUC and MONUSCO in the Democratic Republic of Congo. During their Indian premiere in Sierra Leone three Mi-35s were deployed and they engaged in multiple clashes with rebels, firing the S-8 rockets and machine gun. The deployment was quite dramatic, especially in the Congo.

The UN mission had no mandate for attack sorties unless under direct attack, so the Hinds were called for when the UN camps were attacked. The local UN commander on the ground radioed the helicopters with the positions of UN ground forces. The friendly Congolese army, unable to communicate on UN radio channels, identified its own positions using smoke and white flags. Rebel positions were confirmed by the helicopter crew using visual observation and the Mi-35's sensors. Typically, the helicopter carried out dummy dives to warn and deter the opponent. When the rebels continued to threaten UN forces, the helicopter fired a warning shot. When rebel firing continued, salvos of rockets were launched on their position. Typically, missions were accomplished without any collateral damage thanks to the accurate firing from the attack helicopters. Indian Hinds were shot at numerous times with a perfect safety record.

The Indian air force operated two squadrons until 2019 when the AH-64E became the major attack type and all Hinds remained with 104 Helicopter Unit only, with 125 Helicopter Unit transferring to the Apache Guardian. Although the overhauls were regularly performed by 3rd Base Repair Depot, in 2022 it was agreed the Mi-24V and Mi-35 fleet would undergo general overhauls in Russia due to the need to extend the original service life, a task only OEM can do. Due to the Israeli components of the ships the Israeli industry likely participated in it. The extended service life was scheduled to allow the type's operation with single squadron till 2030 at least. By that time Hinds will be replaced by domestic HAL Prachand type.

An Indian Mi-35 freshly after overhaul in Russia. The number 42 is a call sign and was deleted prior to redelivery. (*Vertolet*)

Right: The Mission 24 Israeli prototype displayed at Paris Air Show. The HMOSP FLIR is clearly visible as well as exhaust outlets with different shapes for better cooling of the exhaust gases. (*Jan Čadil*)

Below: Detail of the Mission 24 prototype wing with 70mm rockets, NT-D ATGMs and original 9M114 ATGMs. Note the empty gun camera housing, deleted RHAWS sensor and new NVG compatible position light. (*Jan Čadil*)

Although the Mi-24V model finally included all the desired systems, army aviation commanders started to complain about the effectiveness of the 9A-624 machine gun. Most service aircraft, apart from training types and helicopters, had switched from machine guns to cannons over the years. It became obvious that a 12.7mm machine gun, while an excellent choice in terms of weight and capacity for integration into a movable turret, was effective only against unprotected or lightly protected targets, with little effect against newer armoured vehicles and reinforced bunkers. Also, in dusty environments the gun was prone to jam because of its sensitive mechanics. For these reasons, the idea to integrate a cannon type of armament was adopted. After evaluation, the best available gun was considered to be the Gryazev Shipunov GSh-30K (internal designation 9A-623K), which was duly selected. This was shortly before the weapon's integration into the Su-25 Frogfoot attack aircraft, which proved successful. However, its installation into a helicopter required completely different approach. Because the huge recoil prevented the cannon from being integrated into a moveable turret, the solution reached was to attach it in a fixed position to the starboard side.

A production Mi-24D helicopter was upgraded with the new gun in 1975, and the type gained the designation Mi-24P (with internal code Izdeliye 243 and Hind F NATO code). The cannon was installed in a fixed U-280 (sometimes referred to as NPU-30) turret on the starboard side of the helicopter. The prototype lacked the DUAS-V air data sensor boom and therefore has incorrectly been labelled as the Mi-24DU model in many publications. On the first prototype the standard GSh-30K gun with 1.5m length was used, but it was soon realised that the muzzle flames damaged the ATGM guidance optics under the nose and dazzled the crew. More seriously, the gun tended to transfer very severe vibrations to the airframe, causing many problems with the avionics and guidance system. Some instruments' needles shook so much during firing that it was impossible to read them, and often they failed to return to their original position after firing concluded. Hence, the aircraft barrels were replaced by longer ones with new total length of the gun of some 2.4 metres. Both barrels were capped by large muzzle dampers. Also the U-280 turret was modified with two large ribs reinforcing the fuselage above it, helping to better distribute the recoil forces.

Tests were conducted to establish the best position and angle of attack of the gun. Unlike the moveable machine guns, with the GSh-30K turret it was the pilot who aimed the gun by positioning the whole helicopter through the ASP-17V gunsight. Therefore, the ideal position of the gun on the airframe was essential for firing accuracy. The ammunition box, originally holding some 1,470 12.7mm rounds, was redesigned to hold 750 30mm shells. The rear end of the ATGM sighting system housing was modified in order to allow the enlarged ammunition box to be opened freely. Because the gun was meant to be fixed, but would move during the loading of ammunition, special platforms were installed behind the pitot static tubes, with rails holding laser pointers for optical harmonisation of the proper position of the gun. Because there was no moveable turret, the WSO cockpit lost the KPS-53AV gunsight station, and the operator consequently had an excellent view from the cockpit with an instrument board in front of him containing all essential flight instruments. This was one of the reasons why the Mi-24P was popular among the crews, because in case of any problem the WSO was able to control the helicopter fully. And this is the reason why Mi-24P operators never asked for a Hind training model—they could use the standard Mi-24P model quite well.

For aiming, an easy-to-use PKV gunsight was installed on the front cockpit frame. On production helicopters the same improvements as on the Mi-24V models were introduced, only the Mi-24P was equipped with TV3-117V engines from the start of production. The first series production helicopters were finished in April 1981 and they were soon widely deployed in Afghanistan. Here they proved their excellent qualities, but also showed that for some missions the 30mm cannon was excessive, and that aiming the whole helicopter to aim the gun could limit the usefulness of the aircraft. However, the crews liked the gun because the effect in the target area was several times higher than with the previous 12.7mm shells. Fortified firing posts, armoured vehicles or shelters in rocks were easy targets for the new gun. Pilots even learned how to fly the Hind for best accuracy and were able to hit a selected car in a convoy at more than 2km with a single shot. There were primarily ground threats in Afghanistan, for which the fixed gun was no problem as other unguided weapons were used in the same manner. It was the later Soviet pilots from European units who complained about lack of flexibility for engaging aerial targets. For example, during area or border patrolling, Mi-24Vs were able to track even much more agile helicopters and aeroplanes using the moveable 9A-624 machine gun, but with a fixed cannon the Hind was unable to outmanoeuvre almost any lighter type.

From 1981 to 1990 some 620 helicopters were finished, with 608 units produced to 1996 for Soviet and then Russian armed forces. It was so important for the Soviet army in Afghanistan that no export was considered for several years. With the Soviet air force the Mi-24Ps served with the above-mentioned units and were also deeply involved in expedition operations. Mi-24P also became the last Hind lost in Afghanistan, when, on 1 February 1989, the crew of one ship was checking the weather on the route selected for other ships' withdrawal and crashed in bad visibility. The Mi-24P became the major produced type for the Soviet army and each unit used it in a way that complemented the Mi-24V in service. Gradually, the Mi-24P prevailed and many units had a 2:1 ratio of helicopters.

The very first Mi-24P prototype. Note the GSh-30 cannon barrel shape and the 9M17P missiles from the Mi-24D model with Mi-24D guidance system. (*MVZ Mil*)

Detail of the GSh-30K twin-barrel gun on the Mi-24P nose with the fuselage reinforcement ribs visible above it. (*Author*)

Instrument board of the weapon system operator in the Mi-24P. No wonder the Mi-24P operators never needed the training model. (*Author*)

Above: A Soviet Mi-24P in typical 'shamrocks' camouflage is flying over Afghanistan. It features the IR jammer, EVU exhaust gas coolers and ASO-2V flare dispensers against MANPADS. (*Vertolet*)

Below: Another shot of the Soviet Mi-24P flying low pass over the runway shortly before a plane takes off. Hinds were repelling mujaheddin from attacking planes. (*Vertolet*)

Above: A Soviet Mi-24P in Afghanistan armed with two 9M114 ATGMs and atypical S-24 heavy-calibre unguided rockets. (*Vertolet*)

Left: Promotional picture of Soviet pilot in winter uniform leaning on the Mi-24P in Afghanistan. Note the combat knife and shortened AKS-74 assault rifle. (*ITAR-TASS*)

A Russian Mi-24P helicopter with 9M114 ATGMs and B-8V20 rocket block during an open day at Mahlwinkel airbase. (*Thomas Girke*)

The remaining twelve units were provided to the East Germany, which refused the Mi-24V and insisted on the Mi-24P model. East Germany became the only foreign operator of the model during Soviet era while having a huge dispute with Moscow about making the type available. German ships were delivered in 1989 and further twenty-four were scheduled to be delivered, but the order was cancelled early in 1990 together with the order of one Mi-24V for planned conversion of older Mi-24Ds to the newer standard. Given by the date of delivery East German Mi-24Ps saw only limited service with assignment to KHG-5 at Basepohl airbase because they came when the regime fell. Those brand-new ships were soon transferred under the united Luftwaffe with 96+xx tail codes, and two with 98+xx codes as those were intended for flight testing with WTD-61 unit in Bavaria. One helicopter was following the path of Mi-24D provided to the OPTEC programme in the US and was operated there in 2006. The US army later attempted to overhaul it but failed, so the ship was grounded and used as instructional airframe.

Six helicopters were provided to the Hungarian air force, which did not operate them and used them for spare parts. Two of them, with fuselage codes 335 and 336, entered overhaul locally in 2003 and were introduced into the service a year later. The first of them in Luftwaffe service was painted with highly visible blue, yellow and red stripes and nicknamed Golder Hind for its apparel, but in Hungary they served with standard camouflage. The remaining helicopters were stored within MH 86 Helicopter Regiment at Szolnok airbase, and in 2018 were sent to Russia for overhaul connected with slight modernisation such as the integration of NVG-compatible lighting, or new radio and navigational systems. All six Hinds were therefore operated with the Hungarian air force, but all were eventually withdrawn from service in February 2026. The remaining five German Hinds were donated to museums, although none of them had logged more than 200 flight hours.

Above: East German Mi-24P flying over the countryside—East Germany became the sole operator of this variant before the collapse of the USSR. (*MVZ Mil*)

Below: Beautiful shot of the East German Mi-24P shortly after delivery with almost untouched camouflage. Note the covered flare dispensers. (*Thomas Girke*)

Above: An originally East German Mi-24P with united Germany Luftwaffe roundels with a special 'Fly Out' scheme. This ship was recently finally grounded in Hungary. (*Thomas Girke*)

Below: The very last delivered East German Mi-24P was later transferred to the USA where it was operated as a 'red air' ship. Note the blinded cannon. (*US DoD*)

Based on the Mi-24P experience another project was launched in 1984. One year later, the Mi-24VP (Izdeliye 258, by NATO recognised as Hind E, together with Mi-24V) prototype was revealed for the first time and joined state trials. It was basically an Mi-24V with new NPPU-24 moveable turret, mounting a GSh-23L (9A-4454) 23mm twin-barrel cannon—the gun which was originally proposed for the V-24 project by Mikhail Mil himself in the late 1960s. Such a weapon proved to be an ideal compromise between the less effective but moveable 9A-624, and the powerful but fixed 9A-623K. The GSh-23 cannon was originally used in some variants of MiG-21 and MiG-23 fighters and L-39 trainers, and became a standard Soviet airplane weapon from the 1960s. Its creators, designers Gryazev and Shipunov, wanted to ensure the ability to hit the enemy in the fleeting moment when it flashed in the gun sight, ideally with the first shot. Therefore they came up with the concept of a twin-barrelled weapon powered by pressurised firing gases.

Post-shot gases from one barrel initiate the mechanism of the other and vice versa, which was a novel concept at the time, but was originally introduced by the German designer Karl Gast at the end of the First World War. Along with the cannon, a new ammunition of 23mm x 115mm calibre, with increased penetration capability and an electric ignition was also developed. The result of the work was a weapon with an empty weight of only 56kg and a rate of fire of 3,400 rounds per minute (less than 9A-624 but still more than 9A-623K). In the USSR, where all equipment usually weighed a multiple of analogues from the West, these were almost unbelievable values that allowed the weapon to be easily built into moveable turrets as well as in a fixed position. The weapon did not have significant recoil.

The cannon reached mass production in 1959, but it was not officially accepted into service until 1965 after a series of tests and the removal of some defects. The turret had a horizontal rotation of some 60° on both sides, and +10° up and—40° downward movement. The control system and gunsight were identical to the 9A-624 model using the KPS-53AV station in the front cockpit. The GSh-23 ammunition box held 450 rounds. Because the cannon required significant changes both to the cannon itself and the turret, the tests were not finished until 1989 when two prototypes were cleared as standard for serial production. The baseline model included provision for the R-60 air-to-air missiles and also PNV-57V night vision goggles. The R-60 was aimed by the pilot via an ASP-17V gunsight, requiring the helicopter to be aimed at the target until the missile seeker achieved a lock and an audio tone was clearly heard. During 1989 and the beginning of 1990, only twenty-five helicopters were manufactured.

The first series of these machines was transferred to the Torzhok training centre, which was responsible for the adoption of new armament. The Mi-24VP was considered at that time as the future standard for the Mi-24. After the USSR's breakup, almost all Mi-24VPs remained in Russia where they became a visible part of army aviation, as some of them served with the Berkooty flight display team. A few helicopters remained in Ukraine and still serve there. During operation some issues appeared relating to barrel cooling and the belt linkage, which was prone to jamming. Hence the later Mi-35M model used a modified liquid-cooled GSh-23V variant instead of the air-cooled version, and link-less belts. The Mi-24VP became the very last Soviet-era Hind ending the type's development under the Soviet empire. The

Berkooty flight display team, sometimes dubbed as 'Vertikal-T' in the early years, also operated a single model called Mi-24T. It was a standard Mi-24V with ATGM and weapon guidance system completely removed for weight reduction purposes. It was painted in a special display scheme. The team started in 1989 under the lead of general Boris Vorobyov, an active army pilot commanding the 344th Helicopter Training centre at Torzhok. The team participated in major Russian airshows until 2012, when it changed the type for Mi-28N.

Right: Detail of the GSh-23L twin-barrel 23mm calibre gun in the NPPU-24 movable turret. Note the spent case sleeve. (*Author*)

Below: A Russian Mi-24VP belonging to the Berkooty air display team from the 344th centre. It was frequently used as solo ship during displays. (*MVZ Mil*)

A Russian Mi-24VP belonging to the Berkooty air display during display over the city of Moscow. Note the extended landing light. (*MVZ Mil*)

After the collapse of the USSR, the Mi-24 production practically stalled. The 1990 delivery to Afghanistan became the final Soviet export of the Mi-24V or Mi-35 model with eighty-three Mi-24Vs and 158 Mi-35s ships delivered to the countries mentioned above, and over 500 to the USSR. At that point production was temporarily ceased, with only four helicopters delivered to the Russian air force in 1995. The Mi-24V/Mi-35 serial production was then renewed only briefly between 2003 and 2006 when the Czech Republic received seventeen Mi-24Vs/Mi-35s. The first export operator became symbolically also the last one. The breakup of the USSR caused the passing of more than 600 Hinds of various models to newly independent CIS states, with details provided later.

The Arsenyev production plant entirely abandoned the model production as it was getting ready for manufacturing of the type's replacement in the form of Ka-50. The Rostov-based production line, focused on Mi-24P and Mi-24VP models, remained intact but was not operational from 1991 due to lack of orders. It produced twelve Mi-24Ps and fifty Mi-35Ps for export, and 608 Mi-24Ps for the Soviet air force. The Russian Ministry of defence accepted a very limited number of Soviet-era production contracts, and the Mi-24 was considered as obsolete platform with planned replacement by Ka-50 or Mi-28. However, a decision was made to keep the production in Rostov available primarily for export purposes. Because the production gap created some issues, the Russian air force ordered eight Mi-24Ps to be produced in 1994 and 1995, of which four were finished in the Mi-24PN model standard described below. In 1995 the Russian air force also bought four Mi-24Vs.

It took several years to draw up an initial contract with Sri Lanka and when it was finally concluded in 1994, the production line was already running thanks to the small domestic orders. Six Mi-24Ps, named Mi-35P when delivered, were selected by the Asian state, combating Tamil insurgents in the lengthy civil war. Sri Lanka originally procured two second-hand Mi-24Vs and a single Mi-24RKhR with NBC set deleted from Ukraine in 1995. New helicopters became a backbone of 9 Squadron based at the Hingurakgoda airbase, from where they supported the operations in the north of the country. Acquisition of further Mi-24s was necessitated by the difficulties in maintaining the light attack IA 58 Pucará airplanes airworthy. Both financially and time-wise the ex-USSR acquisition was the best available solution, but some issues with the quality of the overhaul occurred. The initial introduction into combat operation, with Ukrainian mercenary pilots experienced in Afghanistan working as advisors, proved the type may be extremely effective against the rebels.

The victory in the Operation Riviresa may be attributed mainly to the three Mi-24s which flew 280 hours on seventy-two combat missions. A contract was therefore signed with Russia in 1995 for delivery of two new Mi-35Ps, which were delivered in 1996 became the first newly built ships in Russia. A year later another four ships were ordered, with two being delivered in 1998 and finally, the last two in 1999. All were coming from the unfinished production for the Soviet army and all were widely deployed in civil war operations, with over 1,000 combat flight hours logged to the end of 2001. Several helicopters were shot down by MANPADS systems during the fights, and at least one ship by heavy machine gun fire. Especially the ground-to-air guided missiles eventuated in Sri Lanka, equipping its fleet with the Israeli defence suite and guidance kit.

The Elbit Company provided what was probably the first upgrade to the Sri Lankan air force in the late 1990s as part of a solution for several types of aircraft. Its Mi-24Vs and Mi-24Ps were equipped with a FLIR ball turret attached to a special structure on the portside of the cargo cabin. The Israeli made CoMPASS IV (Compact Multipurpose Advanced Stabilised System) FLIR, was coupled with a display in the cargo cabin where a special operator monitored the area of interest and guided the crew. The defence suite was augmented by the Israeli ELTA EL/M 2160 Missile Approach Warning System, working on the Doppler principle, against UV/IR guided missiles and, in limited way, against RPGs. Those helicopters were used in local conflict and acquitted themselves well. No. 9 Squadron played a major part in the final years of the civil war providing close air support, transport ship protection and search and rescue missions. The unit operated detachments from forward airbases at Anuradhapura, Elara, Vavuniya and Palay. During the war the unit lost twenty-seven service members in combat, highest number of all Sri Lankan units.

After Sri Lanka, Zimbabwe became the second operator of the Mi-35P. Six ships were delivered in 2000, all equipped with American InfraMetrics IRTV 445MHH FLIR devices attached to the left outer wing pylon. The cockpit systems were supplemented by a GPS Garmin 115 navigation system. This became the very first production Mi-24 delivered to a customer with a modern surveillance system. However, given that the installation under the wing limited the number of available hard points, it is evident that it was a product of rapid development shortly before delivery of the helicopter to the customer. Nevertheless, those helicopters were used

A Sri Lankan Mi-35P freshly after an overhaul performed by the LOM PRAHA facility in Prague. Note the late-style tail rotor shaft fairing. (*Lukáš Syrový*)

extensively over the territory of Democratic Republic of Congo and saw a significant combat service, with one damaged during a hard landing in 2021. All were assigned to 7 Squadron at the airbase at the capital of Harare.

In 2000 six Mi-35Ps were delivered to Nigeria, which subordinated them to 97th Special Operations Group (later reorganised into 115th SOG) at the Port Harcourt airbase. The original order was followed by two Mi-24Vs and three Mi-24Ps from Ukrainian surpluses between 2008 and 2014, and two from Belarus in 2010. The Ukrainian-origin helicopters belonged to the earliest production standard although the customer was told those are almost new. Although the Mi-35Ps were brand new, their standard was equal to the original Soviet series, except for the added GPS navigation. Five helicopters were later damaged by storms, with two made airworthy again by the Czech Republic overhaul teams. The Hind fleet was actively deployed in the combat with Boko Haram Islamists, providing close air support and also special forces insertion including roping down, which is not often seen with Hinds.

In 2021, the country considered upgrade of three ships into the Mi-35P Phoenix standard described below, but the plan failed. In 2024 the fleet of legacy Hinds was grounded and helicopters were offered to Ukraine in their conflict with Russia but were eventually rejected due to poor technical condition, and the new Mi-35M model is used instead. In 2001 the Cypriot National Guard received its black-painted twelve Mi-35Ps, which were in original standard only with shortened wings with Ataka missiles capability, NVG-compatible lighting and GPS navigation system. All were assigned to the 450th Squadron at Paphos airbase and were used primarily for patrolling duties; their delivery was kept a secret for almost a year. Budget difficulties led to the decrease of operational ships and it took until 2014 before the fleet—minus one crashed ship—finally passed the general overhauls in Russia. However, lack of budget and poor Russian support left only four or so ships operational in the long term.

In 2023, Cyprus agreed to deliver eleven ships to Serbia where they were assigned to the 714th Antitank Helicopter Squadron (Protivoklovna Helikopterska Eskadrila) located at Kraljevo-Ladevci airbase. Two Mi-35Ps were delivered in 2001 to Angola. In 2003, seven Mi-24Vs, the last of the type, were finished for the Czech Republic which received them as a part of the Russian debt compensation. Those were followed by ten more NVG-compatible Mi-35s in 2005 and 2007, finally ending the Mi-24V/35 production line. The Czech Republic insisted on the Mi-24V/35 model due to its similarity with the already fielded Mi-24Vs, and so some airframe structures from the Soviet era were used and finished for the ships in a form of exemption, as the production line already worked on the Mi-24P/Mi-35P model only.

In 2003, two Mi-35Ps were delivered to Indonesian 31st Helicopter Squadron at the Semarang airbase, followed by six more in 2008 and a final three in 2010. In 2007, one Mi-35P was delivered to Senegal, a year later two Mi-35Ps to Niger and in 2010 one Mi-35P to Myanmar. A small Israeli company, Controp, upgraded at least one Senegal air force Mi-24P with its DSP-HD FLIR ball turret, with day and night camera and laser range finder. Unlike the upgrades referred to above, the Controp programme only included the FLIR installation into the nose, with a dedicated display and control grip in the front cockpit.

In 2011, the Mi-35P model was delivered in one copy to Myanmar and two to Peru, with those being the final Mi-35Ps produced. At that time the production line had

Another visitor to the LOM PRAHA facility in Prague—a Nigerian Mi-35P during an engine run after its overhaul, which included a repaint. (*Lukáš Syrový*)

run the Mi-35M model (described below) for several years. Peru assigned them to the 211 Squadron, flying with the Mi-25s and used them to fight the drug cartels in the rainforest. Myanmar deployed the Mi-35Ps with the helicopter squadron at Meiktila airbase and used them for patrolling purposes with temporary detachments on other bases as well. The Kachin independence army rebels belonging to various separatist groups were aiming at the helicopters and at least one ship was shot down in 2021.

Above: A Nigerian Mi-24P at Port Harcourt airbase is roped down to the ground. It was originally an ex-Soviet ship of early series. (*Lukáš Syrový*)

Below: A Senegalese Mi-24P upgraded with Controp DSP-HD FLIR in the nose. Such an upgrade, although simple, significantly increased combat effectiveness. (*Controp*)

5

Special Missions in Tough Conditions

Not Only for Combat

The Mi-24 was quickly identified as an ideal platform for many special missions within the army air force. In particular, the fact the cockpit could be pressurised which, with inlet air filtration, gave numerous options to use the helicopter for nuclear and chemical reconnaissance. For those tasks the Soviet army used the Mi-8VD model designed in the late 1960s. However, the crew had to wear protective clothes with masks, which made operating the piloting and special systems more difficult. The lightweight model Mi-2RKh (produced as Mi-2RS in Poland) tested in early 1978 showed this type was not ideal for the work in a battle area fully penetrated by NBC agents due to low performance once the special equipment was installed, and also due to the lack of cockpit filtration and sealing.

This led to a requirement for a dedicated NBC reconnaissance Hind variant issued in 1978, with the first prototype modified in the same year. This was assigned a designation Mi-24R (sometimes referred to as Mi-24RKhR) with internal code Izdeliye 2462 and Hind G1 NATO code. Extensive testing followed. The prototype was fitted with a special camera housing on the tail boom for monitoring the operation of special devices on the wing ends. The prototype differed from the production Mi-24V by deleting the entire ATGM and bombing system, including complete removal of missile launch rails, guidance antenna and optics under the nose. Because no ATGMs were used and the weapon range was limited to only UB-32A-24 and UB-16-57 rocket blocks, the ASP-17 gunsight from the rear cockpit was entirely removed and replaced by an easy PKV gunsight attached with gun camera to the frame. The front cockpit retained the KPS-53AV station for machine gun control but lost all the optics and guidance system on the right side, replaced by radio system controls. Curiously, the KPS-53AV gunsight station was equipped with a special NVG-compatible module on some models.

The air system was improved with installation of a special ventilation and filtering unit called SZhO, identifiable by a large intake on the portside of the fuselage in front of the cargo cabin. This system provided not only cleaning of the air for the crew, but also sample-taking for analyses. The end pylons were equipped with hydraulically operated claw-shaped devices for taking soil samples. On the prototype those were turned in the opposite way to those of production models. The left outer pylon was equipped with special wiring for carrying a KPO-1 container with analytical device. It included DP-5B roentgen meter, KPO-1 sample-taking set, MK-3 meteorological research set, TDP decontamination device, R-147 personal radio station, SKhT-40 set of signal flares, and RDG-46 smoke grenades. The container composition was later changed in regular service.

In addition to the helicopter's capabilities, the operators on board could leave the helicopter while in the combat area and take samples using devices from the container. The first prototype had special signal flare dispensers attached to the devices on the end pylons. During testing it was revealed that firing the signal flares might heat the device and have a negative impact on sample quality. Therefore all production helicopters had only one dispenser, which was attached to the tail skid. The skid braces lost their aerodynamic covers. Under the tail boom a special orange flashing beacon light was installed. This was turned on during the sample-taking process. Inside the cargo cabin were two adjustable seats equipped with parachutes. Both were occupied by special systems operators controlling the large console with a computing device in the forward part of the cockpit. The device allowed not only the samples testing, but also data transfer to other helicopters or ground command stations.

On its left side, a large Roentgen meter gauge was installed. Other special devices were located on the rear wall of the cabin. For crew protection, a KKO-LS special protective set was included, consisting of Kompat-L protective suit, Yasen-L mask and individual oxygen masks (two extra cylinders are located in the cargo cabin for the special systems operators). Some helicopters were shielded by special lead material for radiation protection. As well as the missing optics and antenna under the nose, the Mi-24R may be recognised by a large window on the starboard side door allowing downward visibility for both special systems operators. In some later models the door is missing entirely, with the window installed directly in the fuselage.

The helicopters were equipped with some Mi-24V standards such as provision for PTB-450 auxiliary fuel tanks on the inner wing pylons. Later, EVU exhaust gas coolers, ASO-2V flares and L-166V IR jammer were also added as a standard fit. In this modification state the model was adopted for service and from 1983 until 1989, approximately 152 helicopters were built at the Arsenyev and Rostov plants (some sources state only 110) with at least two helicopters of this sub-type assigned to each helicopter regiment and some helicopters assigned to other army air force units. The role of the model with every OVE was to provide NBC reconnaissance with high damage tolerance and own combat capability.

In 1989, a special Mi-24RA variant was introduced with more advanced special systems requiring only one special systems operator instead of two. This helicopter was also equipped with more a powerful datalink system, but lacked the sample-taking devices on the wing-end pylons. Allegedly, only eight of these machines were manufactured until the end of 1990. All Mi-24R/RAs were assigned exclusively to the Soviet army and were never exported, although some were deployed with Soviet units in Central European countries, namely East Germany and Czechoslovakia. During the Chernobyl nuclear plant catastrophe they played a significant role in helping to monitor the area. Mi-24Rs replaced the unprotected Mi-8s and the crews were flying directly over the melted reactor, with some forty flights designed as a maximum before the ship was grounded due to high radiation at one of the compounds near

Above: Mi-24R prototype. Note the end sample-taking devices in a different position from production models, and also with signal flare cartridge attached to it instead of the tail boom. (*MVZ Mil*)

Below left: Detail of the Mi-24R claw-shaped sample-taking device for gathering soil samples in the production variant. A container for detection is behind. (*MVZ Mil*)

Below right: Detail of the Mi-24R signal flare cartridge in the tail skid. The struts are missing typical aerodynamic fairings. (*Jiří Matoušek*)

Above: A Russian Mi-24R model captured at Werneuchen airbase in Germany. Note the double-sized blister in the cargo door. (*Thomas Girke*)

Below: Another Russian Mi-24R at Brandis airbase. The metal sheets on the parking spot were a standard part of the Soviet inventory. (*Thomas Girke*)

to the nuclear plant. It was no surprise the on-board equipment was soon showing maximum limits.

After the breakup of the USSR many helicopters were transferred to Russia, Ukraine and Belorussia, with a few ships in Armenia, Azerbaijan and Kazakhstan. A single aircraft was delivered from Ukraine to Sri Lanka in 1995, but it lacked the chemical equipment and was used for the attack role with unguided armament only. It was designated Mi-24DM by the Ukrainian overhaul facility, as were some downgraded Mi-24Vs. The same designation was used in case of helicopters re-exported from Ukraine to Guinea, all of which had the ATGM system deleted entirely. In 2009 ten Mi-24Rs were delivered from Ukraine to Azerbaijan, all after general overhaul and ready to be rebuilt into the Mi-24G SuperHind standard. Russia still operates the type in its original NBC reconnaissance role; other operators either ceased the operation or use the ships in a combat role.

In 1979, another special variant called Mi-24K, with internal designation Izdeliye 201 (Hind G2 in NATO code) entered state trials. This was a special artillery-spotting and guidance variant, based on the Mi-24V model. The Soviet army required an effective means to increase the accuracy of long-range artillery, and this helicopter was intended to replace the ageing Mi-8TARK model in that role, being a better fit for the role with its high speed, own armament and armouring.

The main role of the new helicopter was to direct and correct artillery fire, gather data on the position of the enemy forces and provide aerial photography for reconnaissance. As it was expected that the helicopter would fly in the combat zone, the unguided weapons were fully retained. The original project was based on the Mi-2KR introduced in 1975, but which had failed. The USSR modified three helicopters, but the performance of the type was not as required. Therefore, the decision to upgrade the much more powerful helicopter was taken. The main difference of the Mi-24K prototype was the lack of entire ATGM system, replaced by an OPN Iris surveillance system under the nose, consisting of a wide-angle AFA-87PV camera with 1,300mm fixed focal length. A 60-metre-long film reel was carried. The camera was in a special moveable housing which could turn through 110°, with the camera device itself moving an additional +15° to −20°. The lens of the camera was protected by a special remotely operated upward hinging cover. This camera was operated by the weapon systems operator through a special panel on the right side of the KPS-53AV station.

In the cargo cabin, another AFA-100 (sometimes AFA-110–280) camera was fitted, covering the area to the right of the helicopter. Its installation necessitated removing the door, and the camera can be identified by a small window located in the fuselage wall. In the cargo cabin a special Ruta reconnaissance and spotting system and data processor were placed. A few helicopters had two places for system operators. Going by the fact the Ruta system also included an Orbita-20-9K computer with datalink, the Mi-24K was evidently able to transfer the revealed data from the air without need to land for picture evaluation and material processing. In the mid-1980s an improved Mi-24KD variant with laser rangefinder instead of the AFA-87PV camera was introduced, but only a small number of helicopters were finished to this standard.

From 1983 to 1990 some ninety-two helicopters (some sources say 163) were manufactured at Arsenyev and Rostov with all of those serving under the soviet army

Above: An Mi-24RA model serving with the Russian Army. It lacks the wing sample-taking devices. Note the repainted fuselage number, a typical feature of ships returning from European deployment. (*MVZ Mil*)

Below: The very same Mi-24RA is taxiing, followed by an Mi-24P. Each Soviet helicopter regiment operated this NBC model. (*MVZ Mil*)

with individual OVEs. Allegedly some of the helicopters were converted from the first series Mi-24Vs undergoing deep overhaul and rebuild at the Arsenyev plant. The Soviet Union deployed those helicopters at air force bases in Eastern Germany and these operations became the initial foreign experience for the type. After the breakup of the USSR some helicopters were transferred to Armenia, Belorussia, Kazakhstan, Russia and Ukraine. In 2001, Ukraine sold two refurbished Mi-24Ks to Macedonia, which operated them for several years as the single export customer. Currently, a few ships are still operated by Armenia, Belorussia and Russia in their original role.

The Mi-24K was not the only recce model of the family. One of the special variants, unofficially called the Mi-24EN (sometimes Mi-24VEN), appeared in 1991 as a conversion of a standard Mi-24V. It was intended for ecological survey and especially for monitoring forest damage and water pollution. The modification was led by the Mil Design Bureau and several scientific ecological organisations participated in it. The helicopter lacked the ATGM system and even the USPU-24 turret. In their place were special sensors, with a day camera to take pictures of the area under surveillance in a spectrum close to UV. The outer wing-pylons carried special containers like those introduced on the Mi-24RKhR. Only one helicopter was updated, and it was even offered for export. It was used for less than a year by various Russian state organisations before being grounded.

Prototype of the Mi-24K model with PTB-450 auxiliary fuel tanks. An early Mi-24V model was used for the conversion. (*MVZ Mil*)

Above: Serial Russian Mi-24K of late series captured in Germany after the reunification. Soviet helicopters left the country in 1994. (*Thomas Girke*)

Below: The very same Russian Mi-24K taxiing at Werneuchen airbase. Note the turret with camera and small window for oblique photo shooting. (*Thomas Girke*)

In 1995, when the Mil Design Bureau was trying to find any new role for the legacy model, a variant intended for police missions was prepared in response to a request by the Ministry of Interior. It was given the designation Mi-24PS with Izdeliye 352 as its internal code. The first prototype was essentially a converted Mi-24P minus weapons systems (although the first prototype was initially displayed with the GSh-30K cannon), with shortened wings and outer pylons only. All weapons were removed, with only PTB-450 fuel tank capability retained for extending the ferry range and endurance. However, on some pictures the PKV gunsight was visible and so the weapons could likely have been carried. Instead of the antennae under the nose a special FPP-7 search lamp and loudspeaker were installed as well as weather radar in the nose.

The second prototype, displayed at MAKS 1995 for the first time, was derived from the Mi-24V model and featured a small forward looking infra-red (FLIR) sensor in the place of the original USPU-24 turret. Close to the cargo cabin doors, rails were fitted to enable rappelling for quick disembarkation of personnel from the helicopter during police missions. Inside the cargo cabin was an LPG-4 hoist with a lifting capacity of 120kg. For hoisting and rappelling operations the front cockpit was equipped with external mirrors allowing the WSO to observe activity outside the cargo cabin. The navigation system was augmented with GLONASS satellite navigation system. Both helicopters were tested by the Ministry of interior for several months, but were rejected due to the very high cost of operation and failure to fully comply with the operator's requirements, although modifications of three dozen ships from the army inventory were proposed.

In the late 1990s the second prototype was rebuilt to a different standard, again called Mi-24PS (with 'S' now referring to 'saloon' instead of the original 'search and rescue'). The cargo cabin was upholstered with installation of four comfortable sofas! The upper side of the door windows was equipped with single enlarged blisters and the lower door part was covered with carpet. This helicopter lacked the FLIR and rappelling rails, but retained the search lamp and loudspeakers, as well as many other systems. Curiously, the tail boom was painted with the word 'conversion', replacing the original 'police'. This prototype was again tested by the Ministry of Interior for the rapid transport of its top-ranking commanders, but was soon grounded. No wonder that the 11-tonne heavy VIP transporter failed to gain traction before 2015, when the dedicated VIP transport Mi-24 model reach operational use, as the Mi-35MS (described below).

Although the Mi-24's A-10 model speed-record-setting days were over, another high-speed concept was introduced at the MAKS 2015 show. This was a technology demonstrator called PSV (Prospective [Future] High-speed helicopter), intended for testing components for a new generation of Russian helicopters with a planned cruising speed in excess of 450 km/h. However, both Mil's high-speed projects, Rachel and X-1, and Kamov's Ka-92, were later frozen for economic reasons. The PSV project was not cancelled as its results could still have been implemented in the design of rotors of aircraft such as the Mi-171, Mi-35 and Mi-28, with expected growth in maximum speed of some 13 per cent in the case of Mi-35M. The PSV project was divided into several subprojects. The main one was the modification of

Above: The very first Mi-24PS prototype modification intended for police support. Note the loudspeakers and rails for rappelling. (*MVZ Mil*)

Left: Later Mi-24PS modification with large-area blister in the upper segment of cargo cabin doors. The tail boom title says 'Conversion'. (*MVZ Mil*)

Later Mi-24PS modification interior—would you like a 'comfy' ride in an attack helicopter with a top speed of 330 km/h? (*MVZ Mil*)

the Mi-24 helicopter, equipping it with brand new, more aerodynamic single-seat front fuselage and newly designed wings with no pylons. The PSV was equipped with a new rotor system with blades of new section and reshaped tips. The powerplant was two Klimov VK-2500-01 engines with a take-off power of 1,789kW each. The first demonstrator displayed at MAKS 2015 was just a static test vehicle, while the real first prototype flew for the first time on 29 December 2015, from Mil's test airfield at Moscow. In November 2016 the PSV named LL-PSV (Flight Laboratory) reached an unofficial speed record of 405 km/h. At that time it wore the code 271 on the tail boom.

This helicopter is probably an upgraded new-build Mi-35, although it is sometimes referred to as a rebuilt Mi-24K model because of the small window on the left side of the cabin—this window actually covers a high-speed camera for measuring the movement of the rotor blade tips during high-speed flight. Further tests also comprised the verification of the new VK-2500M engines with their output increased by some 20 per cent, and with new parts such as a redesigned compressor and control system. Due to complete lack of funds, the PSV project never became a substantial source of research information.

PSV demonstrator—still an Mi-24 but with a brand new nose section, streamlined wing and modified main rotor. (*Author*)

6

Would You Mind a Hind?

The Post-USSR Shopping Spree

When the Iron Curtain fell, the huge Soviet Hind fleet, being gradually pulled out of East Germany, Czechoslovakia, Hungary and Poland, was retrieved back to Soviet territory with the majority of units stationed in Belarus, Ukraine and European part of Russia. With the USSR collapse in 1991, newly independent ex-Soviet republics took over significant a portion of the fleet. Over a few years the number of foreign operators doubled, and the type became the symbol of a cheap rotary-wing warhorse. In 1991 Russian army aviation declared a total of 890 Hinds in the inventory, of which some 100 were of the oldest Mi-24A and Mi-24D types.

The Mi-24 fleet was, over several rounds of reorganisations, split between 45th OVP Oreshkovo, 55th OVP Korennovsk, 237th OVE Bobrovka, 319th OVP Chernigovka, 332nd OVTBP Pribylovo, 337th OVP Berdsk, 364th OVP Srednebeloye, 440th OVP Dvoevka, 487th OVP Budyennovsk and 490th OVP Tula-Klokovo. Those units, originally belonging to the army aviation command, were incorporated into the air force (and now air and space force) in 2002. A separate Hind fleet was operated by 484th Helicopter Training Regiment (UVP—Uchebnyi Vertolyotnyi Polk) at Syzran, and 626th UVP Pugachev, where all the army aviators passed training. The Torzhok-based 344th Centre for Combat Use and Retraining of Flight Personnel of Army Aviation used Hinds, with the Berkooty demonstration team and further helicopters for training of the instructors. Several OVEs were subordinated to the naval aviation units such as the 288th OVP belonging to the Baltic fleet, and few Hinds were used by GRU—the military intelligence.

Few helicopters were also operated by the FSB, a follower of the Soviet-era KGB, and its ships wore civilian registrations sprayed over the camouflage. The quantity of the Hinds soon dropped as only limited overhauls were performed because the majority of overhaul facilities rested in the newly independent Ukraine. The cannibalisation of the fleet was soon the main method of keeping the selected ships airworthy. The Mi-24P model was prioritised with army aviation, both due to its firepower, low service life and embedded training capability. The training and operational plans dropped to 30 per cent only due to lack of funds.

In 1991 the Mi-24 units were engaged in the Georgian civil war and South Ossetian civil war, and in conflict between Armenia and Azerbaijan described

An Mi-24V fresh from production and yet without a customer—after the breakdown of the USSR, the Rostvertol production plant had to seek for new buyers. (*MVZ Mil*)

below, as well as being deployed in Abkhazia, Transnistria and Tajikistan in 1992. A pair of Mi-24Vs aired worldwide in a 1993 newsreel, with both ships overflying the Russian Federal Government building in Moscow during the failed coup. In early 1994 some Hinds with repainted red stars appeared in the region of Chechnya, flown by Russian government-contracted mercenaries, with their deployment focused on oppressing the rebels. Some two dozens tanks were documented to be destroyed by this Russia-backed fleet, mixed with regular Russian units located in the area. Of all the attack sorties, the air raid of the Grozny-Severny airport became particularly famous for destroying several aircraft, including a civilian Tu-134A airliner parked there. Hinds also attempted to seize the capital of Grozny in November 1994 but the operation failed. The official Russian involvement started in December 1994 in the so-called 'First Chechen War', when the then-president Boris Yeltsin sent Russian troops to Chechnya to 'establish constitutional order' in the provincial republic.

Russian ground invasion was supported by two dozen Mi-24Vs and Mi-24Ps providing aerial cover, of which the very first Mi-24P was lost on 9 August 1994 after being hit at the military airport near the combat area. Hinds were used for aerial fire support and were engaged in several sorites per day. The Russian tactics did not differ from its Afghan deployment and the majority of the pilots were Afghan war veterans.

Above: A Russian Mi-24V during the second Chechen war with the tail code repainted. Mi-24Ps were preferred by the Russian air force due to the possibility of using them as trainers. (*MVZ Mil*)

Below: Armourers loading the B-8V20 block with S-8KOM rockets. Note the upper side of the inner weapon pylon damaged by the crew climbing to the engine inspection. (*ITAR-TASS*)

Above: A Russian Mi-24P with a shark painted on the fuselage and a repainted fuselage number. This was during the second Chechen war. (*MVZ Mil*)

Below: A Russian Mi-24P at the Slatina airport in Kosovo. The KFOR title is on the tail boom, despite the fact that the ship never served with the contingent. (*ITAR-TASS*)

of newer Mi-28s and Ka-52s, of which more than 300 were delivered. Legacy Hinds were assigned to 17th Guards Army Aviation Brigade at Kamensk-Uralskii, 30th Independent Mixed Composite Aviation Regiment at Rostov on Don, 98th Independent Mixed Composite Aviation Regiment at Monchegorsk, 330th OVP at Novosibirsk, 337th OVP at Tolmachevo and 440th OVP at Dvoevka. The crews' training was still maintained by the 484th UVP at Syzran, 626th UVP at Pugachov and newly also by the 92nd Instructor and Research Helicopter Squadron at Klin airbase. Several legacy Mi-24Ps were also deployed in Armenia with the Russian crews. The majority of the helicopters belonged to the Mi-24P model, with very few Mi-24Vs in service. The 112nd OVP at Chita and 549th OVP at Kluchevoye operated the Mi-24PN upgraded model. The Russian national guard operated Mi-24Ps with 142nd OVP at Mozdok airbase in Chechnya, 685th OVP at Rostov on Don and 70th Independent Composite Aviation Regiment at Yermolino. The Mi-24VP model was solely operated by the 125th OVE at the Tchkalovsk airbase and the unit belonged to the naval aviation command, being the only one with Hinds in the inventory.

The Russian Mi-24Ps were also deployed in Syria. Although Western intelligence expected the involvement of the most modern Ka-52 and Mi-28 helicopters after the start of the Russian army's operations in Syria, the first contingent sent to the

Two Russian Mi-24VPs operated by naval aviation. The PZU filters are removed on a hot day to increase the engine thrust. (*RIA Novosti*)

Above: The Russian air force still operates a few Mi-24Ps from the Soviet era. The calendar life can be extended, and the flight hours limit has still not been reached. (*MVZ Mil*)

Below: The Berkooty flight demonstration team flying six Mi-24Ps in close formation. Note the non-standard camouflage of the leading ship. (*Author*)

A Russian border guard Mi-24P during a low pass over the ridge. Note the darker camouflage still retaining the 'shamrocks' motif. (*Russian MoD*)

Arab country in September 2015 included only twelve aged Mi-24Ps, most of which lacked elements of the protection system, such as the L-166V-11E infrared jammers. The helicopters came from the 337th OVP from the Siberian base Tolmachevo. The choice of the unit, despite the climatic differences between Syria and Siberia, was not accidental as the unit had been operating for a long time in Chechnya, Armenia and Tajikistan. Some of the Mi-24P helicopters were in the standard from the seventies, except for additional satellite navigation. Relatively shortly after unloading, the Russian national emblems and inscriptions were painted over on all of them. The only modernisation that some helicopters underwent during the last overhaul was the expansion of the armament with 9M120 Ataka anti-tank guided missiles launched from the same containers as the 9M114 Shturm.

Due to the hot weather, the weight of the carried armament was limited, and the helicopters most often carried 350 to 400 pieces of 30mm shells for the GSh-30K cannon, two B-8V20 blocks with 80mm S-8 unguided rockets and two to four 9M114 or 9M120 anti-tank guided missiles. The main role of the detached pair of Mi-24s was to patrol the area of the Khmeimim base of the Russian forces, especially at the time of aircraft arrivals and departures. Combat missions were always carried out by at least a pair of helicopters and were mainly about searching for enemy positions. The aim of the deployment was to gradually clear the areas around the base, and only after a few weeks did the crews engage in combat activities for the benefit of the Russian army. The usual tactic was to fly the leading ship only 5 to 15 meters above the terrain, followed by another helicopter with an elevation of 5 to 10 meters behind it. The opponent on the ground usually failed to hit the first helicopter, and if he revealed his position, he was attacked by the second ship.

Mi-24 attacks with unguided rockets took place after gaining altitude with the firing of salvos of S-8 missiles during the descent from a height of 100 to 200 meters, to the surface of the recess of about 30 meters. The UPK-23-250 cannon proved to be very powerful and effective against lightly protected targets. The command order required the elimination of any resistance with a return after the ammunition was used up. The GSh-30 cannon was usually not used in combat and was considered as a safety weapon for return. In the first six months, the Mi-24 dropped FAB-250 and FAB-500 bombs weighing 250 and 500kg. Compared to the Su-24, Su-25 and Su-34, they allowed drops with the greatest accuracy. In 2022, legacy Hinds were deployed in Ukraine after catastrophic losses of the more modern Mi-35Ms with at least four being shot down. Russian Mi-24s were deployed in several UN missions in Africa.

Because of its odd relation to Ukraine, where two major overhaul plants were located, Russia had to launch its own overhaul programme in domestic conditions and in the early years the Rostov-based overhaul facility worked also as overhaul

Legacy Mi-24Ps captured in the Syrian Khmeimim airbase. Note two ships are missing the IR jammer despite the risk of MANPADS in the area. (*Russian MoD*)

Ukraine became the second largest Hind operator in the world with an incredible 360 ships retained on its territory in 1991, of which a major part belonged to units pulled out of European countries. Some four dozens Hinds were seized at the Konotop and Lugansk overhaul facilities in various stage of the repair process. The new government was unable to maintain the number of helicopters with seven OVPs in operation, and in 1993 a constant spree of reorganisations started with only 260 Hinds declared as active in 1993, and 120 in 1995.

Unlike from other ex-USSR countries Ukraine retained the army aviation as a separate force with major bases at Brody airbase, Kherson airbase and Novyi Kalyniv, with each base having two mixed squadrons equipped with Hinds. Only less than thirty of Mi-24Vs were subordinated to the air force and were operated under the Bela Tserkva squadron of National guard. Prior to the war in the east of the country in 2014 the number of available helicopters was constantly dropping. Despite domestic issues Ukraine participated heavily in the UN peacekeeping missions with contingents deployed in Slavonia, Liberia and Democratic republic of Congo.

The UNTAES mission in eastern Slavonia became the Mi-24 premiere in UN colours and helped to maintain peace between the separatist Serbs occupying the area, which formally belonged to newly established Croatia. Six Mi-24Ps together with four Mi-24Ks were deployed to Klisa airport near Osijek close to Serbian border. Hind crews were patrolling the demilitarised zone and provided reconnaissance with Serbian guns less than 2 kilometres away. Yet in the first two months the squadron logged 288 hours in 237 sorties, of which all were with armed helicopters carrying also ATGMs; no weapon use occurred. While the UN routinely operated transport helicopters, deploying a dedicated attack type like the white-painted Mi-24 was atypical. Ultimately, the firepower of these aircraft prevented the conflict from reigniting in the region. Later UN missions in Congo and Mali were supported by Ukrainian choppers and the latter was abandoned after the Russian invasion.

In 2010 the country launched a fleet overhaul and upgrade programme. The Ukrainian aerospace industry largely consisted of two major companies: the Antonov design bureau and Motor Sich, the largest engine manufacturer in the region. The latter company conducted their own development of the TV3-117VMA engine into the more powerful TV3-117VMA-SBM1V-02 variant. This engine was installed in many Ukrainian army helicopters and was also widely promoted for export, with the upgraded helicopter being designated as Mi-24V-SBM or Mi-24P-SBM. Belarus, for example, has modified the majority of its Hinds with those engines.

In 2010, the Ukrainian Ukroboronprom holding, which managed several domestic overhaul and scientific plants, launched a project for the upgrade of Mi-24P legacy models. The result was named Mi-24PU and offered in two variants. The basic upgrade, called Mi-24PU1, was equipped with new and more powerful TV3-117VMA-SBM1V-02 engines made by Motor Sich. The original defence suite was replaced by the new Adros KT-01AV infra-red jammer and KUV-26-50 flare dispensers with 50mm rounds under the tail boom. The original SARPP-12DM analogue recording system gave way to a new, digital BUR-4-1-07 unit able to track more data and also record voice and sound. The weapon system was added with a modernised ASP-17VPM-V gunsight, offering higher precision, coupled with an

Adros FPM-01KV laser designator. The combination of those instruments allowed weapon guidance even at night. The avionics core included a new Garmin GPS MAP 695 satellite navigation system, VHF radio Bendix King KY-196B, digital Garmin GTX-327 transponder and emergency radio beacon EBC-406AFHM. This model entered service in at least three aircraft in 2012. From the outside view, the main distinguishing feature was the FPM laser designator device located on the starboard side of the helicopter, close to the cannon muzzles. However, this location proved to be problematic due to dust, flames and vibrations during GSh-30K firing damaging the sensitive optics of the laser FMP seeker. Later, therefore, the device was relocated to the port guidance antenna fairing. At least one of the upgraded helicopters lacked ATGM launching rails and guidance optics.

Later, in 2015, a more advanced variant called Mi-24PU2 was introduced. It was a project for which French company Sagem utilised its experience with the below-mentioned Mi-24PUz project from Uzbekistan. It incorporated the improvements noted above with a laser designator being installed in the port-side guidance antenna fairing, and a Sagem EuroFlir 410 FLIR under the starboard side of the nose. The detection range of the FLIR enabled targets the size of a tank to be identified up to 18 kilometres away, and people up to 14 kilometres away. The image from the FLIR was displayed on a dedicated MFD in the pilot's and WSO's cockpits. (In the pilot's cockpit, the MFD replaces the original map indicator screen).

The major Mi-24PU2 improvement was the installation of BAR'ER-V anti-tank laser guided missiles with a range of up to 7.5 kilometres. Missiles were stored in tube launchers using the same attachment points and wiring as the original 9M114 type. The weapons array was also extended with the VSM-1 aerial mining system. Curiously, the prototype had the original, obsolete, defence suite. So far only two prototypes have been identified as being subject to the upgrade, although the modernisation project is currently referred to as standard for army aviation Mi-24s. However, political tensions led to the organisations involved in the project looking for alternative non-Western equipment, such as Polish Cenzin THL-5NV helmets with PCO PNL-3 Bielik night vision goggles. Helicopters came from overhauls just in time to be deployed in combat activities in the Crimean Peninsula and east of the country, invaded by pro-Russian forces. Each Ukrainian unit deployed crews and spare parts to support the selected combat-deployed Hind fleet used widely in close air support in the Donetsk and later Lugansk separatist republic. In April 2014 first two Hinds were shot down with Strela-2 missiles near Sloviansk and many more were hit in the air.

The pro-Russian invasion caught Ukrainian army aviation unprepared and very quickly any suitable Hind was sent to the frontline, including the highly visible, white-painted ships returning from UN missions. In May, another Hind was shot down by heavy machine gun fire, and in August Ukraine lost one more. In total five ships were reported as lost and seven more as heavily damaged but repairable during the Donbas war. The Konotop-based overhaul facility, performing Hind overhauls in USSR's time, launched a wide overhaul programme and started to return ships into service. When Russia invaded Ukraine, some two dozen Hinds were immediately deployed to repel the enemy with the first loss declared on 4 March 2022. Hinds were used for close air support as well as for special forces insertion and resupply of troops near the front. At least seventeen ships had been lost within the operation so far, primarily due to heavy machine gun fire and MANPADS, and so the army aviation deployed any available type, including Mi-24Rs and even Mi-24Ks.

Ukraine later increased its fleet by at least seven Mi-35s from Czechia, twelve Mi-24Vs and Mi-24Ks from North Macedonia, twelve Mi-24Ds and Mi-24Vs from Poland, of which only all Czech ships were all airworthy, and the remaining ships were a mix of operational helicopters and sources for spare parts. Due to the ubiquitous MANPADS risk and radar coverage, the crews mastered ultra low-level flights just some 5 meters above the ground when approaching or departing the combat area, with unguided rockets fired from a short climb to ensure a longer range, although with lower precision. Hinds were stationed on improvised airfields close to the combat area and in some cases the crews performed ten attack sorties per day. The major weapons used were S-8 rockets and cannons. The ATGMs were used only till the stock of missiles was available. From late 2023 Hinds were frequently engaged in the Russian Shahed drones shootdowns, where door gunners, and especially the 9A-624 machine gun, played key role.

Several Ukrainian Hinds were updated with US-made blocks for Zuni rockets of 130mm calibre, or Soviet-origin B-13L blocks with S-13 rockets of 122mm calibre. Those rockets proved to be far more effective when hitting the enemy and were used for hardened shelters and armoured vehicles. Later the 2.75 inch Hydra rockets were also used, due to lack of the original S-8 type.

Before the war with Russia, Ukraine had become the shopping mall for surplus Hinds. In 1993 the local Konotop company, one of the largest helicopter overhaul

The Ukrainian Mi-24PU differs visually by the FPM-01KV laser designator installed close to the GSh-30 muzzles. It worked as target pointer with no designation or guidance functionality. (*Ukroboronprom*)

facilities in the USSR, delivered two Mi-24Ds and four Mi-24Vs to Croatia, followed in 1995 by four Mi-24V. In the same year the first export contracts to non-European customers were fulfilled with two Mi-24Vs delivered to Angola and two Mi-24Vs with single Mi-24R to Sri Lanka and twelve to Peru. In 1996 one Mi-24P and three Mi-24Vs were delivered to Kongo, one Mi-24P and two Mi-24Vs to Sri Lanka and one to Israel where it served as a prototype for local upgrades offered to Hind operators.

In 1997 two Mi-24Vs were smuggled to Serbia although the country was then under UN embargo, in 1998 one Mi-24V to Guinea, and in 1999 twenty-eight ships in total were refurbished for Algeria, three Mi-24Ps for Angola, one for Uganda and two Mi-24Vs for Sierra Leone. In the new millennium a further Mi-24Vs were delivered to Afghanistan, Angola, Azerbaijan, Burundi, Chad, Central African Republic, Democratic Republic of Congo, Equatorial Guinea, Georgia, Guinea, Sri Lanka, Macedonia and Nigeria. The advantage of Ukrainian industry in those mainly poor countries was the ability to deploy maintenance and even flight teams directly in the country with combat flights performed by mixed or even entirely Ukrainian mercenaries in several countries. Some 149 Hinds were re-exported from Ukraine.

The independent Azerbaijani air force was created in February 1992 and its first unit was composed of Mi-24s. During the Soviet era multiple units equipped with Hinds were based in Azerbaijan territory—the 362nd OSAE at Kirovobad airbase, 381st OVE at Nakhchivan airbase and 386th OVE at Sangachal airbase. In 1992, some of Azerbaijani ex-Soviet crew members flew one Mi-24V to the Zabrat airbase shortly followed by eight more Mi-24Vs, all from 386th OVE, while the 381st OVE retrieved to the newly independent Russian federation. As a part of compensation, in late 1992 Azerbaijan received ten (some sources say eight) Hinds from ex-Soviet inventory, all except one in non-airworthy condition.

Since the country entered into war with neighbouring Armenia, Hinds were immediately engaged in convoy protection and airstrikes, usually from the Sangachal

An Mi-24V from Ukrainian surplus freshly after overhaul at the Konotop facility with new desert paint showing the new customer is Algeria. (*Ukroboronprom*)

airbase which acted as safe base from where ships were flying to rearming and refuelling points close to the combat area. The first combat flight of a pair of Mi-24s consisted of an escort of Mi-8MTs evacuating civilians from the Nagorno Karabakh area. Both crews were shot at but were able to return fire and safely fly away. Escort of transport types became a regular task, because for pure attack sorties the air force lacked stocks of missiles and rockets. Only after ex-Soviet storage areas were looted and later formally taken over was it possible to launch attack missions.

In May 1992, multiple air raids were launched, with Hinds systematically supporting the ground troops and also the Armenian air force started to use its Hinds, of which three ships were downed by Azerbaijani fire in June, one Mi-24P was eventually repaired on site and taken into service under Azerbaijani troops with just its roundels repainted. In late 1992, Hinds were performing primarily close air support with some ships flying six sorties per day, and in September, six Hinds were supporting large insertion of ground troops. Among other tasks the Combat SAR missions to evacuate downed pilots were performed exclusively by Hind crews. In July 1993, the government sent troops to Ganja to suppress General Suret Huseynov, a former military commander who had broken away from the government to form an internal armed opposition despite pursuing the same overall national goals. The Hind crews sent there refused to fight with the popular commander, actually considered as father of the Azerbaijani air force, and four Hinds landed at Ganja to fight under the general's command. Huseynov later became a prime minister of the country.

Flights in the Nagorny Karabakh mountains with elevation up to 3,000 metres were definitely not an easy task. Due to faults in navigation and enemy actions at least eight Mi-24s were lost. Two surviving Mi-24Ps with some Mi-24Vs were assigned after the war to the 1st Helicopter Squadron at the Baku-Qala airbase east of the capital. In 1993, a batch of ten Mi-24Vs was procured in Ukraine. In 2009 Azerbaijan bought from Ukraine ten Mi-24Rs and two Mi-24Ps, which after overhaul were assigned to the 1st Helicopter Squadron at Baku-Qala airbase with the legacy ships transferred to 2 Squadron. The surprising number of Mi-24R NBC reconnaissance models had a clear meaning—Azerbaijan agreed with the Ukrainian company Konotop on the delivery of helicopters intended for upgrade to SuperHind standard. Since that model was expected to use Ukrainian BAR'ER-V ATGMs with the new guidance system, the lack of original 9M114 missiles was no problem at all. And since the ships delivered from Ukrainian surpluses were produced in the very late 1980s and usually flew less often than attack models, they were promising in terms of remaining service life.

Konotop facility cooperated with the South African ATE company and they called the SuperHind Mi-24G. It featured the SuperHind nose section with 30mm cannon and EO/IR system. Unlike the full SuperHind standard in Algeria (mentioned below), the Azerbaijani ships retained original wings as the BAR'ER-V missiles were using the same attachment pods. The BAR'ER-V ATGM had an effective range of 7.5 kilometres and could penetrate up to 800mm of homogeneous rolled armour. Azerbaijan became the launch customer of this missile. The avionics was a mix of South African components with some commercially available items such as Chelton MFDs. All helicopters were painted in black with large white fuselage codes, but not all Mi-24Rs were upgraded to the Mi-24G standard immediately and some photos prove at least four ships temporarily operated in the plain configuration with the upgrade provided later in service. In total, eight ships are positively identified to be upgraded to Mi-24G standard.

The remaining two Mi-24Ps were delivered in the Mi-24PU-1 variant with laser range finder and avionics upgrades. The experience with the Mi-24G, especially after economic problems of ATE, caused plans for the upgrade of further ships to be put on hold. It seems the ships were not flown beyond 2016, all being stored in a hangar without rotors three years later. In 2016 one Mi-24G was shot down by the Armenian army with an RPG from short range; it was the single operational loss of the variant. The second ship was extensively damaged but managed to land back in own territory. In 2010 Azerbaijan signed an agreement for twenty-four Mi-35Ms, of which four were delivered in December 2011, and the last three years later. They were assigned to 1st Squadron of the border guard but later were transferred, at least the majority of them, to the army air force and replaced Mi-24Gs. Some of them are documented to have operated from the Nakhchivan autonomous republic, an enclave separated from Azerbaijan. Helicopters were used in multiple wars and clashes with Armenia such as in 2016 and 2020, when the disputed areas originally conquered by Armenia in 1993 were captured back by Azerbaijan. Around 2016 Hinds started to be upgraded with Turkish avionics by TAI company.

Armenia inherited a very limited number of aircraft from the USSR as no large units were located on its territory, except the 65th Independent Transport-Attack Helicopter Regiment (OTBVP) returning recently from Afghanistan. At the Erebuni airbase in the capital of Yerevan only seven Mi-24Ps, two Mi-24Ks and one Mi-24R were seized before they had a chance to fly to Belarus, where the 65th OTBVP was sent within the USSR break-up. In 1992, two more Mi-24Vs were captured at the Gyumri airbase, and earlier twelve helicopters had been retrieved from Russia in return of other military equipment, with two more ships provided by independent Russia. Immediately after gaining its independence the country entered the war with Azerbaijan, in which its Mi-24s were deployed and at least seven ships were shot down between June 1992 and February 1993 and one was captured by Azerbaijan forces.

Armenia attempted to gain control of areas populated by ethnic Armenians which, during the Soviet era, had been subordinated under the Azerbaijani republic. During combat activities Russian Hinds were also involved in a crash of an Mi-26 in March 1992 while evacuating Armenians from the combat area. Hinds were escorting the Mi-26 bringing supplies to the area and taking citizens back. En route they were forced to drive off Azeri-operated Mi-8MT with unguided rockets and managed to do so, but the Mi-26 was shot down seconds later by a MANPADS fired from the ground, with twelve passengers dead and two dozen wounded after an emergency landing.

Armenian Mi-24s were used mainly for combat reconnaissance and escort missions and the army managed to seize significant areas with a truce signed in 1994 between the two nations. In 2013 another Mi-24P was shot down by Azerbaijani ground forces, who claimed it had violated the ceasefire conditions in the hot zone. Current Hind helicopters belong to 15th Mixed Aviation Regiment at Erebuni. In 2020 the Russian air force unloaded eight of their own Mi-35M helicopters from An-124 cargo planes, to be stationed at the Erebuni airbase. Helicopters were sent to the country to

Mi-24Vs and two Mi-24Ps. The fleet size exceeded the need of the new republic, so in 1995 fifteen Mi-24Vs were sold to India, and one Mi-24D to Sudan. In 2000 two Mi-24Ds were attempted to be sold to Liberia, which was then under sanctions. They were shipped to Slovakia, where one ship was seized by the national authorities and much later became an exhibit at the Košice museum. The air force kept only five Mi-24Vs for its own needs, of which two only were operated from the Frunze airbase under the Combat helicopter squadron. In 2016 two Mi-24Vs after overhaul were donated to the country from Russia.

There were no Soviet Hind units in Kazakhstan until 1989, when 486th OVP was formed from the 241st OVE, 311st OVE and 345th OVE, originally located at East German airbases, but the units remained in Europe and came to their new location in 1991 when the Soviet troops pulled out. The unit was located at Usharal airbase in the very east of the country. However, the extreme isolation of the Usharal airbase made it an undesirable posting, prompting the majority of the crews to leave the service shortly after relocating there. The newly constituted Republic of Kazakhstan seized some forty-two Mi-24Ds, Mi-24Vs, Mi-24Ks, Mi-24Rs and Mi-24Ps, which were enlisted into the air force inventory under the 607th Airbase. All helicopters were grounded in the new millennium and were flying only seldomly. In 2005 the first four ships returned after overhaul performed in Russia, and this date could be considered a resurrection of the Hind fleet. Gradually, at least twelve helicopters, including one Mi-24P, were overhauled with a few more exhibited in museums. The rest of the fleet was stored and proposed for sale in 2014, when the active unit removed to Semey airbase. Helicopters were used for training purposes and were engaged in multiple military exercises. Rotations were sent to the border region until they were replaced in service by Mi-35Ms, described below.

Tajikistan became another new republic with ethnic clashes present before its independence was declared. It also did not have any Mi-24s, and Hinds were operated in the country in the early the 1990s by the Russian air force as a military support for the new republic, being stationed at the airport in the capital of Dushanbe. Hinds were engaged in the combat operations from 1992 until 1994 in the border areas, where they attacked the Islamist rebels' position. The opponent, supported by the Taliban, managed to fire several Stinger missiles on the Hinds and other planes, but shot down only one Su-24 plane. In 1992 regular war operations were launched by the Dushanbe government, backed up by Russian Mi-24s. One helicopter was shot down by a heavy calibre gun around 1995, but the control was regained and rebels were pushed beyond the border to Afghanistan. In total, six Mi-24Vs and Mi-24Ps were later handed-over to the Tajik air force with operation from two airbases near the capital of Dushanbe and Khudzhand airbase. All were overhauled in Russia in the new millennium. In 2006 and 2017 four more Mi-24Vs were delivered from Russian surpluses.

Uzbekistan seized some forty-five Mi-24Ds, Mi-24Vs and Mi-24Ps on its territory, some of which were undergoing general overhaul at the Chirchik-based repair facility north of Tashkent. The maintenance capability was used for overhauls of further ships, and twenty-four helicopters were eventually introduced into the service. They were used for support of the army and border patrolling and belonged to the 66th OVP at Chirchik. In June 2000 the French company Sagem signed a contract with Uzbekistan's state company Uzmashsusimpeks for the upgrade of its twelve Mi-24P and twelve Mi-8MT/MTV helicopters. The new modification was unofficially referred to as Mi-24PUz, basically being a standard Mi-24P with a NAD 1M FLIR under the nose. The FLIR allowed area surveillance at night and in adverse weather conditions and worked primarily for target localisation and designation, with a secondary role in flight navigation. Each cockpit was equipped with a dedicated MFD.

The NAD 1M device was a derivative of the FLIR used on NH 90 helicopters and some UAVs. Both cockpits are painted black, and the crew can use Sagem CN2H night vision goggles. The navigation suite was extended by an inertial navigation system with a Sigma 95L GPS receiver. As an option, a helmet cueing and display system was proposed, but this feature was not selected by the customer. The work was performed at Tchkalov Aviation Repair Plant, Tashkent, while the Uzbek side was responsible for the airframe and systems overhaul, and the French company for the delivery and integration of new FLIR system. The first Mi-24PUz prototype was displayed at the Paris Air Show in 2001. Allegedly, fewer than the originally planned dozen helicopters were upgraded. Mi-24PUz served in the border regions as the main platform for counter insurgency operations against Islamic rebels.

When it became independent, Georgia had almost no Mi-24s on its territory, originally operating four Mi-24Vs and two Mi-24Ps only. They were assigned to special forces and were used in clashes during the early 1990s in the separatist republics of South Ossetia and Abkhazia. Mi-24s were used in support of ground forces when the latter separatist republic was attacked in 1992. On 14 August 1992, the first attack sortie was performed by Mi-24Vs attacking rebels' position, but hitting a civilian hospital complex where military personnel were recovering. The area of combat operations had been a holiday resort and consequently several civilian targets and casualties were documented, including a civilian ship sailing under the Russian flag which was hit three days later. The rebels were subsequently reinforced by internationalists and the combat clashes became more severe.

In October the Georgian forces were on the defensive and Hinds were deployed daily to support the armed forces, with first ship lost to MANPADS fire on 4 October 1992. Hinds stationed at Suchumi airbase were attacked by Abkhazian rebels. The war eventually ended in October 1993 with Abkhazian forces regaining control of its territory. Russia deployed its Mi-24s in the country as well supporting the separatist republics. In around 2003, Elbit modernised several Georgian Mi-24s with new NVG goggles of the ANVIS/HUD type. This modernisation included new lighting but did not affect any other systems.

In 2005, Georgia bought three Mi-24Vs and three Mi-24Ps from Ukraine. Freshly overhauled from Ukrainian surpluses, they were assigned to the attack helicopter squadron at the Marneuli airbase, close to the capital of Tbilisi. Georgian Hinds were not actively used in the Russian invasion in 2008, although Russia deployed over thirty Hinds and some remained after the short war, stationed permanently in South Ossetia and Abkhazia. Two Mi-24s on the ground were destroyed by the Russian air raids. The Delta company in the capital performed later overhauls of Mi-24s.

Turkmenistan had sixteen Mi-24Vs and Mi-24Ps at the Mary airbase with the majority of them not being in airworthy condition. They were overhauled in the new millennium at Georgia and are still operated, although only half are serviced.

Above: Uzbek Mi-24PUz with a French-made NAD 1M FLIR under the nose. The helicopter was displayed at the Paris Air Show. (*Jan Čadil*)

Left: Detail of the NAD 1M FLIR under the nose. It was used for navigation and target area surveillance with the original sight used for ATGM guidance. (*Jan Čadil*)

Lithuania became the very last Soviet country to seize one Mi-24D and one Mi-24V on its territory, both in non-airworthy condition. Neither were introduced into the service and the Mi-24D was eventually sold to the UK company BAE Systems, which used it as demonstrator of potential Mi-24 modernisation. The project was focused on augmentation of the original avionics with integration of Mil-Std-1553 architecture allowing easy navigation, weapon guidance and flight data display. Both cockpits were expected to be fully NVG compatible.

The top variant included an Italian three-barrel Oto Melara TMB197 20mm cannon (a licenced copy of the General Dynamics M197 type) in a moveable turret designed as a direct replacement for the original USPU-24 unit. Other options for extending the weapon array included 70mm unguided rockets of Western origin, and even Euromissile HOT ATGMs in later stages. A mock-up of the front cockpit with single MFD screen was displayed during several industry shows between 1999 and 2005. The upgraded non-airworthy Mi-24D from Lithuania was presented at the Farnborough International Airshow in 2004, a year after the upgraded Hind's official roll-out at the company premises. It featured modified cockpits with an MFD and joystick in the front cockpit dedicated to the control of the Italian Titan 385 FLIR, which replaced the original Raduga system under the right side of the nose.

The Titan 385 included an electro-optical camera working in the infrared spectrum, and also Low-Light-Level TV. In the rear cockpit two MFDs were installed. Both cockpits were also fitted with the FMS system with separate control box. Sky Guardian 2000 radar warning receivers were installed on the wing ends in special housings with 360° coverage, linked to the eight new chaff/flare dispensers on the fuselage sides with total of 120 cartridges. BAE updated the avionics core with new V/UHF radios and VOR/ILS navigation and IFF communication system. Under the wings, two Belgian-made 68mm FFAR blocks with nineteen launch tubes each were installed. In the cargo cabin, new crashworthy seats for troops were presented as an option. This helicopter demonstrator was used basically as ground test rig. In mid-2004, BAE announced it had won a tender in Poland, but for various reasons the project did not progress well. Later all the systems were removed from the prototype and the helicopter was loaned to the Midland Air Museum in Baginton, Coventry, UK, where it currently resides with no customer selecting the upgrade.

Croatian Air Force and Air Defence, officially established in December 1991, was soon dragged into a war eventuating in a UN arms embargo limiting the options for delivery of armament into the country. So, in 1993, two Mi-24Ds and four Mi-24Vs were smuggled from Ukraine and initially were even supported by Ukrainian mercenaries. Because proper inspections by experts were not carried out, huge efforts had to be made to keep helicopters in flying condition. In spring 1994 five more Mi-24Vs were introduced into the service with some ships being of early production series and some relatively fresh. Some were delivered via An-124 to Krk airport with follow-on transport on a truck to ZTZ facility in Velika Gorica, where they were checked and assembled. Before long, both Mi-24D were selected as a source of spare parts to ease the problems caused by shortages of spares.

UN observers at that time were located at nearby Pleso air force base and they noticed previously unseen Mi-24s. They suspected that the embargo was being

Above left: An Mi-24D modernised into a new variant by UK company BAE Systems. Note the Italian Titan 385 FLIR replacing the original guidance set. (*Miroslav Gyűrösi*)

Above right: Pilot's instrument board in the ex-Lithuanian Mi-24D upgraded by UK company BAE Systems. The gunsight is missing entirely. (*Miroslav Gyűrösi*)

broken and officially asked the Croatian government for background information on the origin of the Mi-24s. The official answer was that the Croatian government bought these helicopters in the summer period of 1991, before the embargo was officially launched, with their main purpose being to serve unarmed for MEDEVAC operations. To prove this, machine guns were removed from most of the helicopters during UN forces surveys, and large red crosses on white roundel bases were applied on the fuselages of three Mi-24V. As there were no objective arguments in opposition, the UN were satisfied with this explanation. All helicopters belonged to the 29th Combat Helicopter Squadron (Eskadrila Borbenih Helikoptera) at Zagreb-Pleso airport. Combat helicopter squadron has used its Mi-24s since 1993 mostly as close air support against the Serbian-backed militia.

One of classic engagements of the Mi-24 was deep strike missions into the enemy positions, destroying army communications. Mi-24s were effective at this and became very popular in the role. In combat actions Mi-24s mostly were escorted by MiG-21 fighter aircraft. Besides playing a direct role in the combat actions, Mi-24s were on readiness for Combat Search and Rescue duties, with one ship lost due to a piloting error in formation flight.

Right: A Croatian Mi-24V with full weapon array consisting of four UB-32A-24 rocket blocks, four 9M114 Shturm ATGMs and a 9A-624 machine gun. (*Daniel Vuković's collection*)

Below: A Croatian Mi-24V with what is likely the oddest Hind armament—four Mk.44 torpedoes delivered from licenced production in Italy. (*Daniel Vuković's collection*)

After the war Hinds remained in the inventory for some time and one ship was equipped with an IR camera for surveillance and ELINT missions. Furthermore, for the Croatian navy and ability to repel attacks from the sea, one Mi-24 was equipped with integrated systems for carrying Mk.44 torpedoes. The torpedo-equipped Mi-24V was never engaged in a real combat situation over the sea, although it was the only true 'naval Hind'. Tests were scheduled to evaluate the impact of flight vibrations on both the torpedo itself and its explosive warhead. As all foreign ships left the area of the Adriatic Sea that was Croatian territory, this project was postponed and at the end no launch of the torpedo was done. Croatia even considered further upgrades to Hinds but never found the budget; the fleet was grounded in the summer of 1998, and eight years later was officially withdrawn from service.

In 2001 Macedonia procured ten Mi-24Vs and two Mi-24Ks from Ukraine, subordinated to the 201st Anti-armour Helicopter Squadron located at the Skopje airbase in the capital city. In April 2001, soon after delivery, they were used in response to assaults by Albanian insurgents on the town of Tetovo in northern Macedonia, where government forces launched a full-scale offensive in order to neutralise and eliminate them. They were flown by the Ukrainian mercenaries day and night and became the most frequently used assets of the Macedonian air force. The crews used all the S-5 missiles available in the storage within a week of operation, as well as four dozen of Shturm ATGMs and dozens of FAB-250 bombs.

The conflict ended in late 2001 with the total victory of the government forces, which planned a large upgrade of Hinds. Israeli company Elbit, being major after-market supplier, offered its upgrade to several customers from the late 1990s. An important full-scale modification was selected by Macedonia in 2003, with the upgrade process commencing the following year. In total, two Mi-24Vs were selected for the upgrade together with two Mi-17s. The initial project, named Jasmin, entailed those aircraft receiving various lighting upgrades in order to comply with NVG requirements, and the ASP-17V gunsight in the rear cockpit was replaced by an ANVIS HUD-24 (Aviator's Night Vision Head Up Display). Both modifications enabled the use of AN/AVS-9 night vision goggles.

In a later stage of the project, named Alexander, both helicopters received two 6 × 8-inch MFDs in each cockpit, of which one worked as primary flight display and the second as a multifunctional display with the option to display a digital map. The original avionics were augmented by new Mil-Std-1553 architecture, allowing integration of GPS/VOR/ILS/DME systems and also of the Rockwell Collins RT-8200 V/UHF radio and ATE IFF. The major part of the upgrade, which significantly extended the capabilities of the helicopter, was the CoMPASS V generation FLIR ball turret with thermal camera, colour TV camera, laser rangefinder and automatic tracking capability. Elbit successfully coupled the FLIR's movement with the USPU-24 turret. The unit was installed on the port-side of the fuselage. Curiously, the anti-tank weapons were removed and both helicopters lost their launch tube holders, and the guidance pod and optics under the nose. This was partly driven by a plan to reduce the weight of the helicopter. The bombing system was also entirely removed. All grips in the cockpit were modified in order to make them close to HOCAS standard. A very important item was the Helicom planning and debriefing digital system. An inseparable part of the project was the general overhaul performed by the Ukrainian Aviakon Company.

Above: A Macedonian Mi-24V with EVU exhaust gas cooler shortly after delivery. Note the repainted tail number and Ukrainian roundel as well as the warning sign under the tail boom. (*Lukáš Syrový*)

Below: Another Macedonian Mi-24V during inspection. Note the weathered camouflage due to open-air storage. (*Lukáš Syrový*)

Serbia took note of Croatia's combat experience with the Mi-24s and took actions to procure their own ships, although they too were under embargo at that time. With the cooperation of some Russian politics, Serbia was able to ready pilots and technicians for training. It was planned for helicopters to be subordinated to newly created 199th Aviation Brigade at the Niš airbase. However, because Serbia had supported the failed coup in Moscow the acquisition never took place, and Yeltsin's government froze any activities to support them. It was only in 1997 that Serbian State Security, a paramilitary organisation, obtained two Mi-24Vs from Ukraine through illegal channels due to the embargo. Both were delivered in what seems to have been hand-painted camouflage, with a small Serbian flag on the tail fin only. They were briefly used for support of the Serbian security forces over Kosovo in 1998. Due to many technical issues, they were not further used and formally became subordinated to the air force. The air force never used them due to their outdated components, with none of the overhaul plants willing to refurbish them into an airworthy condition.

Among the exported Hinds, the Algerian helicopters resold from Ukraine are worthy of comment. All were assigned to the 421st, 441st, 450th and 451st combat helicopter squadrons located at Biskra airbase in the north of the country. Those helicopters, being relatively new when purchased, were all selected for upgrade to SuperHind standard. The SuperHind project was officially launched in late 1996, when the South African ATE company finished its participation in the AH-2 Rooivalk project and had spare capacity. The upgrade concept was originally designed as a solution to the lack of significant programmes approved by the original equipment manufacturer at that time.

In 1997, ATE bought its first Mi-24V (registered ZU-BOI) from an unidentified country, which was used for several years for performance monitoring and testing. In total, five stages of upgrade were laid down. The initial SuperHind Mk.I featured just minor avionics upgrades with NVG capability, while the SuperHind Mk.II introduced a brand-new sensor turret with Cumulus Argos 550 FLIR and Kentron F-2 20mm single-barrel cannon, derived from a Denel-type. The cannon, with 840 rounds, could be fed with different types of shell from two ammunition boxes on the sides of the redesigned fuselage. The FLIR allowed laser range finding and thermal or LLLTV imaging of the target area with automatic detection and surveillance of the target. Other features of the weapon system remained unchanged. The SuperHind Mk.III introduced South African Denel Ingwe 127mm anti-tank guided missiles, which could be carried on the redesigned end pylons (each pylon carrying up to four), with tilting capability for better look-down view.

The Mk.III SuperHind included also brand-new defence suite of South African origin. Both Mk.II and Mk.III SuperHinds featured one MFD for the FLIR in both cockpits. The SuperHind Mk.IV added a HUD display for the pilot and FMS system. The HUD display significantly increased the effectiveness of the helicopter operation, given that the original gunsight could only be used for weapons guidance with no capability for displaying flight data. The Mk.IV model introduced for the first time a more powerful Cumulus Argos 410 FLIR, with two displays in each cockpit. This variant was the first in which the original avionics relating to the primary flight instruments were fully replaced. As a major improvement brand new composite

Right: A South African prototype with all the features of the Super Hind Mk.III upgrade programme—the most sophisticated modernisation to date. (*ATE*)

Below: The very same helicopter in the Super Hind Mk.V standard with a completely redesigned nose section. This radical rebuild never flew. (*ATE*)

blades, allowing a wider flight envelope, were offered as optional equipment. The SuperHind Mk.V was supposed to incorporate a brand-new front fuselage with tandem seating, where the pilot was expected to sit in the front cabin with the WSO in the back seat. The original armour was to be replaced with a lightweight ceramic type, with further weight savings from removing the retractable undercarriage. Also the main and intermediate gearboxes were to be redesigned in order to further reduce weight. The reason for those radical changes was the increased empty weight of Mk.III and Mk.IV variants, which reached 8,792kg and 8,672kg respectively, exceeding the original weight of the model with no improvement of the powerplant.

Before withdrawing from the market, ATE displayed a mock-up of the SuperHind Mk.V variant, which has apparently never flown. After several years of works the first prototype ZU-BOI was revealed in Mk.III standard at the AAD Air Show in 2002. At that time the Algerian air force had already selected the SuperHind Mk. II upgrade project. Based on the contract between ATE and Algeria, thirty-four helicopters in total were updated in between 1999 and 2002. Some were later updated to Mk.III standard with Ingwe missiles and brand-new PALL particle separators on the engine inlets. Because the upgrade required significant disassembly of the airframe the upgrade was carried out at the Ukrainian overhaul facility premises. However, those helicopters suffered from many post-delivery issues caused partly by the design drawbacks and partly by the improper overhaul of components such as engines. In spite of those issues, the performance of the newly installed systems exceeded the original configuration significantly and crews liked the all-weather and night capability. In the first years of operation only one helicopter was lost for technical reasons.

In around 2010, the majority of the helicopters underwent an overhaul in Ukraine, where the systems were boosted by new Argos II HDT and IPZ Titan 410SD FLIR replacing the original Argos 550. In total, ATE has acquired three Mil Mi-24 helicopters. After ZU-BOI, a second machine, ZU-GAL, was acquired from Algeria. Both were Mi-24V models. In 2003 the company bought a third Mi-24D, ZU-SOV from Bulgaria as a part of the attempts of ATE, Thales and the local Terem plant and Liconex company to win the local tender for Mi-24 upgrades. The ZU-GAL model was intended to be rebuilt into the SuperHind Mk.V variant, but with ATE experiencing financial difficulties, the project was placed on hold.

7

New Times for Hinds

Once a Warhorse, Always a Warhorse

The Mil Moscow Helicopter Plant and Rostvertol production plant were both aware of the Mi-24's obsolescence from at least the mid-1980s. In navigation, weapons and sensor engagement in particular, Hinds were significantly behind their Western counterparts designed for nap-of-the-Earth low-level flying, with full night- and adverse-weather-capability. However, the state-planned economics afforded both Mil and Rostvertol limited options to systematically upgrade the type, especially when new models such as the Mi-28 and Ka-50 were being considered as prospective replacement for all Hinds. However, the USSR's breakup, along with radical drop of production rates of both old and new models, forced Mil's plant to reconsider an option to modernise the existing fleet of Hinds, especially as many newer systems had been designed for, and tested on, the Mi-28 type. Additionally, Russia had to find a way to offer attractive solutions to many countries operating Mi-24s, but which now had fully independent political and procurement systems with no obligation to follow Moscow's recommendation.

Russia became newly obliged to compete on the market against other platforms and even in the area of Mi-24 upgrades it had to compete with entities from Israel and Western Europe. In a situation where the full-scale production and introduction into service of the Mi-28 or Ka-50/52 did not seem feasible in the short term, the survivability of the domestic helicopter industry was discussed. The solution was a new generation of Hinds—the legacy airframe was to be equipped with new items benefiting from the development of the Mi-28. Therefore a large upgrade project, Mi-24VM (for export Mi-35M, by NATO referred to as Hind J), was prepared.

For easy introduction it was proposed in five consecutive stages. The designation Mi-35D also appears in some sources. The first stage was a service life extension of the airframes for 4,000 flight hours and/or thirty years, together with a full overhaul in Russia. This solution was supposed to enable Hinds to survive beyond 2005, as all Mi-24D/Mi-25 models were to reach their end of service life around that date. The original service life had neglected issues of corrosion and fatigue, as all helicopters were expected to receive only one overhaul in service, which was intended to be performed on a relatively new airframe with no critical issues likely to be encountered. However, exceeding the original service life was accompanied by an expected increase of fatigue and corrosion problems on the airframes serving longer than expected. Hence, an overhaul to cater only for relatively new airframes was not enough.

The second stage focused mostly on weight reduction in order to attain better performance in hot and high conditions. This was clearly a result of the Afghan experience, where transport Mi-8MT/MTVs performed better than Mi-24s. The main rotor of the Mi-24 was therefore to be replaced by a new one with fibreglass composite blades and with self-lubricating hinges on the rotor head. The diameter and profile of the blades remained untouched, although the section attaching the blade to the rotor head had a different, thicker profile. The tail rotor of 'X' shape from the Mi-28 was offered. Engines were replaced by the TV3-117VMA and later the improved TV3-117VMA-SB3 variant offered by Ukrainian Motor Sich company. All in all, the weight reduction totalled 300kg, which resulted in an increase of service ceiling by some 600 metres, and an improved rate of climb. On the other hand, the more powerful engines needed a new and improved main gearbox oil cooling system and the hydraulics' boosters had to be replaced by a more powerful KAU-115 type.

The third stage upgrade proposed deleting the undercarriage retraction system, bringing an additional 90kg weight bonus, and significantly increasing flight safety. Hind crews in combat zones often flew with the undercarriage down during low level flight, as this helped absorb the impact if the helicopter was shot down and hit the ground. Therefore it was considered a safety measure which helped bring the safety of the type closer to the new models, and was favoured despite the drag penalty and slightly reduced top speed. Another major feature of the third stage were new BDZ-UV weapon hardpoints, allowing carriage of APU-8/4U multiple racks for up to eight 9M114 Shturm ATGM missiles each. The total capacity of sixteen ATGMs on two pylons allowed the end pylons to be deleted, a further weight benefit. The avionics were boosted by a R-999 secured voice radio.

The fourth stage updated the weapon system; the 9M114 Shturm ATGMs could be replaced by the more effective 9M120 Ataka type, which used identical hardware for operation. Another upgrade included replacing the USPU-24 turret and 9A-624 gun, with a NPPU-24 turret and GSh-23V twin-barrel 23mm cannon with liquid cooling. This variant proved to be more effective than the Mi-24VP's air-cooled GSh-23L variant, which suffered from overheating during long-burst firing. A brand new feature was the lightweight 9M39 Igla-V air-to-air missiles for self-defence. The Mi-35M's avionics were augmented by two BVK-24 mission computers. One of the lesser-known features was the integration of IFF identification with the weapon control system. This solution eliminated unintentional friendly fire. In total the modifications doubled kill-probability and the distance for attack.

The final, fifth, stage introduced ONV-2 night vision goggles (NVG), with necessary upgrades to the lighting system, and a GOES-342 FLIR ball turret with thermal imaging, TV camera and laser pointer and range finder. The GOES ball turret was originally installed on the port-side of the nose, while at the 1997 MAKS show, another prototype based on the Mi-24V with 9A-624 machine gun was displayed with the GOES on the starboard side. However, in both cases the FLIR was just an addition to the existing Raduga system. Later, a sixth modification was introduced with PNK-24 (sometimes referred to as PrVK-24) automatic flight, navigation and weapon guidance system derived from the PrPNK-28 model introduced on the Mi-24, and OPS-24N weapon guidance system instead of the original Raduga type.

It was the first variant where the ball turret was located on the site of the original optics under the starboard side of the nose with Raduga system entirely deleted as useless. In addition, a Mak-UFM warning system coupled with UV-26 26mm flares was introduced. Later, a variant with the more powerful Klimov VK-2500-02 engines derived from the TV3-117VMA and produced in St Petersburg was offered.

Those stages were proposed either as an upgrade or as a base standard for brand new helicopters. Contrary to the specification above, the Russian manufacturer started to offer the Mi-35M worldwide in three simplified final variants: the Mi-35M1 with GSh-23L cannon, composite main rotor and 'X' shaped tail rotor, TV3-117VMA engines, KAU-115 boosters and BDZ-UV pylons and ONV-3 NVG goggles; the Mi-35M2 featured 9M39 air-to-air missiles and GSh-23V cannon; the Mi-35M3 combined the majority of all the above-described upgrades.

The first prototype representing the stepped upgrade scheme debuted at the Paris Air Show in June 1995. At that time, it was an updated Mi-24VP and, surprisingly, it was not yet equipped with the electrooptical system and featured only shortened wings with multiple racks, new rotors, improved engines and updated avionics. The main upgrade features were the French made Sextant Avionique/Thomson CSF NOCAS (Night Operation Capable Avionics System) and Nadir 10 navigation system, portside-mounted Thompson thermal CSF Chlio imager and a VH-100 HUD display in rear cockpit. The same helicopter appeared at the domestic MAKS-95 Air Show, and because of its green paint scheme it was frequently called 'the new model' even if it was built on a ship several years old. It addressed many drawbacks of the original Hind concept but struggled to find a customer, mostly due to dozens of available surplus Mi-24Vs and Mi-24Ps—of which some were resold by Russia itself. During MAKS-97, another prototype Mi-24V conversion was present with the full suite of upgrades, including GOES-342 FLIR. A door gun of 12.7mm calibre was also introduced, though this limited internal cargo capacity. Despite a massive marketing campaign, both helicopters seemed to be just static demonstrators.

The first flight took place on 4 March 1999 near Moscow. The first prototype was converted from an Mi-24VP operated by the 344th combat and conversion training centre, Torzhok, and after the maiden flight and some public demonstration it entered state trials. The helicopter was close to Mi-35M2 standard, excluding the FLIR system and designated multi-function display in the front cockpit (in the rear there was a display acting as a primary flight indicator in place of the ASP-17V gunsight and another display for the digital map instead of the original map indicator). The prototype with full equipment, close to the full Mi-35M3 standard, flew for the first time around 2001 and was displayed at the 2003 Paris Air Show and MAKS show.

The first prototype was fully funded by Mil Moscow Helicopter Plant and the selection of the air force helicopter for modification was driven by a wish to persuade the Russian Ministry of Defence to upgrade more helicopters in service. However, only a very limited number of helicopters were updated. The Mi-35M prototype state tests were finished in 2006. Some of the modifications were later available for export separately, with new designations for downgraded variants Mi-24O or Mi-24VO and Mi-35O respectively. The Mi-24O designation was seen during MAKS-99 with the display of an old Mi-24V and with fuselage code 16 with NVG gear and moving map LCD in the rear cockpit. It was announced that FLIR would be added later.

Above: The second Mi-35M prototype with FLIR turret installed on the starboard side as an addition to the original sighting system. This helicopter was converted from an Mi-24V and lacks the 23mm cannon. (*MVZ Mil*)

Below: The same helicopter from the opposite side. Note the rotor system has not been modernised. The ship was converted from a serial Mi-24V. (*MVZ Mil*)

Above: The first Mi-24VM prototype, converted from an operational Russian air force Mi-24VP assigned to 344th Flight Centre. (*MVZ Mil*)

Below: The first Mi-35M prototype after modification, with GOES FLIR installed instead of Raduga sighting system. Note the Igla AAGMs under the inner pylon. (*MVZ Mil*)

Above: Detail of the Mi-35M's main rotor head with all-composite rotor blades of modified chord, and the vibration damper on the top. (*Author*)

Below: An Mi-35M wing with eight 9M120 ATGMs and B-8V20 rocket block. Note the fixed main landing gear with no openable doors. (*Author*)

Right: Pilot's cockpit of the Mi-35M with two MFDs covered by ground covers and a visible HUD display instead of the original gunsight. (*Author*)

Below: Front cockpit of the Mi-35M with single MFD used for guidance of the weapons. In spite of all the upgrades, the hand controllers are still of original shape. (*Author*)

The massive marketing campaign consisting of an Mi-35M flight display in some twenty countries eventuated in the first success in a country not having any previous experience with Hinds: Venezuela. The South American country, under the leadership of Hugo Chavez, refused to continue procurement of US armament, and placed a massive armament order with Russia for thirty Su-30MKV fighters and thirty-eight helicopters, including ten Mi-35Ms. Venezuela, became the launch customer for the new Hind generation, receiving the slightly downgraded Mi-35M2 model (with internal code Izdelyie 658) with initial deliveries in 2006 and spanning to 2008. Those helicopters also differed in having Bendix King KHF-950-10 HF radios (replaced by KHF-1050 type on later machines), two KTR-908 VHF radios and Reutech ACR500 multiband UHF/VHF digital radio. Hinds were assigned to the 716th Combat Helicopter Squadron (Batallón de Helicópteros de Ataque) located at the Barinas airbase close to the Colombian border. Two ships were later transferred to 722nd helicopter squadron at the Caracas La Carlota airbase where they were used for training purposes. They are known as Mi-35M Caribe and are used for border patrolling and combating the narcos crossing the border from Colombia. The ships regularly fly with IR jammers active due to the risk of MANPADS and are engaged in several combat clashes every year.

In 2014, the fleet passed overhaul in Russia, during which the helicopters gained a new paint scheme. After the success in Venezuela, Brazil also decided to buy the new Mi-35M standard (again Izdeliye 658) and received twelve ships, delivered between 2010 and 2014. All were named AH-2 Sabre in the country and were stationed with the attack helicopter squadron at Porto Velho airbase in the middle of Brazilian Amazon. Helicopters were used against various armed groups in the area and were frequently used to pursue light aircraft operated by drug cartels. For that purpose later the helicopters had highly visible 121,5 codes on the side of the front cabin Plexiglass, showing the proper radio frequency to the pursued plane. One helicopter was lost but the remaining continued to serve to end of 2022, when a sudden decision to ground all of them was taken. Although many media houses linked this decision to sanctions imposed on Russia, Brazil (as a member of BRICS organisation) was not directly affected and had legal means to continue in the support. The official air force explanation mentioned the need for extensive and expansive overhauls in Russia as the reason and the country likely decided to buy a newer light-type for a cost equivalent to a full overhaul of the legacy Hinds.

In 2010, Russia ordered Mi-35Ms (Izdeliye 758) for its own use. There are no records of how many ships were delivered, but the estimates mention almost sixty ships, with small deliveries going on in the past years as war-attrition replacement. As of now, the Mi-35Ms remain in active service with 332nd OVP at Pushkin airbase, 487th OVPBU at Budyonnovsk airbase, 549th OVP at Pribylovo airbase, 39th OVP at Dzhankoi airbase, 55th OVP at Korenovsk airbase, and the 15th Army Aviation Brigade at Ostrov. Hinds are deployed alongside with transport Mi-8MTVs/AMTShs models and Mi-28Ns and are considered as more than ideal for Spetsnaz special operations teams and combat search and rescue missions. The Russian air force has deployed the Mi-35M in combat in several places. The first action was to patrol the airspace of Armenia, as this activity is provided by the Russian air force on the basis of an intergovernmental agreement.

Above: A Brazilian AH-2 Sabre helicopter used for air interdiction of drug smugglers over Amazonia. Note the emergency radio frequency on the blister. (*Agência Força Aérea Brasiliera*)

Below: A Brazilian AH-2 Sabre taxiing prior to another flight over the Amazonian rainforest. (*Agência Força Aérea Brasiliera*)

Helicopters located at the Erebuni base were used to guard the borders against illegal crossings by smugglers and troops of neighbouring countries.

In December 2015, the first four Mi-35Ms were delivered by Il-76 aircraft to Syria. One of the helicopters had the most modern Vitebsk self-defence system but returned to Russia after four months. Evidently, this was a test of the novelty, as the subsequent Mi-35Ms sent to Syria in mid-2016 already had this system. It was the Vitebsk system that caused the Mi-35M to take over the security of the Khmeimim base. Ships with the new defence suite were sometimes called Mi-35MD. The selected Mi-35Ms had mostly a camouflage scheme, but the special forces liked to use all-grey helicopters, because they flew them primarily at night and the dark colouring was ideal for such deployment. Initially, Mi-35M flights were dominated by escorts of transport helicopters. As the fighting progressed and the Islamists were pushed out of their positions, micro-teams of special forces and intelligence services also began to be actively supported by the Mi-35M. In both cases, it was a pure combat deployment with dozens of clashes with rebels. Helicopters were particularly deployed in the vicinity of Palmira, where one helicopter was destroyed on the ground. The machines usually carried a full supply of ammunition for the GSh-23V on-board cannon, two blocks of S-8 unguided rockets and two to eight 9M120 Ataka ATGMs.

The optics of the targeting system worked very well in Syria, which allowed the search for and destroying of targets even at night. Although it did not have a large multiple of magnification, the sensor made it possible to distinguish the thermal contrast between enemy units and the background very well. A large part of the action took place at night or in the evening, when helicopters flew around the conquered territories and checked the enemy's movements based on intelligence information. The insertion of the Spetsnaz commandos took place mostly without landing with forward flight at a low altitude of up to 2 meters, during which the soldiers jumped out of the cabin. Landing in the sand was almost never carried out in order to protect engines, and even to prevent sand getting into the open cabin.

Mi-35Ms were also intensively involved in the destruction of selected targets. In combat over cities Hinds were flying ultra-low to reduce the chance of being hit. All the time helicopters fired flares to confuse any enemy missiles. Newer PIKP-26 flares in UV-26 cartridges were used in several machines, which offered longer burning time and higher temperature compared to the original PPI-26 type in the ASO-2V exchangers. At night, crews used an interesting tactic whereby the lead helicopter usually shot at areas out of the enemy's zone of interest to distract them, and only the second machine attacked the real target. This approach was devised because ISIS fighters were constantly improving their tactics, with most of them hiding in buildings or underground tunnels; patrols only came out to check what was happening on the surface, and it was the shooting that usually lured the patrols.

Having gained superiority in combat areas, the Mi-35Ms were actively used to bomb underground shelters, and the most widespread weapons became the 100 and 250kg FAB bombs, as well as the incendiary variants of the ZAB bombs. The biggest change, which was introduced in mid-2016, was the new S-8OFP missiles. These have been put to the test in Syria and represent a new version of the extended S-8 family. While the most widely used S-8K or S-8M use a warhead weighing 3.6kg, the S-8 warhead weighs 9.5kg and, thanks to a modified high-energy rocket engine, offers a range of up to 6 kilometres, which is a third more than the original model. S-8OFPs have been tested in Syria and have shown a significant increase in effectiveness.

Russian Mi-35Ms have been widely deployed in Ukraine since 2022, with at least fourteen ships destroyed by the anti-aircraft fire. The type was used primarily for protection of transport helicopters and at least three ships were shot down during the very early stages of the Russian occupation. Later, the Mi-35Ms were engaged in close air support, especially when the Ka-52 fleet suffered heavy losses. After Ka-52 the Mi-35Ms were the best equipped in terms of defence suite and were prioritised over attack Mi-28Ns. The tactics of deployment did not significantly differ from the Syrian experience, including ultra-low flights necessitated by the omnipresent risk from MANPADS. In 2016 at least five Mi-35Ms are recorded to have been delivered to the FSB intelligence agency for border area operations.

With the domestic operator ordering Hinds, some foreign customers followed suit in 2010. In 2010 Azerbaijan selected new Hinds. The initial four ships (Izdeliye 558), delivered in 2011 and painted all-white, were assigned to State Border Guard and its No. 1 Squadron at the Baku-Qala airbase, with time-limited detachments to Tanriqulular airbase. The remaining sixteen ships in green colour were also ordered for the border guard, but at least eight were later assigned to the 1st Helicopter Squadron of the air force at the Baku-Qala and replaced the Mi-24Gs and legacy models. Later Kazakhstan, Uzbekistan and Belarus opted for Mi-35M as well.

Iraq became one of the largest purchasers with immediate deployment of the helicopters in combat against ISIS. Hinds were assigned to the 35th assault helicopter

A Russian air force Mi-35M is disembarking a special forces commando unit during a MAKS airshow at Zhukovsky near Moscow. (*Author*)

A Russian air force Mi-35M in a camouflage paint scheme. The grey-painted helicopters were assigned to support special forces, while camouflaged ships performed combat tasks. (*ITAR-TASS*)

squadron at the Al Kut airbase and were extremely active in the combat operations. They proved to be equally, if not better, suited for the combat sorties when compared to newer Mi-28NEs also delivered. The combat sorties included anything from attacks on armed Toyota pickups, to convoys or the elimination of snipers. Mi-35Ms destroyed hundreds of targets from armed pickups to infantry vehicles, tanks and bunkers. In contrary to other Iraqi air force types those helicopters were flying close to the enemy and battle damage was nothing unusual, with two confirmed battle losses and one unconfirmed. However, the value of the type for the Iraqi air force is undoubted, and its generals were talking about Hind with great respect. It became one of the few types which was eventually overhauled and remained in service even after withdrawal of US support.

Curiously, Pakistan had ordered and received five aircraft, although the country operates Bell Cobra helicopters and at that time had been approved for delivery of AH-1Z type, although in the end none were provided. It had also recently received Chinese Z-10 helicopters. Pakistani helicopters were engaged in combating various armed groups in Baluchistan province with operation from the Quetta airbase. Hinds managed to repel several terrorist attacks on the base and proved to be superior to legacy AH-1F fleet. Neighbouring Afghanistan also expressed interest in the Mi-35M model in the time of coalition operations in the Asian country, but the deal was limited by fact that the funding must be provided by US and there were some legal limitations in place for the purchase of Russian military equipment due to the tremendous corruption scandals linked with previous deliveries.

Since 2015, Mi-35Ms has also supplemented legacy Hinds with Nigeria, Myanmar, Mali and Togo. Rwanda received Mi-35Ms in 2022 as a new type, with all being stationed at Kigali airbase. Serbia became a surprising operator of four Mi-35Ms delivered in 2019 to the 714th anti-armour helicopter squadron at Kraljevo airbase. More ships were planned to be delivered, but later instead the ex-Cyprus Mi-35Ps were introduced into the service and the country plans domestic fleet upgrade. In the last years Belarus became the last operator with allegedly two more operators negotiating delivery of new Mi-35Ms.

At MAKS-2015, an advanced Mi-35M prototype, benefiting from solutions developed for other attack helicopters, was displayed. This was essentially the full Mi-35M configuration with a brand-new defence suite consisting of large housings with UV sensors on the fuselage sides in front of the cargo cabin doors, covering the front hemisphere, and two more sensors in the housings on the tail boom for the rear hemisphere. The L-166V Ispanka IR jammer was removed, although the mounting pad remained in place. Instead, a small ball with DIRCM beam against UV/IR-seeking missiles can be found under the tail boom. The ASO-2V flare dispensers in triple cases were mounted on both fuselage sides. At the Army 2018 exhibition this model was displayed with large DIRCM gimbals under the fuselage sides and pods on the stub wings for additional protection equipment. New multiple racks allowed the ship to carry not only sixteen Shturm or Ataka ATGM missiles, but also the 9A-4172K

An Iraqi Mi-35M flying over the desert. The camouflage is very dirty from exhaust gases. (*Agence France-Presse*)

Vikhr-M laser-guided ATGM missiles originally developed for Ka-50. Those missiles were designed for laser beam-riding guidance instead of typical laser designator spot guidance and proved to be very effective due to their high speed of flight. The weapon array was further extended by the 9M324 Igla-M self-defence anti-aircraft missiles of the Strelets system. Such upgrade shall be possible to be performed during general overhaul of legacy Mi-35Ms.

In 2015, three very unique helicopters called Mi-35MS were finished (registered RF-13345 to 13347) to the federal protection service FSO. Those are based on Mi-35M standard and are customised for VIP transportation. They were built using Mi-24PS expertise. All three were assigned to the presidential fleet and carry the president and prime minister. The cargo cabin is redesigned for passenger transport with soundproofing and a luxury finish. It includes a sofa and three to four chairs with TV screens on the wall.

The vertical-split entrance doors were completely redesigned and are now narrower, are one piece and hinged on the bottom edge with built-in steps. The windows are also bigger. The place of the original USPU-24 station is occupied by a weather radar antenna under an aerodynamic cover. All systems associated with ATGMs were removed, but the end wing-pylons were retained and hold special fairings with UV detectors of missiles launched with the Vitebsk system, and also position lights. Also the infra-red jammer is a brand-new type, with different housing. All helicopters can carry EVU exhaust gas coolers. Under the tail boom there is a small ball containing a DIRCM countermeasures system. Curiously, no flare dispensers were spotted on the helicopters yet. On the majority of pictures the Mi-35MS helicopters carry PTB-450

An extremely weathered Mi-35M showing its latest improvements in the form of added defence suite elements. The VKS ROSSII titles refer to air and space force. (*Russian MoD*)

Above: Wing of the latest Mi-35M variant with DIRCM housings visible. Under the fuselage is the DG-64 underslung hook. (*Miroslav Gyűrösi*)

Right: Wing of the upgraded Mi-35M variant with B-8V20 rocket block and six 9A-4172K Vikhr-M laser-guided ATGM missiles. (*Miroslav Gyűrösi*)

A Russian prototype of the Mi-35P Phoenix variant with promotional digital camouflage. Note the defence suite housing on the wing end pylons. (*Rosoboronexport*)

auxiliary fuel tanks, but apparently they can be armed with unguided weapons as well, which makes them very interesting 'presidential helicopters'. At least two of those miss the DUAS system on the frame of the front cockpit. The power plant is shared with the Mi-35M model with vibration damper on the main rotor head but no 'X' shaped tail rotor is used and a conventional three-bladed type was selected. All helicopters have brand new composite armouring of both cockpits and VIP cabin walls and floor.

At the Army 2020 exhibition another model called Mi-35P Phoenix was introduced for the first time. Although marketed as brand new, it is actually a downgraded variant of Mi-35M. It comes with original transmission and rotor system with VK-2500PS-02 engines and anti-vibration damper on the main rotor head. Surprisingly, the original wings with end pylons carrying new housings for the Vitebsk defence suite were reintroduced as well as the retractable landing gear. The multiple racks allow sixteen Ataka ATGM missiles, ten 9A-4172K Vikhr-M laser-guided ATGM missiles and four 9M324 Igla-M anti-aircraft missiles to be carried. The troops' cabin can be equipped with pintle mounts for Kord-12.7 machine guns. Guidance is performed through OPS-24N-1L electro-optical system with a GOES-321MK gimbal allowing detection of tank-sized object at a range of 10 kilometres. The avionics were augmented by a new VIM-95-35 navigational system, working as VOR/ILS navigation as well as with

VND-94 as DME. The Mi-35P also received a new PKV-8-35 autopilot integrated in the pilot and navigation suite KNEI-24-E1. Apparently, this model is aimed at African and Asian countries.

Alongside the above-described Mi-35M project, which reached series production, were several Russian programmes which were not so successful. At MAKS-1999 a prototype Mi-24N (referred to in some materials as Mi-24VN or Mi-35MO) was introduced as a low cost alternative to Mi-35M project. This helicopter, developed jointly with the scientific organisation NPO Geophysika, featured the GOES-342 FLIR with a new targeting and surveillance system. The FLIR was located under the starboard nose instead of the original Raduga system optics. Allegedly six Russian air force helicopters were updated prior to 2001 with live firing tests passed in July 2000 and flight tests completed in August the same year.

In October 2000, another project called Mi-24PN (Izdeliye 543) was revealed (sometimes referred to as Mi-24PM or even Mi-24M) as an option for upgrading the existing fleet of Mi-24Ps within a limited budget. This helicopter featured a Zarevo 9S475N sighting and guidance system based on the Noktyurn IR seeker as an add-on to the original Raduga optical station. The Noktyurn device was originally developed for infantry vehicles and although its performance was not the best available, it could be fitted for a very low price due to mass production. The whole system was installed in a beam on the nose of the helicopter, which ensured the best field of view, but also made it prone to dust and insects obscuring the lens. The reason for retaining the original system was driven by the requirement to reduce costs, its minimal impact on other systems, and also due the acceptable performance of the Raduga system during daylight operation. Both weapon systems operator and pilot had a dedicated multifunctional display in the cockpit. The helicopter was also equipped with ONV-1 NVG gear and also with BREO-24 piloting and navigation system. The weapons system was strengthened with the addition of a 9K113N Shturm VN system with infra-red seeking system for new guidance of ATGMs, using a laser rangefinder for better accuracy. All weapons were stored on modified BDZ-UV weapon racks with in-built cranes.

After several years of testing in 2004, the Rostvertol company started to upgrade Russian air force helicopters. In total sixteen Mi-24PNs were adopted by the Russian air force up to 2008, with a few being brand new and the majority refurbished Mi-24Ps. The refurbished helicopters were given a remaining service life of some fifteen years and 1,000 flight hours. All Mi-24PNs were delivered to the 487th OVP at Budennovsk and to the 344th conversion training centre at Torzhok, with all ships later transferred to 112nd OVP at Chita airbase and 549th OVP at Pribylovo. In spite of some improvements, the type suffered from being overweight, as the new systems and associated ballast to restore the correct centre of gravity added some 280kg.

In 2004, news of an order for six Mi-24PN helicopters by Uganda appeared in the media with a single helicopter seen, apparently already in the country. This machine was converted from a surplus Mi-24P and delivered by Russia with two standard Mi-24Ps. The African country therefore became the sole foreign operator of the type. In late 2000 another upgrade project called Mi-24VK-1 was unveiled. It was a standard Mi-24V equipped with GOES-321 FLIR ball turret with infra-red imager and laser rangefinder installed instead of the original Raduga system, and

NVG compatibility. Because the FLIR was not fully integrated at the beginning of development, and was used for unguided weapons firing and navigation only, the first prototype helicopter lacked holders for guided anti-tank weapons tubes, and also the guidance antenna under the port side of the nose.

The prototype fuselage code 17, displayed to Russian air force officials in March 2001, was in this configuration. The following stage, dubbed Mi-24VK-2, would feature a new GOES-342 model FLIR with daylight camera, thermal camera and laser rangefinder, BDZ-UV weapon racks and 9M120 Ataka ATGMs, R-999 secured radio and Glonass satellite navigation system. However, this variant did not materialise and instead all those improvements were presented on an Mi-24P-based model with the designation Mi-24PK-2. An analogous Mi-24VK-1 and Mi-24VK-2 variants for the Mi-24P were marketed as Mi-24PK-1 and Mi-24PK-2, but neither reached the hardware stage. For export, the Mi-24VK-1 and Mi-24PK-2 modifications were labelled Mi-35VN and Mi-35PN respectively. Although the Russian air force decided to upgrade some of its Mi-24Vs in this way, when contracts for new Mi-35s, Mi-28s and Ka-52s were signed, the modernisation plans were frozen.

In 2006, two more projects were mentioned in the press with the Mi-24VP-M and Mi-24VP-I designation. Both were intended to be variants of upgrades for the Mi-24V/P serving with the Russian army. Both should have been based on Mi-35M

An Mi-24PN prototype with nose-installed sensor. It utilises some Mi-35M features such as shortened wings. (*MVZ Mil*)

configuration with Igla missiles and new sensors, but neither went ahead. Some Russian air force Mi-24s were upgraded during overhauls with new Prima system radios and BUR flight recorders, but in both cases this was to mitigate obsolescence rather than true modernisation. At MAKS-2019 airshow another modification was introduced under the designation Mi-24P-1M by the Russian KRET avionics consortium. It used the DIRCM protection suite from the latest Mi-35M model for self-protection. For navigation and target engagement it featured in the nose the B006E radar with active electronically steered array. The OEM stated the detection range allowed identification of a tank at 15 kilometres, and a bridge at 80 kilometres, with up to ten targets tracked simultaneously. For optical detection the OPS-23N-1L electro-optical gimbal was installed. The on-board avionics were completely redone with large MFDs in both cockpits, with HUD display in the rear cabin. The prototype, converted from legacy Mi-24P, was never intended for serialisation in Russia, but rather to show the capabilities of the industry.

Although the Hind had always a good reputation, it is only now that it can fully show its qualities. The transport-attack capability is ideal for many asymmetric conflicts. There is no doubt that the latest Hinds will remain in operation more than seventy years after the V-24 maiden flight, fully acknowledged as one of the best attack helicopters ever to shape attack strategy and defence policy in many countries.

Detail of the Zarevo 9S475N sighting and guidance system on the Mi-24PN model. Note the NVG-compatible taxiing light. (*Miroslav Gyűrösi*)

Above: Serial Russian air force Mi-24PNs taking off. These were the very first ships to be built for the domestic air force after the breaking up of the USSR. (*MVZ Mil*)

Below: An Mi-24VK-1 prototype displayed at MAKS airshow. This particular ship lacks ATGM launching pads for unknown reasons. (*MVZ Mil*)

Above: GOES-321 FLIR ball turret with infra-red imager and laser rangefinder installed instead of the original Raduga system of the Mi-24VK-1. (*MVZ Mil*)

Below: The sole prototype of the Mi-24P-1M helicopter with the B006E radar unit and the OPS-23N-1L electrooptical sensor on the nose. (*Miroslav Gyűrösi*)

Appendix A

List of Mi-24 Production

Arsenyev and Rostov Production Plants

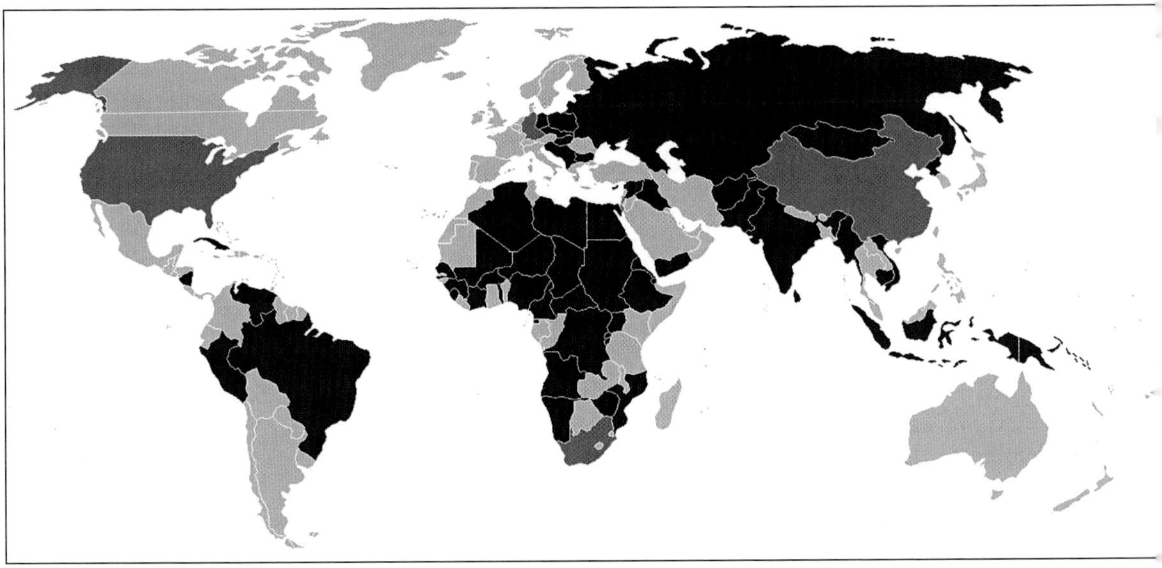

To capture the Hind operators over the time, this map ignores state changes. Dark grey indicates Mi-24 regular operators and medium grey indicates countries using Mi-24s for testing purposes only.

List of Mi-24 Production for Soviet Army/Air Force

Year	Variant	Qty	Comment
1970	Mi-24	5	Two for static and fatigue tests
1971–75	Mi-24A	204	
1973–75	Mi-24U	25	
1973–74	Mi-24B	10	Exact number unspecified

Year	Variant	Qty	Comment
1975–81	Mi-24D	199	
1976–89	Mi-24V	500	Exact number unspecified
1977–91	Mi-24DU	99	
1981–96	Mi-24P	608	
1983–89	Mi-24R	152	
1983–90	Mi-24K/KD	92	
1989–90	Mi-24VP	25	
1990	Mi-24RA	8	

List of Mi–24 Production for Russian Army/Air force/Security Bureau—Rostov Production Plant

Year	Variant	Qty	Comment
1994–95	Mi-24P	8	Four completed as Mi-24PN
1995	Mi-24V	4	
2011	Mi-35M	6	
2012	Mi-35M	16	
2013	Mi-35M	8	
2014	Mi-35M	16	
2015	Mi-35MS	3	For FSO
2016	Mi-35M	5	For FSB
2017	Mi-35M	4	Unconfirmed
2022	Mi-35M	6	Unconfirmed
2023	Mi-35M	8	Unconfirmed
2024	Mi-35M	8	Unconfirmed
2025	Mi-35M	3	Unconfirmed

List of Mi-24 Exports—Arsenyev Production Plant

Year	Variant	Qty	User
1975	Mi-24A	6	Libya
	Mi-24A	12	Algeria
1976	Mi-24A	6	Libya
	Mi-24U	2	Libya
1977	Mi-24A	10	Ethiopia
	Mi-24U	1	Ethiopia

List of Mi-24/25/35 Exports—Rostov Production Plant

Year	Variant	Qty	User
1978	Mi-24D	4	GDR
	Mi-24D	4	Hungary
	Mi-24D	4	Czechoslovakia
	Mi-24D	4	Poland
	Mi-24D	31	Iraq
1979	Mi-25	7	Afghanistan
	Mi-25	17	Iraq
	Mi-24D	16	Bulgaria
	Mi-24D	4	GDR
	Mi-25	24	North Korea*
	Mi-25	4	Kampuchea
1980	Mi-24D	4	Czechoslovakia
	Mi-24D	16	Hungary
	Mi-25	20	Algeria
1981	Mi-24D	10	Czechoslovakia
	Mi-25	1	Nicaragua
	Mi-24D	4	Bulgaria
	Mi-24D	18	GDR
	Mi-24D	4	Poland
	Mi-25	12	Syria
	Mi-25	12	Cuba
1982	Mi-25	27	Syria
	Mi-25	13	Libya
	Mi-24D	4	Bulgaria
	Mi-24D	6	GDR
	Mi-24D	10	Czechoslovakia
1983	Mi-25	11	Peru
	Mi-24D	10	GDR
	Mi-25	12	Angola
	Mi-24D	4	Bulgaria
	Mi-25	13	Libya
	Mi-25	7	India
1984	Mi-25	1	India
	Mi-25	6	Mozambique
	Mi-25U	1	Mozambique

Year	Variant	Qty	User
1984 (*Cont'd*)	Mi-25	8	Iraq
	Mi-25	10	Syria
	Mi-25	5	Nicaragua
	Mi-25	12	Angola
	Mi-24D	4	Bulgaria
	Mi-24D	6	Poland
1985	Mi-25	2	Mozambique
	Mi-25	2	Peru
	Mi-25U	1	Peru
	Mi-25	1	Libya
	Mi-24D	10	Hungary
	Mi-24D	2	Poland
	Mi-25	12	Syria
	Mi-24D	6	Bulgaria
	Mi-24DU	2	Czechoslovakia
	Mi-24V	10	Czechoslovakia
	Mi-24V	10	Hungary
1986	Mi-24V	6	Bulgaria
	Mi-24V	16	Poland
	Mi-24V	12	Mongolia
	Mi-35	1	Sudan
	Mi-35	18	Afghanistan
1987	Mi-35	12	Angola
	Mi-24V	10	Czechoslovakia
	Mi-35	12	Mozambique
	Mi-35	9	Afghanistan
	Mi-35	10	Ethiopia
1988	Mi-35	5	Afghanistan
	Mi-24V	8	Czechoslovakia
	Mi-35	12	Angola
	Mi-35	12	Libya
	Mi-35	13	Afghanistan
1989	Mi-25U	4	India
	Mi-24V	3	Czechoslovakia
	Mi-35	6	South Yemen
	Mi-35	20	India

Year	Variant	Qty	User
1989 (*Cont'd*)	Mi-24V	1	Poland
	Mi-24P	12	GDR
1990	Mi-35	18	Afghanistan
1995	Mi-35P	2	Sri Lanka
1998	Mi-35P	2	Sri Lanka
1999	Mi-35P	6	Zimbabwe
	Mi-35P	2	Sri Lanka
2000	Mi-35P	6	Nigeria
2001	Mi-35P	12	Cyprus
	Mi-35P	2	Angola
2003	Mi-24V	7	Czech Republic
	Mi-35P	2	Indonesia
2005	Mi-35	7	Czech Republic
2006	Mi-35	3	Czech Republic
	Mi-35M2	3	Venezuela
2007	Mi-35M2	5	Venezuela
	Mi-35P	1	Senegal
2008	Mi-35M2	2	Venezuela
	Mi-35P	6	Indonesia
	Mi-35P	2	Niger
2010	Mi-35M	6	Brazil
	Mi-35P	3	Indonesia
	Mi-35P	1	Myanmar
2011	Mi-35M	4	Azerbaijan
	Mi-35P	1	Myanmar
	Mi-35P	2	Peru
2012	Mi-35M	3	Brazil
	Mi-35M	8	Azerbaijan
2013	Mi-35M	4	Iraq
	Mi-35M	8	Azerbaijan
2014	Mi-35M	3	Brazil
	Mi-35M	8	Iraq
	Mi-35M	4	Azerbaijan
2015	Mi-35M	4	Iraq
	Mi-35M	4	Pakistan
	Mi-35M	1	Myanmar

Year	Variant	Qty	User
2016	Mi-35M	2	Nigeria
	Mi-35M	4	Kazakhstan
	Mi-35M	4	Iraq
2017	Mi-35M	4	Nigeria
	Mi-35M	4	Kazakhstan
	Mi-35M	2	Mali
2018	Mi-35M	4	Nigeria
	Mi-35M	4	Pakistan
	Mi-35M	1	Mali
2019	Mi-35M	2	Nigeria
	Mi-35M	4	Serbia
2020	Mi-35M	4	Uzbekistan
2021	Mi-35M	4	Uzbekistan
2022	Mi-35M	4	Rwanda
	Mi-35M	1	Mali
	Mi-35M	4	Uzbekistan
2023	Mi-35M	4	Kazakhstan
	Mi-35M	4	Belarus
	Mi-35M	3	Togo
2024	Mi-35M	4	Belarus
2025	Mi-35M	4	Belarus

* Not fully confirmed (likely redistributed to other users—see text)

Appendix B

List of Mi-24/25/35 Re-exports

Year	Variant	Qty	User	Origin
1978	Mi-24A	18	Ethiopia	USSR
	Mi-24A	3	Vietnam	USSR
1979	Mi-24A	1	Afghanistan	USSR
	Mi-24U	1	Afghanistan	USSR
	Mi-24A	3	Vietnam	USSR
1980	Mi-24A	6	Vietnam	USSR
	Mi-24U	1	Vietnam	USSR
1984	Mi-24A	12	Vietnam	USSR
	Mi-24U	2	Vietnam	USSR
1985	Mi-25	2	Pakistan	Afghanistan*1
1986	Mi-24D	6	Nicaragua	USSR
1987	Mi-25	1	USA	Libya*2
1988	Mi-25	1	Honduras	Nicaragua*1
1989	Mi-35	3	Pakistan	Afghanistan*2
1990	Mi-25	1	Nicaragua	Honduras*3
1991	Mi-24D/V/K/KD/R	15	Armenia	USSR*4
	Mi-24D/V/P/R	18	Azerbaijan	USSR*4
	Mi-24A/D/DU/V/P/R/K	76	Belorussia	USSR*4
	Mi-24V/Mi-24P	6	Georgia	USSR*4
	Mi-24D/K/V/P/R	42	Kazakhstan	USSR*4
	Mi-24U/D/DU/V/P	28	Kyrgyzstan	USSR*4
	Mi-24A/U/D/DU/V/P/VP/R/RA/K/KD	890	Russia	USSR*4
	Mi-24V/P	16	Turkmenistan	USSR*4
	Mi-24A/D/DU/V/P/VP/R/RA/K	360	Ukraine	USSR*4
	Mi-24D/V/P	45	Uzbekistan	USSR*4
	Mi-24D/V	2	Lithuania	USSR*4
	Mi-25	2	USA	Iraq*2

Year	Variant	Qty	User	Origin
1992	Mi-25	7	Peru	Nicaragua
	Mi-24D	1	USA	Germany
	Mi-24P	1	USA	Germany
	Mi-24V	2	Armenia	Russia
1993	Mi-24D	18	Poland	Germany
	Mi-24D	14	Hungary	Germany
	Mi-24P	6	Hungary	Germany
	Mi-24D	2	Croatia	Ukraine
	Mi-24V	4	Croatia	Ukraine
	Mi-24D	16	Czech Republic	Czechoslovakia*[5]
	Mi-24DU	1	Czech Republic	Czechoslovakia*[5]
	Mi-24V	19	Czech Republic	Czechoslovakia*[5]
	Mi-24D	8	Slovakia	Czechoslovakia*[5]
	Mi-24DU	1	Slovakia	Czechoslovakia*[5]
	Mi-24V	10	Slovakia	Czechoslovakia*[5]
1994	Mi-24V	5	Croatia	Ukraine
1995	Mi-24V	2	Sierra Leone	Belarus
	Mi-24V	15	India	Kyrgyzstan
	Mi-24D	1	Sudan	Kyrgyzstan
	Mi-24V	2	Angola	Ukraine
	Mi-24V	2	Sri Lanka	Ukraine
	Mi-24RChR	1	Sri Lanka	Ukraine
	Mi-24D	12	Peru	Ukraine
1996	Mi-24V/P	6	Tajikistan	Russia
	Mi-24V	6	Sudan	Belarus
	Mi-24P	4	Eritrea	Russia
	Mi-24P	1	Dem. Rep. Congo	Ukraine
	Mi-24V	3	Dem. Rep. Congo	Ukraine
	Mi-24P	1	Sri Lanka	Ukraine
	Mi-24V	2	Sri Lanka	Ukraine
	Mi-24V	1	Israel—IAI	Ukraine
	Mi-24P	2	Abkhazia	Russia

Year	Variant	Qty	User	Origin
1997	Mi-24V	2	Serbia	Ukraine
	Mi-24P	2	Papua New Guinea	Belarus
	Mi-24V	1	South Africa—ATE	CIS country*[6]
1998	Mi-24V	2	Rwanda	Belarus
	Mi-24P	2	Uganda	Belarus
	Mi-24D	2	Chad	Russia
	Mi-24V	1	Guinea	Ukraine
1999	Mi-24V	2	Ethiopia	Russia
	Mi-24V	28	Algeria	Ukraine
	Mi-24P	3	Angola	Ukraine
	Mi-24V	2	Sierra Leone	Ukraine
	Mi-24P	1	Uganda	Ukraine
	Mi-25	6	Sudan	Libya
2000	Mi-24P	2	Ethiopia	Belarus
	Mi-24V	4	Dem. Rep. Congo	Ukraine
	Mi-24V	3	Guinea	Ukraine
	Mi-24V	2	Sri Lanka	Ukraine
	Mi-24V	1	South Africa—ATE	Algeria
	Mi-24D	1	Slovakia	Kyrgyzstan*[7]
2001	Mi-24V	2	Angola	Ukraine
	Mi-24V	2	Central African Republic	Ukraine
	Mi-24V	2	Chad	Ukraine
	Mi-24V	2	Equatorial Guinea	Ukraine
	Mi-24V	10	Macedonia	Ukraine
	Mi-24K	2	Macedonia	Ukraine
	Mi-24P	7	Sri Lanka	Ukraine
2002	Mi-24V	2	Cote d'Ivoire	Belarus
	Mi-24V, P	5	Afghanistan	Russia
	Mi-24P	6	Angola	Russia
	Mi-24V	1	Burundi	Ukraine
	Mi-24D	2	Namibia	Libya

Year	Variant	Qty	User	Origin
2003	Mi-24V	3	Uganda	Belarus
	Mi-24D	2	Cote d'Ivoire	Bulgaria
	Mi-24P	2	Uganda	Russia
	Mi-24PN	1	Uganda	Russia
	Mi-24P	2	Equatorial Guinea	Ukraine
	Mi-24D	1	South Africa—ATE	Bulgaria
2005	Mi-24P	2	Djibouti	Belarus
	Mi-24P	2	Burkina Faso	Russia
	Mi-24P	12	Sudan	Russia
	Mi-24P	3	Georgia	Ukraine
	Mi-24V	3	Georgia	Ukraine
	Mi-24P	1	Georgia	Uzbekistan
	Mi-24V	3	Afghanistan	Ukraine
	Mi-24P	2	Afghanistan	Russia
	Mi-24V	1	Afghanistan	Russia
2006	Mi-24V	2	Chad	Ukraine
	Mi-24V	2	Tajikistan	Russia
2007	Mi-24D	2	Mali	Bulgaria
	Mi-24P	2	Equatorial Guinea	Ukraine
	Mi-24V	1	Afghanistan	Ukraine
2008	Mi-24V	3	Afghanistan	Czech Republic
	Mi-24V	2	Chad	Ukraine
	Mi-24P	1	Nigeria	Ukraine
	Mi-24V	2	Nigeria	Ukraine
2009	Mi-24V	1	Uganda	Belarus
	Mi-24V	3	Afghanistan	Czech Republic
	Mi-24V	4	Dem. Rep. Congo	Ukraine
	Mi-24V	1	Afghanistan	UAE*[6]
	Mi-24R	10	Azerbaijan	Ukraine
	Mi-24P	2	Azerbaijan	Ukraine
2010	Mi-24P	2	Nigeria	Belarus
	Mi-24P	4	Myanmar	Russia

Year	Variant	Qty	User	Origin
2011	Mi-24P	4	Myanmar	Russia
2012	Mi-24V	4	Sudan	Belarus
2013	Mi-24P	12	Sudan	Russia
2014	Mi-24P	4	Libya	Belarus
	Mi-24P	2	Nigeria	Ukraine
2015	Mi-25	3	Afghanistan	India
	Mi-24P	2	Myanmar	Russia
	Mi-24P	2	South Sudan	Russia
2016	Mi-24V	2	Cameroon	Slovakia
	Mi-25	1	Afghanistan	India
	Mi-24V	4	Sudan	Uganda
	Mi-24P	4	Angola	Russia
	Mi-24P	4	Syria	Russia
	Mi-24P	4	South Sudan	Russia
2017	Mi-24P	4	Angola	Russia
	Mi-24V	2	Tajikistan	Russia
	Mi-24V	6	Egypt	Russia
2018	Mi-24V	6	Egypt	Russia
2022	Mi-35	2	Ukraine	Czech Republic
2023	Mi-35	2	Ukraine	Czech Republic
	Mi-24D/V	12	Ukraine	Poland
	Mi-35P	6	Serbia	Cyprus
2024	Mi-35	4	Ukraine	Czech Republic
	Mi-24V	10	Ukraine	North Macedonia
	Mi-24K	2	Ukraine	North Macedonia
	Mi-35P	5	Serbia	Cyprus

*1 Defection, *2 Captured, *3 Returned, *4 Heritage after USSR break up, *5 Heritage after Czechoslovakia, *6 Exact origin unknown, *7 Seized during attempt to be sold to Liberia

Appendix C

Mi-24 Technical Data

Variant	Mi-24A	Mi-24D	Mi-24V	Mi-35M
Crew	2 + 1	2 + 1	2 + 1	2 + 1
Troops	8	8	8	8
Overall length with rotors turning [mm]	21,350	21,350	21,350	21,270
Fuselage length [mm]	17,050	17,310	17,310	17,310
Fuselage width [mm]	1,700	1,700	1,700	1,870
Stub wingspan [mm]	6,520	6,540	6,540	5,060
Stabilator span [mm]	3,270	3,270	3,270	3,270
Height with tail rotor [mm]	5,470	5,470	5,470	5,760
Height without tail rotor [mm]	3,970	3,970	3,970	4,440
Clearance [mm]	307	320	320	318
Wheel track [mm]	3,030	3,030	3,030	3,030
Wheelbase [mm]	4,390	4,390	4,390	4,390
Main rotor diameter [mm]	17,300	17,300	17,300	17,200
Tail rotor diameter [mm]	3,970	3,970	3,970	3,970
Empty weight [kg]	7,830	8,450	8,620	8,090
Maximum take-off weight [kg]	10,600	11,100	11,500	12,000
Cabin load [kg]	1,300	1,500	1,500	1,500
Sling load [kg]	2,200	2,400	2,400	2,400
Engines	TV-3-117	TV-3-117	TV-3-117V	VK-2500-02
Maximum power output [kW]	1,640	1,640	1,660	2,013
Cruise power output [kW]	1,045	1,111.1	1,118.6	1,340
Maximum speed [km/h]	315	335	335	312
Cruise speed [km/h]	270	270	270	260
Rate of climb [m/s]	11	12.5	12.5	12.4
Hovering ceiling [m]	1,600	1,200	1,500	3,100

Variant	Mi-24A	Mi-24D	Mi-24V	Mi-35M
Service ceiling [m]	5,120	4,500	4,800	5,400
Range [km]	485	595	595	415
Range with AFT [km]	–	1,000	1,000	1,085
Endurance [min]	140	125	125	125
Endurance with AFT [min]	–	240	240	240

Bibliography

Bašný, J., Brázda, J., Ovčáčik, M., Susa, K., *Mi-24D/V/DU* (Prague: Nakladatelství 4+, 1993)

Fiszer, M., Gruszczyński, J., *Mi-24*, edition 100 lat polskich skrzyeł (Warsaw: Edipresse, 2019)

Fojtík, J., *Bitevní vrtulník Mi-24*, (Cheb: Svět křídel, 2007)

Fojtík, J., *Bitevní vrtulníky* (Brno: CPress, 2022)

Fojtík, J., *Ruské vrtulníky Encyklopedie strojů konstrukčních kanceláří Bratuchin,* Kamov, Kazaň a Mil (Cheb: Svět křídel, 2007)

Fojtík, J., *Mil Mi-4 Hound* (Bedfordshire: Guideline Publications, 2024)

Fojtík, J., *Mil Mi-24/35 HIND* (Warsaw: Stratus, 2017)

Gordon, J., Komisarov, D., *Mil Mi-24 Hind Attack helicopter* (Shrewsbury: Airlife, 2001)

Grozev, K., Andonov, E., Petrov, V., Mladenov, A., *Mi-24 the assault helicopter* (Sofia: Aeropress BG, 2010)

Gunikal, V., *Mi-24V, P v detalyiach* (Kyiv: Vertikal, 2004)

Gyűrösi, M., Stolár, M., Vanga, M., *Vrtuľníky Mi-24 na Slovensku* (Bratislava: Magnet Press, 2011)

Mikheev, V., 'Vintokrilnyi shturmovik Milya', in *Aviatsyia i vremiya*, vol. 3 (1996), Aero Khobby, 1996, pp. 2–17

Moroz, S., Prikhodchenko, I., *Boyevoy vertolyot Mi-24* (Moscow: Exprint, 2005)

Povolný, D., Czvalinga, J., Čepelka, P., Dvořák, F., Fojtík, J., Medzihradský, S., Minařík, P., Špaček, J., Špaček, V., *Historie československého a českého vrtulníkového letectva od roku 1945 po současnost* (Prague: Ministerstvo obrany ČR, 2014)

Rusiecki, M., Senkowski, R., *60 lat innowrocławskiej jednostki śmigłowcowej 1963-2023* (Wroclaw, Ministerstwo obrony narodowej, 2023)

Sekach, N., *Boyevoy vertolyot Mi-24*, edition Voyennyi muzeyi (Moscow: Exprint, 2001)

Sekach, N., *Boyevoy vertolyot Mi-24*, edition Aviakollektsiya (Moscow: Modelist konstruktor, 2010)

Šiška, J., F., *Rudé hvězdy nad Afghánistánem 1* (Bratislava: Magnet Press, 2016)

Šiška, J., F., *Rudé hvězdy nad Afghánistánem 2* (Bratislava: Magnet Press, 2018)

Špaček, J., Fojtík, J., Mezihradský, S., *Pětatřicátník—Vrtulníky Mi-24 na Moravě a v Čechách,* (Prague: Aeromedia, 2014)

Špaček, J., *HIND Mi-24 v československých a českých službách* (Obrnice: Eduard, 2016)
Špaček, J., *Věčka Mi-24V a Mi-35 v československých a českých službách* (Obrnice: Eduard, 2023)
Špaček, J., *Tygři a Hroši v Přerově* (Bratislava: Magnet Press, 2023)
49th pułk śmigłowcow bojowych, *35-lecie śmigłowcow Mi-24* (Pruszcz Gdański: Ministerstwo obrony narodowej, 2016)
Marketing and promotional materials of Aviakon Konotop, Federal Service for Military-Technical Cooperation, Klimov, KRET, Mil Moscow Helicopter Plant, Motor Sich, Progress, Rostvertol, Rosvooruzhenyie, Rosoboronexport, Rostech and Helicopters of Russia agencies